NATURE OF
AUSTRALIA

NATURE OF
AUSTRALIA
A portrait of the island continent

JOHN VANDENBELD

Facts On File®
New York · Oxford

*in association with the Australian
Broadcasting Corporation*

for Margaret, Nadine and Justine, with love

Nature of Australia: A portrait of the island continent

Copyright © 1988 by Australian Broadcasting Company
Published by arrangement with BBC Books, a division of BBC Enterprises Ltd., in association with Australian Broadcasting Corporation.

Library of Congress Cataloging-in-Publication Data

Vandenbeld, John.
    Nature of Australia : a portrait of the island continent / John
Vandenbeld.
      p. cm.
    Bibliography: p.
    Includes index.
    ISBN 0-8160-2006-X
    1. Natural history—Australia.   I. Title.
QH197.V36 1988
508.94—dc19   88-11697
                                                    CIP

Printed in the United States of America

10 9 8 7 6 5 4 3 2 1

FOREWORD

What an astonishing place Australia is turning out to be. Far from the old, worn slab of rock we once took for granted, with not much more than scrub (we called it 'bush') as a covering and some freaky primitive beasts hopping about. Far from the dismal shores that Charles Darwin found so little to his liking. Not at all the forgotten land, a mere sideshow to the main events of natural history.

This book (and the film series that inspired it) shows how the discoveries are being made now as never before. Myths are being shattered. Connections are being made to the global paths of evolution in unexpected ways. The giant continent Gondwana is the key to understanding Australia's ancient origins. Stretches of forest left from that gondwanan landscape still stand in southern parts of the continent, as surprising and indeed precious as living dinosaurs would be.

And that so-called 'bush', a pejorative term used by some scientists and laypeople alike, is perhaps the greatest surprise of all. When Captain Cook and his scientists came to the east coast and when further European natural historians succeeded them, they called Australia 'Terra nullius', meaning that the land was unaffected by human hand. The Aborigines (or 'indians' as they were sometimes described) were thought to be mere wanderers passing through a terrain unchanged since time began.

Now we know that the opposite is true. Some Australian forests are as much a creation of people as are the parks of London and Vienna. One hundred thousand years ago and before, there was oak and casuarina. Then came the human beings, crossing in boats that may have been the very first fashioned by hand.

Lower sea levels and the existence of islands made the passage easier than in modern times when the open ocean stretches further. Those people brought fire, and they used it for hunting and so transformed the forests. The eucalyptus and fire-adapted banksias came to dominate, and with them, other kinds of animal flourished.

The giant marsupials and sundry behemoths that once flourished fell to a new force, probably human beings. But plenty of spectacularly different beasts remained, some of them causing great perplexity and indeed incredulity when they were brought to London for the first time. At first they were greeted as frauds, then as freaks, finally as primitive relics. I don't know which is the worse insult, for the monotremes and marsupials are by no means mere offshoots. And please don't infer that I'm indulging in a kind of biological chauvinism (after all, I was born in Europe myself), because Australia's kangaroos, koala and platypuses turn out to be highly specialised beasts with adaptations of the most sophisticated kind. What's more, as a result of a woeful neglect of native fauna, only now being corrected, our understanding of these animals is quite incomplete. Hence the surprises, many of which John Vandenbeld reveals in this remarkable book.

The deserts, which are in no way a 'Dead Heart'; the tropical seas, containing the richest variety of fish on the planet; the rainforests, containing the world's genetic bank; the hills, in which the smaller, endangered animals still survive — all have been visited in the past three years by crews from the *Nature of Australia*.

The images are vivid: David Parer (who has always struck me as the David Lean of natural history film-making), lying in a cage underwater at Lizard Island in the far north, filming the tiger sharks as they attack turtles exhausted from their egg-laying. Liz Parer-Cook, who forsook her training as a sociologist to study biology and to spend months in all parts of Australasia. Dione Gilmour, who spent so many consecutive weeks on location that her return to the city was nearly as shocking as that of Tarzan in 'Greystoke'. And John Vandenbeld, trying to put it all together to produce this book and a film series that would fascinate both the scientists and the wider community.

I hope their efforts help to kill the myths about the nature of Australia. The true story is so much more surprising and exciting.

Robyn Williams

CONTENTS

Changing colour through
the day as its surface has been
abraded by time, Uluru is a
metaphor for Australia's grandeur and isolation.

PROLOGUE

Skimming it at sunrise, Australia's Centre seems the sea it once was, its dunes re-
ceding to the horizon in waves of deep blue and purple, their crests tipped with
rose. Uluru is a black island, looming against the lightening sky.

Watching the dawn brush away the black, the facts supplied by science fall
short of the reality. The facts add up to a geological oddity: an outcrop of hard
sandstone called arkose, rising 300 metres above the plain, measuring 8 kilometres around its base, yet merely the tip of a formation that may run as deep as
6000 metres. The massive sandstone was compressed from sediments laid down
in seas 600 million years ago, in the dawn of life on earth. Forces released by the
turmoil within the planet twisted and tilted the giant slabs of stone, exposing
them to the grind of time and weather. Like a sculptor releasing his figure from
marble, they wore away the softer rock, and revealed Uluru — Ayers Rock.

Yet to know this seems less than enough. It needs that other dimension of
the human imagination, which sometimes creates gods, and sometimes generates an exultant sense of the importance of being human. In that dimension,
Uluru becomes more than compressed sandstone coloured by the rising sun. It
becomes a potent symbol of time, the essence of the aeons that shaped the continent from whose heart it rises. And standing at its heart, the stone is the right
place to begin the quest for the continent's origins and those of the life it carries.

Worn almost totally flat and repeatedly invaded by the sea, the
land continues to be pounded by the southern oceans.

Driven by storms from the icy south, rain-laden clouds break on the highlands of Tasmania — one of the few permanently moist environments in Australia, and one that contains relics of the continent's ancient ties with Gondwana.

Opposite

Immense forces, acting with immense slowness, have carved the nature of the continent in shapes that, while they have equivalents in other places, contain elements unique to Australia.

A hundred thousand million dawns have washed over Uluru. In those 300 million years, it has seen mountains rise and fall, seas and lakes flood and vanish, great forests spread to the horizon and fade away — and, a few moments ago in geological time, the invasion of the deserts. Much of the drama of Uluru derives from its setting, the way it rears from the flatness of the surrounding plains. The drama is heightened by colour: the dry desert air makes colours hard and bright, and as the sun rises, the dry sky turns intensely blue, the rock a vivid red.

There are other places in the world that are flat and dry, but in Australia it is a pervasive description, defining the character of the continent right to its coastal fringes. It is a far from uniform character, however: to make an aerial journey across the continent as it awakens to the new day, from the great rock at its heart to its coastal margins, is to discover infinite variety in the landscape. Such a journey gives the lie to claims of monotony. The variations are often subtle, sometimes striking, and a closer look reveals that each landform contains its own marvellously adapted company of plants and animals.

Such a journey is at once a celebration of Australia, and an approach to an explanation of its difference. As the sun rides higher in the sky, the blue and purple waves of the night sea are transformed into waves of sand, glistening red and yellow. A little dew still clings to the speargrass that grows in patches between the dunes. A curiously shaped creature is moving stiff-leggedly between the stalks, its camouflage-patterned skin — like armour plating, studded with horns and spikes — giving it the fierce appearance reflected in its Latin name, *Moloch horridus*.

As so often in this continent where little is as it seems, appearances are deceptive: the thorny devil is a mild enough creature whose spiky defences are meant simply to deter potential predators. Even more remarkable is another feature that allows the devil to 'drink' with its skin. During the night, dew condenses on its body. An intricate network of capillary channels draws the moisture to the devil's mouth, and it drinks. Water is scarce in these dry regions, and survival depends on making a little go a long way.

Soon the sand dunes give way to plains of stone, worn remnants of mountains. The stones are called gibbers, polished to a jewel brightness. Very little grows among them, yet there is a bird that thrives here. It takes a cunning eye to distinguish the gibberbird from the gibbers themselves as it crouches motionless over the nest it has made of the stones, shading its chicks from the heat with wings that repeat the pattern of the gibbers. The gibberbird's camouflage deceives the airborne hunters that patrol the vast stretches of sand and stone. Even on the flat plains of pure salt, the beds of the great sea that once filled the inland basins,

There is one constant in the variety of landforms that make
up the continent: in all but the central regions, the landscape
is dominated by eucalypts, uniquely Australian plants that
have adapted so perfectly to the land that they have
become synonymous with it.

there is life. Subtly patterned pale lizards, the Lake Eyre dragons, have made the salt their domain, their markings blending in with the play of light around the miniature ridges and hillocks sculpted from the crystals by the wind.

The inland basin, which is today a series of barren salt lakes, was formed around the same time as Uluru and as part of the same processes. As rock formations in the earth's crust shifted, slid and finally sank, a huge saucer-like depression was created, into which all of Australia's inland waters would eventually drain. As the centre sank, the edges were pushed up, and slabs of ancient seabed were tilted to form what remains only as a chain of rugged hills: the Flinders Ranges.

The layers of sediments laid down in those primordial seas can be seen as bands in some of the sheer cliff faces, and they have preserved some of the earliest life on earth: the delicate spirals of worms and molluscs from an evolutionary line that has long since died out. These same sheer cliffs are also home for some of the latest life forms fashioned by the processes of evolution — surefooted animals that negotiate the craggy cliffs with ease and agility, yet animals that move in a very different way from those inhabiting rocky slopes in other parts of the world. They are rock wallabies — a group of the kangaroo family that is still evolving into new species in widely separated and isolated habitats.

Rivers flow out of these ranges, but like all the rivers in these arid regions of the continent they flow merely with sand. There is water, but it is many metres below the surface, and only the trees can reach it. Their gleaming white trunks line the rivers of sand; their roots draw water from the sands buried far below. To conserve water and to minimise evaporation, the river red gums' tough, hard leaves angle away from the sun. The bare branches of some seem to be festooned with white blossoms: as one moves closer, they resolve into white cockatoos, perched in their hundreds, resting from forays on to surrounding plains. Cockatoos are members of the parrot family, and semi-arid Australia is their stronghold. Yet in other lands parrots are jungle birds, flashing through the lush green in streaks of bright colour.

The aerial journey now approaches the continent's eastern coastline, where the land rises into a series of rounded folds. These highlands, unlike the stark ranges of the inland, are clad in green; in winter, their higher slopes are covered in snow: snow (such a surprise in arid Australia) that recalls more familiar lands. But in the snow-fed streams that tumble out of the highlands live animals the likes of which are found nowhere else.

Moving down the eastern slopes through gradually drier and more open woodland, there is one constant: at every altitude, the dominant trees are eucalypts. Their leaves are rich in pungent and

Typical of jungles in other parts of the world, parrots have colonised some of Australia's harshest environments. Their adaptability reflects the many changes animals and plants had to make to survive.

flammable oils, yet at certain stages of their growth they are food for a unique animal. The koala looks a little like some of the bears of other lands, but belongs to a totally different animal group: the marsupials that have made Australia their heartland, with a range of types and forms to make use of just about every resource the continent has to offer. The combination that recurs most frequently includes the grasses and shrubs of the plains and the open spaces of the woodlands. Such areas support the largest and most numerous of the marsupials, the macropods — the big-footed ones — the kangaroos and wallabies.

The macropods typify the singular nature of Australia, for they represent a line of evolution unique to this continent. To trace their lineage is to trace the making of Australia itself.

The morning's journey across Australia pauses for a moment in a woodland clearing. A small group of tammar wallabies is nearing the end of its morning's feeding. Soon, they will return to the shelter of the trees. To watch them is to become aware of both their similarities to animals elsewhere in the world, and of their great differences. Their heads, with large brown eyes and silky ears twitching at every sound, are rather like those of deer. They are grazers, like many antelope in Africa, pampas deer in South America, and European deer; but instead of walking on all fours, they hop on their hind legs. Groups of tammar wallabies are not as large as the big herds in which grazers gather elsewhere in the world, but they are large enough for a social system to develop.

That system, as in most animal societies, revolves around two primary and universal urges — to survive, and to procreate. Among social mammals, males are usually larger than females: males have to compete for access to females, which leads to selection for greater size and strength. Among the tammars grazing in the morning sun, the process is about to be illustrated.

One of the does has come into season, and has aroused the interest of a young male. Enticed by the scent that signals her readiness to copulate, he follows her. But before he can manage to mate, an older male intervenes: raising himself to his full height, he draws attention to his superior size. On most occasions the larger male's display would be enough to make the young buck turn tail. Not this time, however: the urge to procreate is strong, and the young buck also draws himself up into a fighting stance.

So far it is bluff, but with no sign from either that he is about to give in, the combat escalates from the ritual to the real. It is not antlers or horns that are the weapons, but the powerful hindlegs. The combatants leap full tilt at each other, raking at chest and belly with claws that can inflict grievous wounds. In this bout the injuries remain minor: soon, the young buck is forced to retreat, and the

As Australia became drier, open woodlands and grasslands gradually displaced the forests, and the forest wallabies gave rise to new groups to graze the new, coarser grass food. Tammar wallabies (*Macropus eugenii*) represent one of the early stages of this new radiation.

Some other lands, parts of other continents, are flat and dry;
but these qualities are the all-pervasive essence of Australia.
Surrounded by plains of sand and stone, the legacy of
millions of years of erosion, Chambers' Pillar epitomises the
harshness of the Australian environment.

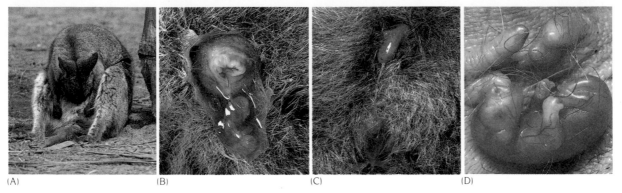

(A)   (B)   (C)   (D)

A remarkable sequence showing the birth of a marsupial, in this case a tammar wallaby. It begins (A) when the female moves away from her group, squats, and cleans her pouch. When the young is born (B) it is only two centimetres long, and weighs half a gram. Yet its front claws are strong enough to haul the embryo on a long and arduous journey (C) through its mother's belly hair, into the pouch where it blindly finds its way to a teat (D) and clamps onto it, to begin suckling and completing its development into a well-formed young wallaby. The milk delivered through the teat changes in composition to match the young tammar's growing needs.

dominant male claims his prize. The doe that triggered the contest stands passively, waiting to receive the victor. He grasps her from behind with his forearms and his flexible penis finds its way into her cloaca. The winner's reward is that his genes are passed to the next generation — thus perpetuating the trend toward larger, more powerful males.

Other aspects of the procreative drive reveal the profound differences that exist between these Australian grazers and their counterparts elsewhere in the world. The first difference can be seen when one of the does moves off by herself, squatting, so her tail and hindlegs extend in front of her, with her cloaca facing upward. She begins to lick inside the fold of skin that forms a pouch on her belly. A few moments later, she gives birth — not to a fully developed young that can run with her almost immediately, but to a barely formed embryo, a pink, naked and blind creature only two centimetres or so long; half the size of a newborn mouse and weighing only half a gram.

It emerges head first, still enclosed in its foetal membranes, from which it frees itself with well-developed forearms and claws. These now become crucial in the first and most arduous of this tiny wallaby's life journeys.

The newborn tammar hauls its way up through the fur on its mother's belly, into her pouch. There, it blindly finds its way to one of the four teats, and clamps its mouth firmly over it. Just how the newborn knows to find its way from cloaca to teat is not certain — possibly through some perception of gravity: up to the pouch, then down inside, where smell may help locate the teat. It is a remarkable feat of both endurance and navigation; all the more so because the birthling receives no help from its mother.

Firmly attached to its mother's teat, the young wallaby grows, safely ensconced while its mother moves about, cropping the coarse grasses she will convert to milk. The milk itself changes in composition to match the needs of the growing young, with a higher fat and protein content and less sugar as the 'joey' grows.

After nine months or so, it will venture out of the pouch for the first time — a kind of second birth. Spells outside lengthen gradually, until it is completely independent of the pouch.

Their hopping locomotion and the use of their hindlegs in social behaviour set these animals apart already: but their development inside a pouch is the one feature that most clearly distinguishes Australia's unique marsupials from the world's other mammals.

Watching the tammars as they gradually move back into the scrub that will shelter them during the day — the adults constantly on the alert, the young skipping at foot or tumbling back into the pouch — the puzzles and paradoxes of the morning's journey across the continent shape themselves into a single question: why *these* animals in *this* place, this place alone? Nature's laws are deemed universal, yet this seems (as Darwin suggested) a separate creation. The answers are not, of course, simple — nothing in nature ever is — but in many ways the story of how and why the marsupials came to make Australia their dominion, of how the most impressive of the marsupials — the kangaroos and wallabies — came to be the way they are is very much the story of how Australia came to be the way *it* is. The search for those origins goes a long way into the past, and a long way outside Australia.

To trace the evolution of the macropods — the kangaroos, wallabies and their kin — is to trace the evolution of Australia itself, for these unique marsupials developed in tune with Australia.

A SEPARATE CREATION

A ledge of rock at Hallett Cove, South Australia, scoured by
glaciers in the Permian epoch 280 million years ago. Since
glaciers only flow downward from higher ground and the
scourings point from the south, it suggests Australia once
was part of a greater landmass.

*T*he first signs of the direction the search should take have nothing to do with
animals, but with the shape of the world that gave rise to them. It begins
where the morning's journey ends — on the South Australian coast.

The signs are engraved in polished sheets of rock that slope to the sea. The
engravings were made by glaciers, through the scouring of boulders trapped low
in the ice sheets as they moved across the rock, carving away the softer layers
and leaving deep scratches in the harder rock. Though they look as if they had
been carved yesterday, they are in fact 280 million years old. Their depth and
shape point them south, across what is now the Southern Ocean.

Far to the south, across the storm-racked Southern Ocean, lies Antarctica
— ice-covered now as it was when glaciers ground their signatures into these
Australian rocks. Off Cape Raoul, on the southern tip of Tasmania, there are
other rocks that tell of a connection. Spectacular formations rise from the sea in
flutes and pipes of brilliant black dolerite, a composition born of geological
events that followed the retreat of the glaciers 250 million years ago. Layers of
sediments thousands of metres deep, laid down in the post-glacial seas,
cracked; molten rock was forced into the cracks like bronze into a cast, and set
into an impermeable hardness. Over the next 100 million years, the sedimentary
rock was worn away to reveal the dolerite sculptures of Tasmania, black against a
cold grey sea.

Opposite

Opposite

Dolerite rock formations off
Cape Raoul, Tasmania: one of
the geological clues that point
to Australia's one-time
connection with Antarctica, as
part of the Gondwanan supercontinent.

Below

The south polar perspective of
the globe at the present time.
Antarctica, in the centre of the
illustration, straddles the south
pole; and Australia lies almost
on the edge of the globe to the
right, its outline distorted by
the unfamiliar angle.

Right

The same perspective 150 million
years ago, when Australia —
together with Africa, South
America and India — were joined
with Antarctica in the
supercontinent of Gondwana.

Two thousand kilometres to the south, the sea is colder and
greyer as icebergs loom and vanish in the spray of gale-whipped
waves. The icebergs calved from glaciers, part of the ice cap that
covers the Antarctic continent up to 3 kilometres deep. Ice returned to Antarctica 20 million years ago, but there are a few places
where it does not reach. The dry valleys are in the part of Antarctica
that lies directly to the south of Australia. A quirk of topography
keeps much of the valley's rock-strewn floors and walls free of ice,
and the result is a landscape of startling beauty, of austere compo-
sitions in black and white tinged with the subtlest shades of pastel
when the sun appears low on the horizon.

It seems a world away from the hot, dry continent to the north,
yet the rocks tell us otherwise. The black cliffs of dolerite that flank
the valleys are identical to those of southern Tasmania. Not far
from the dry valleys are rock pavements with glacial scourings that
match precisely the carvings in that cove on the South Australian
coast, where the journey began.

The glaciers and mountains of Antarctica hold other clues to
Australia's past, when it and Antarctica were joined. In the
Devonian epoch, 400 million years ago, fish swam in shallow seas
where now there is land. Their shapes are imprinted in sediments,
hardened by time into rock; and time has exposed them amid the
ice of Antarctica (and 5000 kilometres to the north, in the dry inland of central New South Wales).

In the walls of rock that flank the dry valleys, seams of coal show
that in the slightly warmer climate that followed the retreat of the

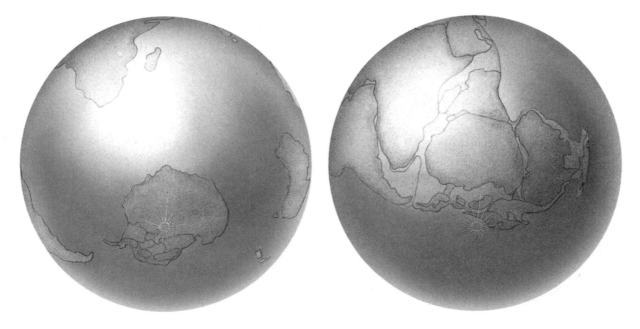

Permian glaciers, Antarctica was covered by forest. Preserved in the seams are the fossilised images of fern-like plants and primitive trees. In places, petrified stumps still protrude from the rock; logs lie as they fell 250 million years ago. It was these fossils that gave scientists their first inkling of a theory that would revolutionise the way we think about how the world was shaped as dramatically as Darwin's theories of evolution had a century earlier.

The fossils' entry into the scientific record was also attended by great drama, for they were collected on Captain R F Scott's last expedition to Antarctica, a lost and fatal race to the South Pole. Specimens collected by the expedition's scientist, Edward Wilson, on the return journey were found with his frozen body, and those of Scott and Bowers, in their iced-over tent. The heroic failure of the race to the pole seized the popular imagination, but it was the humble pile of rock fragments — an almost overlooked aspect of the expedition — that would have lasting significance.

Scott's diary for 8 February 1912 records '. . . We found ourselves under perpendicular walls of Beacon Sandstone, weathering rapidly and carrying veritable coal seams. From the last Wilson, with his sharp eyes, has picked several pieces of coal with beautifully traced leaves in layers, also some excellently preserved impressions of thick stems, showing cellular structure.' The plants were of a kind named *Glossopteris*. They matched almost exactly specimens found in coals and rocks of the same age in South Africa, India, South America — and in Australia.

Not far from the coal seams that attracted Wilson's sharp eyes, later explorers found other fossilised remains — not of plants, but of more recent animals. Reconstructions based on fossil bone fragments revealed large, reptile-like creatures, including a beast

Opposite

These rocks, on the coast near Swansea, south of Newcastle, New South Wales, are the petrified remains of *Glossopteris* — trees that flourished 250 million years ago, and whose fossilised presence in now widely separated locations around the southern hemisphere was the first of the pieces of evidence on which the theory of continental drift was founded.

The present-day distribution of the fossils of *Glossopteris*, a cold-adapted plant of the Triassic period, and *Lystrosaurus*, a mammal-like reptile, is part of evidence that the continents were once linked. The illustration shows the continents re-united, with the possible patterns of distribution suggested by connecting the places where the fossils were found.

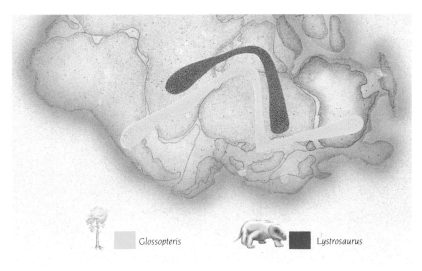

Glossopteris   Lystrosaurus

ERA	PERIOD	MILLION YEARS AGO	CLIMATE (MAINLY AUSTRALIA)	FLORA	FAUNA	MILLION YEARS AGO
CAINOZOIC	QUATERNARY	1 / 2	LAST 10,000 YRS. CLIMATE HAS BEEN RELATIVELY STABLE, ARIDITY A MAJOR FEATURE. ARIDITY OF THE AUSTRALIAN CONTINENT REACHED PRESENT PROPORTIONS IN LATE PLIOCENE/PLEISTOCENE ABOUT 2.5 M.Y. AGO	CYCLIC CHANGES FROM OPEN/DRIER VEGETATION IN GLACIAL PERIODS TO FORESTED/WETTER VEGETATION IN INTERGLACIALS	MARSUPIALS MONOTREMES	1 / 2
CAINOZOIC	PLIOCENE (TERTIARY)	5 / 7	COOL	DEVELOPMENT OF OPEN FORESTS AND GRASSLANDS	ECHIDNA	5 / 7
CAINOZOIC	MIOCENE (TERTIARY)	10 / 20	DRYNESS STARTS TO APPEAR IN UPPER TERTIARY. LATE MIOCENE COOLING. COOLER. WARM	NUCLEUS OF ARID FLORA DEVELOPS IN DRIER AREAS. GRASSLANDS IN THE CENTRE IN LATE MIOCENE	PRIMITIVE PLATYPUS	10 / 20
CAINOZOIC	OLIGOCENE (TERTIARY)	30	PERIODS OF RELATIVE ARIDITY. WARM		ANCESTRAL DASYURIDS; OTHER MARSUPIAL FAMILIES	30 / 38
CAINOZOIC	EOCENE (TERTIARY)	40 / 50	*COOLING*	DECLINE IN RATE OF DIVERSIFICATION OF THE ANGIOSPERMS AFTER RAPID EVOLUTION OF FAMILIES. RAINFOREST IN CENTRAL AUSTRALIA	BIRDS: FIRST PENGUINS; RUNNING BIRDS, FLIGHTLESS	40 / 42 / 50 / 54
CAINOZOIC	PALAEOCENE (TERTIARY)	60	WARM AND WET. SEA TEMPERATURES WARM. *INCREASED RAINFALL*	COAL SWAMPS IN THE SOUTH		60
MESOZOIC	CRETACEOUS	100	AFRICAN EVIDENCE SUGGESTS ABRUPT COOLING IN W. GONDWANA AT END OF THE CRETACEOUS. WARM, EQUABLE CLIMATE. THROUGHOUT THE MESOZOIC, SOUTH POLE ALMOST STATIONARY JUST SOUTH OF TASMANIA BUT CLIMATES TEMPERATE & WARM. LOWER CRETACEOUS MARINE FLOODING WORLDWIDE	MAJOR DIVERSIFICATION OF ANGIOSPERMS WORLDWIDE. RADIATION INTO AUSTRALIA — RAINFOREST. 95 LAST PERIOD OF FERN, GYMNOSPERM DOMINANCE ELSEWHERE IN GONDWANA & REST OF WORLD. 100 EARLIEST ANGIOSPERM POLLEN IN W. GONDWANA — NOT IN AUSTRALIA. ALGAE IN SHALLOW SEAS FORM OIL SHALE	MASS EXTINCTION OF THE DINOSAURS, AND MANY SPECIES OF ANIMALS. BIRDS: FIRST FEATHER (Vic.). TURTLES. PTEROSAURS. DINOSAURS	65 / 69 / 77 / 84 / 88 / 95 / 100 / 109 / 114 / 125 / 135
MESOZOIC	JURASSIC		SUBTROPICAL. WARM AND WET	PODOCARPS. ARAUCARIANS. AGE OF CONIFERS, CYCADS, TREE FERNS	MULTITUBERCULATES ANCESTORS OF MONOTREMES. AGE OF REPTILES DINOSAURS. CICADA	162 / 190
MESOZOIC	TRIASSIC	200	WARM TO HOT. PERIODS OF ARIDITY AND SEASONAL RAINFALL. WARM	DICROIDIUM FLORA	REPTILES (Dinosaurs start in Australia but are rare/common in rest of Gondwana). AGE OF AMPHIBIANS. TRIASSIC LUNG FISH. LYSTROSAURUS ZONE Africa/India/China/Antarctica	200 / 225
PALAEOZOIC	PERMIAN		TEMPERATE DURING COAL FORMATION. ICE CAP ADVANCING AND RETREATING	EXTENSIVE SWAMPY TERRESTRIAL ENVIRONMENTS FOR DEPOSITION OF COAL. GLOSSOPTERIS FLORA	LABYRINTHODONTS	252 / 280
PALAEOZOIC	CARBONIFEROUS	300	GLACIATION. COOLER. WARM	RHACOPTERIS FLORA. LEPIDODENDRON FLORA	FIRST SHARKS. FIRST AMPHIBIANS PROBABLY EVOLVED FROM LUNG FISH	300 / 345
PALAEOZOIC	DEVONIAN	400	WARM AND WET	BARAGWANATHIA FLORA (VICTORIA)	PLATY-HEADED FISH. MARINE INVERTEBRATES	380 / 400
PALAEOZOIC	SILURIAN		HOT. PARTS ARID. WARM	FIRST LAND PLANTS EVOLVED FROM THE ALGAE. ALGAE IN THE SEA	LIFE STARTS ON THE LAND. BRACHIOPODS, GASTROPODS, TRILOBITES	410 / 425 / 440
PALAEOZOIC	ORDOVICIAN	500	WARM		TRILOBITES, GASTROPODS	500
PALAEOZOIC	CAMBRIAN		HOT AND DRY			570

Note (spanning vertically in CLIMATE/FLORA): CLOSED FOREST VEGETATION THROUGHOUT TERTIARY (Angiosperm Dominated)

A CHRONOLOGY OF MAJOR EVENTS IN THE NATURAL HISTORY OF AUSTRALIA'S CLIMATE, PLANTS AND ANIMALS dubbed *Lystrosaurus* . . . one of a group that was to give rise, millions of years later, to the ancestors of the mammals. And as with *Glossopteris*, remains of *Lystrosaurus* have turned up in all the southern continents — except, so far, Australia.

The Gondwanan Connection

There was no way identical species could have arisen independently in what are today widely separated locations, and the Antarctic fossils lent support to a revolutionary theory first put forward by a German astronomer, Alfred Wegener, in 1912: the same year Scott was making his diary entry.

Wegener's theory, now known as continental drift, posited nothing less than the movement of continents across the face of the globe. Once, these continents had been joined in a single great landmass — a supercontinent Wegener named Gondwana, after the Indian people in whose region the first *Glossopteris* fossils (the first piece of the jigsaw puzzle) were found.

His idea provided explanations for many puzzles: the occurrence of highly similar large, flightless birds in widely separated continents — the rhea in South America, the ostrich in Africa and the emu and cassowary in Australia — marsupials in South America and Australia, and the heath-like Proteaceae of Australia mirrored in South Africa.

Appealing though the idea was that all these places were once united, it took a long time to be accepted, for neither Wegener nor anyone else could come up with an acceptable mechanism by which continents could go careering around the globe. Then, in the late 1960s, came the theory of plate tectonics, which states that the earth's crust is made up of a small number of plates, each 50 to a 100 kilometres thick, that move relative to one another and that include both ocean basins and continents. Movements are initiated at huge cracks that zigzag along the ocean floors; where lava wells up from the earth's interior, spreads to each side and (at a rate of up to ten centimetres a year) pushes plates further apart.

With the mechanisms of continental drift locked into place by supporting evidence from a number of quarters, the suggestion of Gondwana firmed into as near a fact as science will allow. Some of that evidence had been observed for a long time, but only now was its true significance established: when aligned along their coastlines, for example, continents fit roughly together. Later, more sophisticated techniques enabled the coastlines as they were during Permian times to be mapped with a great degree of accuracy — and a rough fit became a remarkably precise one.

To bring them together only requires time to spin the world back through the past 150 million years. The continents re-unite;

though not at the same time, or at the same pace. At around 30 million years ago, South America rejoins Antarctica — a relatively short journey. At 45 million years ago, Australia returns from a much longer voyage. India and New Zealand follow 80 million years ago, and with Africa and Madagascar back at 135 million years ago, the reunion is complete: Gondwana has been recreated.

Fifty million years or so earlier, Gondwana itself had been linked with the great northern supercontinent of Laurasia, which incorporated what is now North America, Europe and Asia, to form a single mighty continent; Pangaea. Gondwana and Laurasia had already drifted apart and rejoined twice — their final separation began about 170 million years ago.

It was Gondwana that produced the ingredients time and evolution would eventually meld into Australia and its unique company of animals and plants. Such a huge landmass probably made for a range of climates; but though it was so far south, temperature variations between the equator and the pole were far lower than they are today. The *Glossopteris* that had dominated the vegetation following the retreat of the great Permian glaciation had vanished, and much of Gondwana was now covered by forests of club

Frogs are a thriving legacy of the Age of Amphibians. This pair is spawning: the female has broad flanges on each finger, with which she paddles the water, whipping up the jelly around the eggs into a buoyant foam.

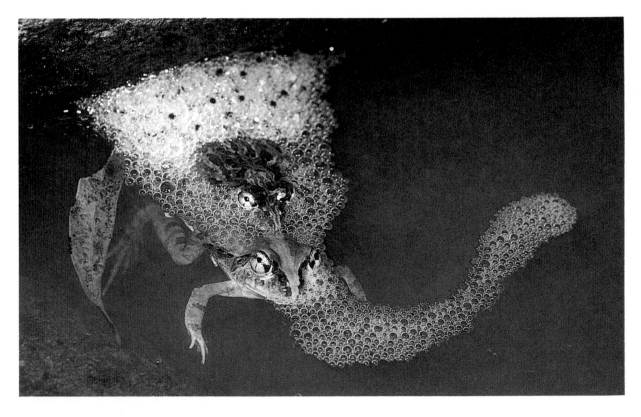

mosses, horsetail ferns and cycads. The club mosses had straight trunks, topped with a small crown of branches carrying seed-bearing cones at their tips. The cycads were palm-like; among their living descendants are the burrawangs (*Macrozamia* spp.) common in eastern Australia. Club mosses and horsetails survive too, though in miniature form: only 60 centimetres high.

There were no birds, but the ancient forests swarmed with insects: butterflies, scorpion flies, brilliantly coloured cockroaches, praying mantises and dragonflies, some of which had wingspans of 30 centimetres. The insects provided food for larger animals: on the edges of lakes and swamps lived amphibians that could live on land, but which had to return to the water to reproduce. Water was essential to the fertilisation of their eggs.

Frogs illustrate amphibians' dependence on water; a dependence that varies from species to species, but one that makes use of the same basic strategy. Marsh frogs of the genus *Limnodynastes* have evolved a particularly refined method of bringing water and eggs together to increase the eggs' chances of survival. Once his bellowing call has attracted a female, the male grasps her waist, leaving her forelimbs free. Half-submerged, she releases a stream of eggs that is then covered by the male's sperm. And while that is happening, the female paddles the water in front of her with her forelimbs, sending water and trapped air bubbles back beneath the emerging eggs, whipping up the jelly surrounding the eggs into a buoyant foam. The foam forms a floating nest, where the eggs will eventually hatch into tadpoles. The nest itself affords the eggs their only protection; the parents take no further interest in their young.

Most of the eggs and tadpoles will, in fact, fall prey to hungry mouths. But the strategy takes this into account: while the mortality rate is enormously high, so is the number of eggs produced, and just enough will survive at least to replace their parents. There are almost as many reproductive variations among amphibians as there are species of amphibians; but all share a dependence on water to bring eggs and sperm together.

The New, Improved Egg

The reptiles began their rise to dominance when they cut their reproductive bond with water — when some groups evolved a way of fertilising the eggs within the female's body. The eggs were more advanced, too; surrounded by protective coats, they came equipped with their own fluid, a miniature sea in which the embryo could develop. An example of a very early stage of this new development survives in New Zealand. The tuatara (*Sphenodon punctatus*) is the last representative of an ancient and once-widespread group of reptiles that made its appearance 200 million years ago, when

Dinosaur tracks at Broome,
Western Australia: lasting
impressions of the giants that
once strode across Australia.
These footprints were left in
mud that solidified; they
belonged to *Megalosauropus
broomensis*, a carnivorous
dinosaur 6 or 7 metres long.

Right
On the other side of the
continent, one of the fossilised
tracks near Winton, in central
Queensland, recording a
dinosaur 'stampede'.

New Zealand and Australia were part of Gondwana. The tuatara's
mating ritual is a primitive one, in which the male and female genital openings are brought together in what can only be described as
a cloacal kiss.

Such a technique involves a good deal of cooperation on the
part of the female tuatara. The natural inclination of any animal is
to keep its distance from others and, if another comes too close, to
flee or fight. As mating requires great closeness indeed, the male
tuatara needs to persuade the female to do neither. He does so
with a primitive form of courtship, many of whose signals are also
part of the aggressive repertoire used to assert his dominance over
other males: he raises his crest, distends his jowl to display its dew-
lap, and his gait changes to a curious kind of lunging high step with
which he circles the female. If these advances prove resistible, the
male becomes more aggressive — lunging at the female's head
and even biting it, until she allows him to mount. They press their
cloacas together for four minutes or so, allowing the male's sperm
to swim directly into the female's oviduct.

Later reptile groups developed a way of getting the sperm even
closer to the eggs, with an organ that could be inserted directly into
the female's genital opening. With the development of the penis,

courtship rituals became more elaborate affairs. Some of the dragon lizards of Australia exemplify this next stage. When the bearded dragon (*Amphibolurus barbatus*) feels the urge to mate, in late spring, he communicates his intentions to a prospective partner by advancing on her slowly, bobbing his head and lifting one arm in a kind of wave to reassure her he means no harm.

Rather than being consigned to the hazards of the water, as in the case of most amphibians, the fertilised eggs of the reptiles complete the first stage of their development within the safety of the female's body. She produces far fewer eggs than amphibians — the bearded dragon, for example, has a 'clutch' of only ten eggs — but their chances of survival are correspondingly greater. When she lays her eggs — all connected by a membrane, like a string of tiny sausages — she makes provision for their continuing safety by burying them in a shallow hole, where the temperature will remain fairly constant to help incubation, and where there is less likelihood of predators finding them. When the young hatch and dig themselves out, what remains of the egg's yolk sac provides them with food for their first few days, while they learn to hunt the grubs and insects that will be their staple diet.

Rise of the Dinosaurs

The really important feature of this new mode of reproduction was that it freed the reptiles from their dependence on water. Once that bond was broken, they could go on to colonise all of the land. They evolved rapidly into a range of shapes and sizes to take advantage of new habitats, and the foods they offered. Earlier, smaller reptiles — like the surviving dragons — fed mainly on insects.

Later, some reptiles turned to plants for food, and grew to massive proportions. They reached their ultimate form in the dinosaurs, a hugely successful group that ruled the earth for 100 million years. Because the Australian part of Gondwana was remote and difficult to reach even then, dinosaurs appeared here much later than in the rest of the world.

By 110 million years ago, Australia's skies were filled with flying reptiles that ranged in size from sparrows to creatures with a wingspan of 15 metres. Most of the flying dinosaurs, or pterosaurs, were probably fish-eaters that hunted over the shallow seas that covered inland Australia. The Australian fossil record is relatively poor, but dinosaurs appear to have existed here in a great diversity of forms and sizes. The most complete remains, found in central Queensland, are those of an iguanadon named *Muttaburrasaurus* — a plant-eater that reached a length of 11 metres.

Muttaburrasaurus probably browsed on foliage, often on all fours, but it could also stand on its hindlegs to reach higher veg-

An artist's reconstruction of *Allosaurus*, one of the great and varied company of dinosaurs that ruled Australia for 100 million years.

etation. It had a hollow chamber above its snout and in front of its eyes, which may have served to amplify sound or to sharpen its sense of smell. Both would have given it warning of the approach of the carnivorous *Rapator ornitholestoides*, which ran swiftly on its hindfeet — leaving its front claws free to grapple with its prey.

Large though *Muttaburrasaurus* was, there were even more gigantic dinosaurs: *Austrasaurus* was 17 metres long, and a sauropod known from a single vertebra found in northern Queensland has been estimated to measure 22 metres from snout to tail. Both had very long necks and browsed on the ferns, pines and cycads that grew in abundance in Australia's warm, moist climate.

Fossilised vertebrae and partial skeletons have helped us build an image of some of the individual inhabitants of that long-ago Australia. Other remains conjure, with vivid immediacy, a detailed portrait of an instant in the lives of some of those inhabitants. Near the outback Queensland town of Winton, a set of fossilised footprints records no more than a minute in the lives of 130 dinosaurs, 100 million years ago. They had gathered around the muddy shores of a freshwater lake to drink, to rest and to browse on the luxuriant ferns and conifers. There were two types — small, saurischian dinosaurs called coelurosaurs, which had feet with three long, thin and springy toes, and which ranged in size from chickens to half-grown emus; and larger ornithopods, up to the size of a full-grown emu, with heavier feet. Their prints in the mud, overlain by sand, clay and other sediments and hardened into sandstone, record what happened in the next few moments.

The peaceful gathering was put to panic-stricken flight — and the petrified mud also records the most likely cause: the slow, measured tread of a large, three-toed carnivorous dinosaur, a carnosaur, stalking the herd as it fed by the lake. Whether he succeeded, or whether all the browsers managed to escape, the rocks do not say: the picture freezes with all the tracks in full flight.

It is a brief glimpse, but enough to convey some sense of that long-ago world of creatures so different from the inhabitants of the present, yet so much the same in their essence: animals that ate and rested, that hunted and were hunted, that lived and died.

The dinosaurs were among the most successful — certainly the largest — forms of life ever. They held dominion over land, air and sea. But there was one region they could not conquer completely; a region not in space, but in time. The night, and all its opportunities, remained closed for the majority of dinosaurs.

For any creature that could remain active at night, there was a wealth of food to be tapped. Natural selection will not leave a niche unfilled for long, and at about the time the dinosaurs began their rise to prominence, other groups of reptiles began to show features that would enable them to maintain their internal warmth.

Muttaburrasaurus langdoni — one of the great diversity of dinosaurs that lived in Australia. This reconstruction is based on part of its skeleton, recovered from early Cretaceous deposits in central Queensland.

From among groups of small, lizard-like reptiles, creatures emerged whose teeth sheared against each other, enabling them to chew food faster and more efficiently (which enabled them to use more energy to generate body heat), and that had skin covered with dense fur to insulate and maintain that heat. From these animals, the modern mammals would arise.

Monotremes: the Early Mammals

The earliest mammals retained many of the features of their reptilian ancestors. The monotremes laid eggs, as do most reptiles, but they also had a very stable internal temperature, fur, and — even more significantly — they suckled their young with milk. Only three monotremes survive, all of them in Australasia: the platypus and two species of echidna, of which one is now found only in Papua New Guinea.

Much about the monotremes remains a mystery. They appeared perhaps 120 million years ago, and probably in the Australian part of Gondwana, for the only fossils have been found here. The oldest is an opalised jaw fragment 100 million years old, and

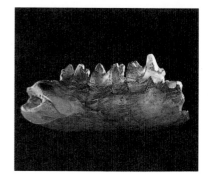

The opalised jawbone of a long-extinct monotreme. *Steropodon galmani*, thought to be an ancestor of the modern platypus.

The echidna's long snout serves it to search crevices and rotting wood for ants and termites.

A baby echidna in its burrow, where it hatched from an egg inside its mother's pouch 35 days earlier. Though its birth is like a reptile's, its infancy is truly that of a mammal, for it is suckled on its mother's milk.

possibly belonging to a more or less direct ancestor of the platypus: the next fossil, only 15 million years old, also belongs to a platypus-like animal. Because both the platypus and the echidna are highly specialised animals, there were probably many other, more generalised monotremes — yet no trace has so far been found of these other, mainstream animals.

The echidna's fur has become an armour of defensive spines; when it is threatened, it curls itself into a spiky and impregnable ball. Like a small, spiny bulldozer, it potters about in a busy search for food, its long tongue flickering out to lick up the ants and termites that are its main food. It has strong curved claws to rip open nests and mounds, and its insect food supplies all its moisture: the echidna is indeed an adaptable animal, at home in cool, temperate coastal regions as well as the hot inland. Its close relative, the long-beaked echidna (*Zaglossus bruijni*) thrives in the tropical rainforests of Papua New Guinea, where it feeds on worms.

One of the most fascinating aspects of the echidna's life is the way it reproduces — and how its reproduction may untangle some of the early threads of evolution. Monotremes can be seen as an early experiment in the mammalian mode of life — successful, but overshadowed by later experiments. It was an experiment that retained some ancestral reptilian features, especially reproduction.

Monotremes, like all true mammals, nurture their young until
they are able to fend for themselves. The young echidna is
now well grown — it is already foraging for termites and ants
in the company of its mother, and soon it will be independent.

The platypus (*Ornithorhynchus anatinus*), together with
echidnas, are the only surviving monotremes. The platypus
hunts crustaceans and other small aquatic animals in the
streams of eastern Australia, stores them in its cheek
pouches and returns to the surface to chew its catch.

In southeastern Australia, echidnas breed once a year in winter. For the male, mating is (understandably) a circumspect affair. The courtship is simple enough: he merely follows a prospective partner until she stops to let him mount. He penetrates her spiky defences with a long, flexible penis, but it is what happens next that marks one transition between reptile and mammal reproduction. After a gestation of about a fortnight, the female echidna retires to a nesting burrow and there, like a reptile, lays an egg.

Platypuses are covered in thick dense fur to insulate them from the often cold waters, and spend much time combing and grooming it with their hindclaws.

Unlike a reptile, however, the egg is laid into a pouch that formed on her belly in the last days of her pregnancy. And — again unlike a reptile — the embryo inside the egg has grown while it was in its mother's uterus. The female echidna remains in the burrow, incubating her egg until, after ten days, it hatches. The baby echidna struggles out of the eggshell with the aid of a special eggtooth, which falls off soon after birth — a temporary appendage it shares with some reptiles, and their descendants, the birds.

The newborn echidna's next move takes it to the feature central to the mammalian way of life. The hatchling is naked and blind but it can smell, and it uses that sense to find its way to a patch of its mother's skin which, stimulated by the birth, is now exuding milk. The two milk-producing, or mammary glands, lie beneath the skin, and the liquid is secreted through the pores (teats only appear in more advanced mammals). The milk feeds the young echidna as it grows inside the pouch for its first 60 days or so, until it develops (soft) spines of its own. Then, the female deposits what is by now a recognisable echidna in a safe place while she looks for food, returning from time to time to suckle her offspring. Eventually, the young echidna will follow her at foot. Maternal care lasts for about three months after the baby leaves the pouch, until it is large enough to fend for itself.

Long-term care of a young nurtured by milk represents an important new strategy for achieving life's most important objective: to perpetuate oneself. Among reptiles, the usual strategy is — and has always been — to produce a large number of eggs, provide them with some degree of protection, then leave them to take their chances, relying on the law of averages for some at least to survive. The monotremes were among the foundation members of a group that would individually produce relatively few young, but which would invest much energy in providing them with care that increases their chances of survival. The principal vehicle for that care is the mammary gland. Through it, mammals provide their young with not only food but protection — and an opportunity to learn to survive in the adult world before being exposed to its risks.

Ornithorhynchus anatinus is a far more specialised animal than even the echidna, and though they are related, the platypus is derived from a different line of evolution. Somewhere along that line it took to the water; which may have been a factor in its survival.

Though one of its earlier scientific names translates as 'paradoxical birdbeak', there is nothing paradoxical about the platypus. Its various adaptations add up to a very sensible solution to the problems of survival in its environment. Its body is streamlined, flattened top to bottom and covered with a dense brown fur to allow swift passage through the water. It swims mainly with its forepaws, which are webbed to form a fan-shaped paddle; the hindfeet act as rudders. The tail is flat and broad, like that of a beaver, and helps the platypus dive and rise. But the most remarkable feature is the snout. Shaped somewhat like a duck's bill but softer and more leathery to the touch, it is the platypus's most important sensory organ.

A clear mountain pool — a pause in the stream tumbling through a forest in the Tasmanian highlands — is a good place to see how that organ works. Late sun flashes on the rippling water as a platypus emerges from its burrow and slips down the bank. With a swift diving lunge and two or three powerful strokes of its forelimbs, it sails to the bottom, trailing bubbles from its fur.

As it moves along the floor of the pool, the platypus's eyes, ears and nostrils are closed, while its bill scoops through the sand and gravel in search of worms and small crustaceans. Pebbles are tossed aside and clouds of silt billow through the water as the platypus shovels its way along, sensing its food not by sight or smell, but with a special organ in the bill, capable of detecting the minute electromagnetic fields that surround its prey.

The hunting platypus stores its catch in cheek pouches; when they are full, it swims to the surface, there to chew and swallow before diving for more. Once it had teeth, but, like the echidna's, they were lost somewhere along the evolutionary road and the platypus does its chewing with horny pads on its upper and lower jaws.

Although its life is very different, the platypus's reproductive system is almost identical with that of its fellow monotreme survivor, with one variation: the female — understandably, given her aquatic home — does not develop a pouch in which to hold her eggs. Instead, she adopts a half-sitting position deep inside her burrow and folds her two eggs between her belly and her broad, flat tail, curling her nose to exhale warm, humid air into the area to help them incubate. She remains in this position, virtually immobile, until the eggs hatch about ten days after they are laid.

A newborn platypus looks almost exactly like a newborn echidna; and its first movement is the same, too: to the patch of skin oozing milk on the mother's belly. There is no teat, and the young sucks liquid from its mother's belly hair: but it is receiving both milk *and* maternal care. That development in the monotremes would open endless rows of evolutionary doors.

The young platypus are suckled in the nest for around three months, and toward the end of that time the mother takes them out for an occasional foray. They travel in her company up and down in the mountain stream, making their way through rapids and back again, swooping to the bottom of pools to search for food, gathering experience in the business of being a platypus. By the time they leave their mother's side, the young platypus are well able to look after themselves.

A Chance of Anatomy: the First Marsupials

The platypus and the echidna are specialised ends of a long line of monotreme evolution that has died out behind them. But there were other early mammal experiments elsewhere in Gondwana — and in Laurasia — the results of which would come to dominate the earth. Not that any observer would have predicted such grandeur of the tiny furred creatures that scurried through the night. That they were there at all was a matter of pure chance, for the reptiles from which they were descended — the synapsids — had all but died out, while the reptiles that were to give rise to the dinosaurs, the diapsids, marched on to become rulers of the earth.

Mammals would remain small and inconspicuous for the next 140 million years, but they underwent some important changes in that time. Because they hunted mainly by night, their senses of hearing, smell and touch became particularly acute, which led to the development of larger brains to process a variety of sensory information. Larger brains meant an increased capacity to learn, which reinforced the need (and the opportunity) for extended parental care and teaching.

The monotremes represent one solution: a combination of reptilian egg-laying with mammalian care. Slightly different solutions evolved in two other groups: the eutherians, or placental mammals, and the marsupials. The eutherians would provide a long period of development inside the mother's body, and a relatively short suckling stage. The marsupials would have a shorter gestation, but a much longer lactation.

Those differences would not become pronounced until some way down the evolutionary track. Primitive eutherians and marsupials were probably very similar, in their appearance as well as in their reproduction. The tree shrews, insect-eating eutherians that live in the forests of eastern Asia, illustrate the appearance of the earliest eutherians, and they also closely resemble a primitive survivor from the other side of the mammalian fence, the marsupial *Rhyncholestes raphanurus*, which lives in the cool mountain forests of South America. Both are small, with greyish-brown fur, a whiskered nose to find their way by touch in the dark, and sharp claws and teeth. Both are fast, voracious hunters of insects and other invertebrate prey, and opportunistic feeders on fruits and seeds.

And both give birth to tiny, naked young, which are then nurtured for some time while they complete their development.

The tree shrew young complete more of their development inside their mother's body than the young of *Rhyncholestes*, in which only the forelimbs are well formed. Their forelimbs enable them to haul themselves to their mother's teats, where they will complete their growth. Marsupial reproduction went on to the ultimate form of the kangaroo's well-developed pouches; the eutherian strategy led to the birth of young so well developed they are able to run with their mothers within a few hours.

What set the early marsupials and eutherians on their separate reproductive paths was simply a chance variation in anatomy. Somewhere among the proto-mammal group, the oviducts of some female embryos fused into a single vagina and uterus. In other embryos, that fusion did not happen, and the ducts formed two separate uteri and vaginae. A single uterus is larger than either of two separate wombs, and can accommodate an embryo to a much later stage of development. This was to become the eutherian reproductive technique. The twin uteri of the marsupials afforded limited scope for growth of the young, and after a relatively brief period inside their mother's body, the embryos completed the remainder of their development outside. And so, a chance reshuffle of perhaps only a few cells laid the foundations for the major divisions of mammals.

Antarctic beech (*Nothofagus cunninghamii*) is one of the earliest flowering plants. It dominated the forests that covered Australia 60 million years ago when the continent was still part of Gondwana, and it was these forests that saw the early radiations of the first marsupials.

Just where the first marsupials made their appearance remains a subject of vigorous debate, with various theories teetering on a few fragile pieces of evidence. The laws that govern science say that where a particular kind of organism is currently most diverse is its most probable centre of origin. That would make Australia the birthplace of the marsupials — but there is no fossil evidence to support this interpretation. The oldest marsupial fossils in Australia are only 23 million years old; older fossils have been found in South America, and show that at one time South America had a greater diversity of marsupials than Australia has today.

Which could make South America the marsupials' centre of origin, except that the oldest fossil so far known was found in Texas. An animal called *Holoclemensia texana* lived there 120 million years ago — though some experts are not convinced it was a marsupial.

Which would put South America back in the running . . . except for a discovery made in far northern Australia in 1985: a tiny fragment of fossil tooth 100 million years old. The fragment is not sufficiently complete for a definitive identification, but it *could* belong to a marsupial.

Until there is more fossil evidence, answers to where the marsupials arose will remain elusive. In the meantime, the tiny *Rhyncholestes* of South America remains as close a living relative of the ancestors of all marsupials as is likely to be found.

Gondwana: the End of the Beginning

The journey that began in an Australian eucalypt woodland, and that traced its way back through evolutionary and geological twists and turns in time and space, pauses now in a forest in the South American division of Gondwana, around 100 million years ago.

Dinosaurs are still dominant, and the ancestral mammals, both marsupials and eutherians, are still confined to the night. The plants among which they live have remained much the same for 100 million years: uniform stretches of conifers that resemble kauri, with understoreys of cycads and tree ferns. All relied mostly on wind for pollination, but a new type of plant was emerging in the understorey — one that set flowers to attract insects, pressing them into service as couriers for its pollen.

Just where the flowering plants first appeared is also a matter of speculation, but it was probably somewhere in the forests of Gondwana. The arrival of the flowers and the new method of reproduction they represented was as much a revolution in the plant world as was the arrival of the mammals and their new way of procreation in the animal kingdom. And, like the mammals, the flowering plants remained for a long time a small and inconspicuous component of a world still dominated by their conservative predecessors. Like actors waiting in the wings, their cue was about to come: a series of cataclysmic events remade the world and set the stage for a new ascendancy.

The supercontinent of Gondwana was breaking up. Massive shifts in the earth's crust sent huge pieces drifting off to form separate continents: Africa broke away first, then India and New Zealand. Then, around 65 million years ago, the dinosaurs that had ruled for so long vanished.

Many possible causes have been advanced to explain the disappearance of the dinosaurs, among them that changes in oceanic current patterns (and consequent changes in world climatic cycles) triggered by the breakup of Gondwana produced a short, sharp cold spell to which the dinosaurs succumbed en masse. Another theory poses an 'asteroid winter', caused when the dust from a huge meteorite impact obscured the sun for several years. (The theory has a certain macabre appeal to a species facing its own extinction in a similar kind of winter, albeit one that is the result of the machinations of its own, improved brain.)

None of the theories advanced to date explain why dinosaurs took several million years to die out. Indeed, recent research has indicated there is nothing particularly remarkable about their extinction: the death of an animal group is as common, given the vast sweep of geological time, as the death of an individual animal.

No matter what, if anything, led to the extinction of the dinosaurs, when the sun rose on a world without the 'terrible lizards', it rose on a world going through other, equally great changes. The equilibrium that had existed for many hundreds of millions of years had been disturbed, and any organism with a reproductive advantage over others would thrive. The mammals and the flowering plants were about to have their day.

The primeval forests of gymnosperms — the conifers and podocarps, with their understoreys of tree ferns — were being swept aside by the advance of the flowering plants. And as the flowers extended their dominion, so did the early marsupials. For them, flowers offered energy-rich nectar and protein-rich pollen, and attracted an abundance of insects. In this new and favourable environment, the omnivorous marsupials spread rapidly through the Americas and deep into Gondwana.

They also reached Europe and northern Africa, by way of connections through the Americas. They did not survive there, however, possibly because of competition from eutherian mammals; nor did they appear to reach Asia.

It was the southern continents — South America, Australia and Antarctica — that became the marsupials' strongholds; in some places, animals and plants survive little changed from those early ages. One such place is a forest of southern or Antarctic beech,

Opposite

In northern New South Wales, past and present come together: eucalypts frame a view of *Nothofagus* forests at New England National Park. Eucalypts now dominate Australia's wooded margins.

Nothofagus, one of the earliest of the flowering plants, in the far south of Chile. Younger plants — bamboos — grow in thickets in open patches of *Nothofagus* forest, and that is where *Dromiciops australis*, the colocolo, makes its home. It belongs to a somewhat more recent group than the shrew-like *Rhyncholestes*, with which it shares the forests; and it looks just like a tiny possum. And that resemblance is significant, for the colocolo is a key figure in the natural history of Australia's marsupials. If *Rhyncholestes* represents the ancient, ancestral marsupial, *Dromiciops* is close to the founding fathers of the Australian families

Keeping its small body warm and moving needs relatively large amounts of food, and the colocolo spends almost every waking moment foraging busily through the undergrowth for insects and fruit. It also uses bamboo leaves to make a roughly spherical nest, and has been seen carrying nesting material curled up in its prehensile tail. When food supplies run low in winter, it curls up in its nest and goes into torpor for a few days, in a kind of suspended animation. Come spring the colocolo breeds, and the female has two to five young in her pouch by December. When the young grow too big for the pouch, the mother carries them on her back while she goes foraging: a scene that in its essentials is little changed from 60 million years ago, when *Nothofagus* spread its green mantle across the southern landmasses of Gondwana in a vast forest that stretched from South America, across Antarctica (where much fossil pollen has been discovered) and Australia. And as it spread, the ancestral marsupials went with it.

Stages of a continental journey: 150 million years ago, Australia was part of the supercontinent of Gondwana, 100 million years ago, the great landmass was breaking up — Africa and India had departed. 40 million years ago Australia had separated, and was moving north. By about 15 million years ago, it had moved into tropical latitudes, close to its position on the globe today.

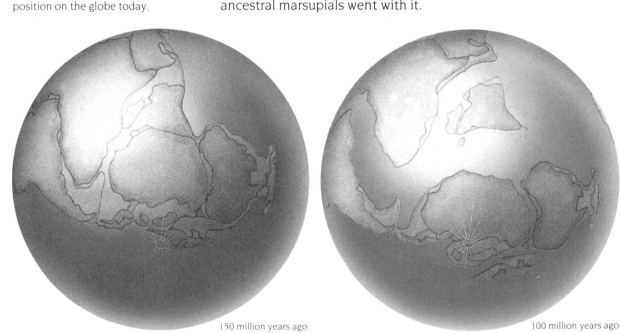

150 million years ago   100 million years ago

Southern beech forest very similar to that of southern Chile still exists in Australia, in Tasmania and in highland pockets on the mainland. To walk through these cool, damp and almost silent forests is to walk back into Gondwana. Green light filters down through the canopy, and the forest floor is covered with mosses, ragworts, rotting logs, ferns and treeferns. In patches of less fertile soil grow proteas, like *Nothofagus* itself among the most ancient of the flowering plants. Animal life is inconspicuous in the beech forest, but the eucalypt and banksia woodlands that have displaced it over most of its former range are alive with stirrings come nightfall.

A whiskered nose emerges from a hollow, tests the air. A pair of bright eyes becomes visible. A moment later, an animal appears that bears a striking resemblance to the colocolo of the Chilean *Nothofagus* forest 12,000 kilometres away across the southern ocean. It is the eastern pygmy (*Cercatetus nanus*), and the likeness is not only in looks, but also in behaviour. Scurrying over the forest floor, up and down trunks and branches, it runs in a tireless quest for food. Like the colocolo, the eastern pygmy possum is an omnivore — as adept at catching insects as it is at reaching nectar-rich flowers or buds and fruits.

And also like the colocolo, it seeks refuge in a nest and goes into torpor in cool weather, when there is not enough food to maintain its high metabolic rate. Curling up tightly, the pygmy possum slows its breathing; its body temperature falls close to that of its surroundings and will stay that way for up to two weeks.

An animal very much like the pygmy possum was among the

Like *Nothofagus*, banksias are among the earliest flowering plants. Now they often form an understorey in eucalypt woodlands, where their flowers provide nectar for eastern pygmy possums (*Cercatetus nanus*).

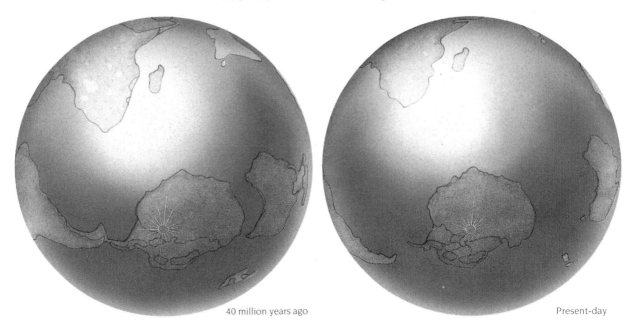

40 million years ago   Present-day

first marsupials to settle in Australia. It was such tiny ancestors that gave rise to the many and diverse marsupials that would make the continent their stronghold. Just why marsupials rather than eutherians came to dominate mammal life in Australia is one of those vexing questions that have several possible answers, but no clear-cut proof for any single explanation. Leaving out the possibility that marsupials originated here, and were already too well established for eutherians to compete, the most likely answer lies in what was happening to Gondwana around the time the marsupials were migrating to its Australian component.

The massive shifts in the earth's crust that were rifting the southern supercontinent, and that had already sent Africa and India on their separate ways, began to sever Australia's ties with Antarctica — its link with Gondwana — about 80 million years ago, when the marsupials were already well established. That they were established in Antarctica at least 40 million years ago was proved with a fossil find on Seymour Island, on the South American side of Antarctica. That is all the discovery proves, however: it provides no help to the question of origins, since the Antarctic marsupials could have been part of a migration from an Australian origin to the rest of Gondwana, or vice versa.

Perhaps eutherian mammals simply did not reach Australia before it was completely cut off from other landmasses 45 million years ago, so the marsupials were free of other mammal competition. In any event, it seems fairly certain that once Australia was cast adrift on its voyage into isolation, the marsupials had the run of the continental raft. Any eutherians that might have been aboard only survived for part of the journey.

The First Australians

The first Australian marsupials were in all likelihood tree-dwellers. The pygmy possum represents one ancestral group — the diprotodonts — from which the kangaroos and wallabies would eventually derive. Another major group is the marsupial carnivores — the dasyurids. Its ancestral members may have looked and behaved very much like the phascogales that live on in forested and wooded country around the edge of the continent.

They are much larger than the pygmy possum. The most common, the tuans, are twice as long, and eight times as heavy: at 200 grams they are still no heavyweights, yet they are ferocious hunters that fearlessly tackle prey larger than themselves. Like their remote ancestors, tuans spend most of their lives in the trees. In daylight hours they shelter in a nest lined with leaves or shredded bark in a tree hollow, emerging at dusk to hunt spiders, centipedes — and virtually anything else that will make a meal. Tuans sometimes

share a nest, and when hunting alert each other to danger by drumming their forefeet.

There is no way of knowing, of course, how much of this behaviour has been inherited from the past, or how much was acquired along the way. The pygmy possum and the phascogale are the end points of two long lines of evolution, but they both retain enough original features to build up a composite portrait of Australia's very first marsupial inhabitants: small tree-dwellers, which fed variously on insects and the more easily digested parts of plants — nectar and fruits. From these basically omnivorous ancestors arose the three main groups of Australian marsupials: the carnivores, the bandicoots (which are still omnivorous) and the largely herbivorous possums, from which would emerge the line leading, eventually, to the kangaroos and wallabies.

Supplies of the original omnivores' diet of nectar, pollen, fruits and insects increased enormously with the advent and diversification of the flowering plants; and as the opportunities increased, so did the number of marsupials. But flowering plants bring with them seasonal variations in food supplies.

An eastern barred bandicoot (*Perameles gunnii*) — a member of one of Australia's main three groups of marsupials. Its forefeet have long claws to scoop out shallow pits from which it digs earthworms and insects.

One way to cope with the occasional shortfall was for animals to go into torpor. Another was to make use of foods available all the year round — leaf-buds and leaves. Leaves are bulky, and require time to digest. They need strong grinding as well as shearing teeth, and a large gut in which to process food. Bulky food required larger animals . . . and the possums were on their way.

Larger size made a difference to the way animals moved around in trees. Smaller creatures, such as the pygmy possum and phascogales, can run fairly conventionally: there is enough room on the surface of the branches for them to use a one-foot-after-the-other style of locomotion. As animals grew larger, there was less room for their feet to move in this way and still keep their balance, so there was pressure toward the evolution of a synchronised pushing with the hindlimbs: a trend reinforced by (or possibly inspiring) a curious phenomenon among the arboreal proto-possums: a fusion of the second and third toes on the hindfeet. This was the genesis of the marsupial hop.

In the forests of southeastern Australia, between the Great Dividing Range and the coast, a mountain brushtail possum or bobuck

The elusive musky rat kangaroo (*Hypsiprymnodon moschatus*) lives in the rainforests of north Queensland. The most primitive of the kangaroo family, and close to its founding fathers, it feeds on fallen fruits, and turns over the leaf litter in search of insects. It also buries food, 'squirrelling' it away for later consumption.

(*Trichosurus caninus*) climbs out of its daytime nest high up in the hollow of a tree. Cautiously, it moves along a branch to the main trunk of the tree, its hindfeet moving together. It is a robust animal, nearly half a metre long. Occasionally it stops, squats on its haunches, pulls a spray of leaves closer with its forepaws and munches awhile. Its teeth make an efficient grinding mill for the tough and fibrous material, and its gut is well equipped to extract what little food value there is in the leaves. Once possum stomachs could cope with leaves, a whole range of other plant food became available as well — much of it on the ground, in the form of buds on low shrubs, fungi and lichens: so animals that once were strictly arboreal began to come down from the trees.

The bobuck's ancestors were among those early venturers. Although it spends the day in its treetop nest, much of the bobuck's active night is spent on the ground, searching for food. It marks out territory with scent secreted from glands on its chin, on its chest and around its anus. An adult bobuck will stand up to an intruder of its own species, but should there be any sign of danger — from a descendant of one of the ancestral groups that took the carnivorous road, or a carpet python hunting at night — the gait it acquired to keep its balance aloft switches into action, and it leaps for the nearest tree, racing up the trunk to safety.

Brush-tailed phascogales (*Phascogale tapoatafa*) are typical of the small marsupial carnivores that thrive in the Australian woodlands. Fierce hunters of insect prey, they are agile climbers, and their hindfeet can rotate backwards, so they can scamper up or down treetrunks with equal ease.

The Proto-Kangaroos

The early possums' first move to the ground opened up a whole new range of adaptive possibilities. From sharing their time between the canopy and the forest floor, some marsupials moved to spend their entire lives on the ground. One such was the musky rat kangaroo (*Hypsiprymnodon moschatus*). Now a rare and elusive animal that inhabits a few isolated patches of Queensland's lowland rainforest, the tiny musky rat kangaroo is of an ancient lineage, with characteristics that put it very close to the direct link between the possums and the ancestors of modern kangaroos and wallabies. It is certainly the most primitive living kangaroo.

One sign that points to its climbing past is the cross-hatched skin on its soles and palms. Another is the possum-like big toe on its hindfeet: later members of the kangaroo family have lost that big toe. Its diet, too, testifies to the musky rat kangaroo's 'primitiveness' — a mixture of insects, earthworms and other small invertebrates as well as fruits and other plant material. The hindleg bound that evolved as an aid to balance in the trees now proves useful for getting around on the cluttered forest floor.

Unusually among marsupials, *Hypsiprymnodon* is an animal of the daylight hours (strictly speaking, it is crepuscular, most active early in the morning and late in the afternoon). It spends the rest of its

A female rufous bettong (*Aepyprymnus rufescens*) with her young in the nest where they spend the day. These tiny animals represent an early stage in the evolution of kangaroos — they feed on roots and tubers, from which they also obtain most of the water they need.

time sleeping in a nest of dried leaves and ferns, which it gathers in a manner reminiscent of its arboreal past — it carries the leaves curled up in a tail that in later kangaroos is a rigid rudder.

When the musky rat kangaroo retires to its rainforest nest for the night, the rufous bettong emerges from its very similar den in the drier forests further south. The rufous bettong (*Aepyprymnus rufescens*) represents the next stage in the development of the kangaroo-like marsupials. With so much food available at ground level (and a lot below ground, too), the early macropods began to specialise. Some, such as the rufous bettong, use their forepaws to dig up underground food — roots, bulbs and fungi. Their gut has evolved a stage beyond that of *Hypsiprymnodon*, to cope with more fibrous plant material.

The first macropods were rather solitary animals. The nature of their food made them so: foraging for a bulb here, a root there, takes time and energy, and it would not do to have other animals around, perhaps snatching the piece of food that has taken so much effort to uncover. Being solitary and small, the natural way to avoid predators is to hide from them rather than to attempt to out-run them. But should a predator chance on an animal in its nest, the quarry needs a reliable escape mechanism: for the proto-kangaroos it was the hindlegged bound, which enabled them to leap away from beneath a predator's nose in an explosive burst. By the time the hunter recovers, the quarry is hidden again.

What began as a means of balance in the trees and developed into a ground-level bound was now a more defined hopping gait, with most of the locomotion left to the hindfeet. This left the forepaws free to manipulate food, to bring choice buds and shoots within reach and to help strip them. With the greater reliance on plant food there was also a trend to greater size, for the larger an animal, the lower its metabolic rate: the amount of food it needs for the energy it uses. Most plant material is very low in proteins and simple sugars, so a larger animal can process more food. There is an advantage in more efficient processing, too: what began as a fairly simple tube-like stomach in the possums and the rat kangaroos be-came a tube with a sac-like section in the bettongs. The tube trans-ports and stores the herbage, while the sac does the digesting in a system that became more complex and efficient in the potoroos, another early group of macropods.

With proto-kangaroo groups similar to bettongs and potoroos adapting to life among the shrubs and groundcover of the early Australian forests — feet used for hopping, forepaws for manipu-lating food, stomachs equipped to handle tough plant food — and the possum groups and some of the dasyurids continuing to colon-ise the higher levels of the forests, all the elements were in place for one of the remarkable events of natural history: the swift radiation of the Australian marsupials into nearly every niche that opened up as the continent drifted north into isolation . . . and was transformed in the process.

The South American Connection

Back where the marsupials had emerged, they would not have such a clear evolutionary run. South America had also become isolated soon after Australia, but by that time some primitive groups of eutherians had become well established — and the marsupials found themselves sharing the continent with rivals. They evolved into a fairly peaceful coexistence, however: while the marsupials continued to feed chiefly on insects, mainly at night, the eutherians moved into the plant-eating niches, many of them daytime opportunities left vacant by the extinction of the dinosaurs.

Typical of these primitive eutherians are the sloths, which move slowly among the foliage of the South American rainforest, feeding on leaves, blossoms and fruits. They never come down to drink since the foliage and the dew provide all the moisture they need. A sloth (there are actually six species) looks like a soggy bathmat — and moves about as quickly. But its virtual immobility is a defence measure, as is the green camouflage created by algae growing on its hair. Between them, they serve to blend the sloth into its background to escape the searching eyes of any predator.

Sloths and their relatives among the primitive eutherians were not only slow, but were also solitary and silent. South American rainforests 40 million years ago were probably not unlike Australian rainforests now — quiet places inhabited by secretive, unobtrusive animals, silent but for the occasional call of early birds. Then, around 30 million years ago, new sounds began to be heard: the screech and chatter of monkeys. Just how they got to South America is still a matter of some debate — either via a temporary land bridge falling sea-levels had opened up across the isthmus of central America, or by an island-hopping route across the Atlantic from Africa, at that time still relatively close to South America.

However they arrived in South America, primates evolved quickly and spread through the forests to dominate the daytime canopy, leaving the marsupials undisturbed in their nocturnal niches. Primate social systems increased in complexity, and so did the visual and vocal signals that held them together.

Among howler monkeys, vocal signals have developed to a remarkable degree. Howlers move about in small troops, each of which has its own feeding range. The dominant males of each troop howl to warn other troops to keep out of the way. Of the two species of howler — the red and the black — it is the red males that

produce the loudest calls. Both red and black howlers have specialised larynxes surrounded by a greatly enlarged hyoid bone that
supports a resonating chamber. The result is a roar that can carry
for 3 kilometres: a device that helps conserve energy, for calling involves much less effort than fighting.

And it is important for howler monkeys to conserve energy,
since half their food comes from leaves that are high in fibre but low
in energy-producing sugars. Their need to conserve energy also
has social consequences: work is divided between the sexes, with
the stronger males settling disputes and defending important food
trees, and the females looking after the young. And this in turn
means more efficient exploitation of the food resources and better
protection against potential predators.

Pouched Hunters and Killer Birds

As the eutherians diversified into the various plant-eating niches
that developed in South America, the primitive marsupial
insectivores evolved into hunters. Collectively they are called
borhyaenids: the lions, tigers and jaguars of their time, hunting
marsupial and eutherian prey alike.

Reconstructions show them to have been rather stocky animals, short-legged and heavily built — more like robust dogs than
sleek cats. There were twelve main genera, ranging from one the
size of a small fox to one as large as a modern lion. Borhyaena, the
species that lent its name to the entire group, was as large as a
brown bear, with a hyaena-like skull and teeth, that enabled it to
crush bones. The borhyaenids were an immensely successful
group, ruling the South American forests and woodlands for some
30 million years.

From one of the borhyaenids arose what was probably the
most spectacular marsupial hunter of all time; Thylacosmilus, a marsupial sabre-toothed tiger armed with large, stabbing teeth that
were probably used to slash the soft throat of its prey. The teeth
were larger, and longer, than those that developed in true cats, and
kept growing, unlike those of the eutherian sabre-toothed tigers.
Thylacosmilus' skull even had a deep flange on its lower jaw, as a
'sheath' to protect the sabres when not in use.

Eventually, most of the sabre-tooth's fellow marsupial hunters
succumbed to competition from an unlikely quarter: large, fast-
running ground birds that used massive beaks to stab and rip their
prey. The phororhacoids were more like latter-day carnivorous
dinosaurs than birds. Their power and speed proved superior to
the borhyaenids, and they took over the role of large predators.

But the sabre-toothed Thylacosmilus and its close relatives survived unchallenged until a great upheaval that completely

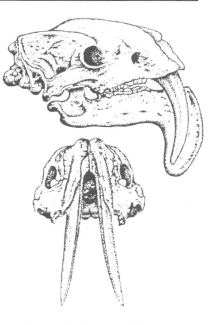

A front and side view of the skull
of the marsupial sabre-tooth,
Thylacosmilus.

changed the make-up of South American life. The upheaval followed a temporary end to the continent's isolation, when sea levels dropped and a land bridge emerged to join North and South America two million years ago. Across the bridge came new types of animals — while South America and its mammals had been in isolation, there had been a great wave of adaptive radiations in the northern continents. Conditions there had fluctuated more sharply, and had led to many more evolutionary experiments. For some reason marsupials did not survive, but the eutherians that had passed the evolutionary tests now began to filter through to South America, there to displace and out-compete many of the original inhabitants.

Whatever chance the South American marsupials might have had of extending their range into daylight vanished again. The more highly developed eutherians simply left the marsupials where they had always been — in the dark. Those marsupials that had managed to carve themselves a daytime niche — the sabre-toothed *Thylacosmilus* and its relatives — were totally outclassed by the eutherian jaguar, panther, ocelot and other members of the cat group; sleek and fast hunters whose physiques had been honed to perfection in the demanding environments of the north.

The herbivores that formed their prey changed, too. The primitive eutherian ungulates — the rabbit, camel and horse lookalikes that had been hunted by the marsupial carnivores — disappeared, and the precursors of the modern South American grazers, the llamas, vicunas and deer, took their place. Bears and raccoons were also among the immigrants. It was not all one-way traffic. Some of the porcupines and opossums made their way north: in North America today, the Virginia opossum is a widespread and successful animal, in fact, its name comes from the Algonquin word for 'white animal'.

Webbed Feet and a Reshuffle

For the marsupials of South America, the night was to remain their chief domain: it continued to offer them plentiful food and living space; there was little need for specialisation, and marsupials generally remained small, all-purpose animals that could exploit their environment efficiently. One opossum did move beyond the forest confines, to become the only marsupial known to have taken to life in the water. The yapok (*Chironectes minimus*) takes its name from the river Oyapok in Guyana.

It is a striking animal, with dense black or dark grey fur striped with silvery-white or light grey. A pouch should be a hindrance for an animal that spends most of its active time in water, but the yapok copes by having one that opens to the rear. While she is

diving it becomes a watertight chamber, sealed off by fatty secretions and long hair around its lip.

Just how the young survive while their mother is underwater is something of a mystery: presumably, there is enough trapped air to last them until the pouch opens again.

Webbed hindfeet moving with alternate strokes propel the yapok through the water while she uses her forepaws to feel for fish and crustaceans. She hunts by touch rather than by sight because the yapok hunts by night: she spends the day in a hole in the riverbank, and that is where she leaves her young — up to six of them — when they grow too big for the pouch.

The yapok has a place of its own, but the other marsupials that survived found themselves sharing the night with some of the newly arrived eutherians.

Typical of these invaders is the kinkajou, a member of the raccoon family, which exploits the same resources by night as monkeys do by day, feeding primarily on large fruits such as figs,

The yapok (*Chironectes minimus*), a South American opossum and the only known aquatic marsupial. Its hindfeet are webbed to provide swimming power, and the fingers are tipped with sensitive pads with which it feels for its prey of crustaceans and fish.

The spotted-tailed quoll (*Dasyurus maculatus*), also called the tiger cat. It hunts through the forests of eastern Australia for birds, reptiles and possums — a living link with Australia's golden age of marsupials, when its ancestors were part of a great company of pouched predators.

avocado and mango — the same food as one of the more common of the opossums, the red woolly opossum (*Caluromys laniger*). Like its marsupial counterpart, the kinkajou relies on smell to find fruit in the dark forest night.

The kinkajou and woolly opossum rarely find themselves in direct competition, however, for rainforests offer some kind of fruit virtually all year round. There is usually plenty for eutherian and marsupial alike.

And, while some of their food preferences overlap, there is enough difference to avoid direct competition. The kinkajou relies almost solely on fruit, while the woolly opossum is also a skilful and agile hunter; insects and other invertebrates make up around twenty per cent of its diet.

Unlike the monkeys whose niche they occupy at night, kinkajous are largely solitary animals. Night promotes solitude, for darkness prevents the visual contact that keeps animals together. Nocturnal animals rely mainly on smell, and the kinkajou lays a scent trail with special chest glands to mark its movements — and to help males find females, come breeding time.

Although there was a degree of overlap in food preferences between resident marsupials and 'invading' eutherians, the pressures of evolution eventually enabled them to reach an accommodation in time, so their peak periods of activity did not coincide, and in space, so that size and greater or lesser climbing ability kept them out of each other's way at the various levels of the forest.

Early Australia

While marsupials were enduring mixed fortunes in South America, very different pressures were acting on their Australian cousins, whose island continent had carried them away from competition with other mammal groups. Parts of Tasmania still evoke what much of early Australia looked like: a land covered in temperate rainforest. Mists swirl through the silent forests of southern beech, with mosses and ferns in the wetter gullies and an understorey of proteas such as *Banksia* and *Hakea* in the drier, less fertile places. In the forests survivors of what in that long-ago age had evolved into a rich and varied company of marsupial carnivores — the pouched equivalents of panthers, tigers and wolves — still roam.

The demands of hunting other animals tend to mould predators into a similar basic shape, and there is a remarkable physical similarity between the marsupial carnivores and their eutherian counterparts. One of the largest of the surviving marsupial hunters is the spotted-tailed quoll or tiger cat (*Dasyurus maculatus*). It looks much like one of the medium-sized hunting cats of South America, with its spotted fur, strong, sharp teeth, powerful claws and a

A smaller relative of the spotted-tailed quoll is the eastern quoll (*Dasyurus viverrinus*), which mostly hunts insects and small mammals. When the young grow too large for the pouch, they cling to their mother's back — even when she goes searching for the night's food.

crouching spring that means swift death for a range of prey, from birds and reptiles to possums, both in the trees and on the ground.

A smaller, more slightly built relative is the cat-sized eastern quoll (*Dasyurus viverrinus*). Although it may share the larger tiger cat's habitat, there is no direct competition: the two match their prey to their size, and the eastern quoll's most important food is insects, supplemented with regular meals of fruits and even grass.

As befits nocturnal hunters, both quolls are solitary animals; they socialise with other members of their species only at breeding time. Copulation lasts up to eight hours, with the male spotted quoll holding his mate in position by grasping her neck.

Her pouch begins to develop almost immediately from a few rudimentary folds to a deep, moist chamber that receives the five or six young after a gestation period of 21 days. When they grow too large for the pouch, the female deposits the young quolls in a den — a nest of plant material in a hollow log or cave — while she goes hunting. She returns to suckle her young, and to introduce them to solid food, until they are large enough to fend for themselves.

The quolls are living links with the golden age of Australia's marsupial kingdom. They are the last direct representatives of what was once a great diversity, just as the Tasmanian forests in which they live are today merely remnants of vegetation that once covered most of the continent.

The course of marsupial evolution and radiation in the first 25 million years of Australia's geographical independence remains a mystery. There are few fossils from this period, so we have hardly any clues about what was happening in those hidden forests. The continent and its inhabitants had drifted off into the unknown; but whatever did happen set the scene for one of the most remarkable chapters in evolutionary history.

A Golden Age

When the fossil record resumes after its 25-million-year interruption, it reveals an Australia rich with life more varied than the continent had ever seen before, or would see again. The evidence lies entombed in rock at Riversleigh, in northwestern Queensland. Now a parched and barren place, Riversleigh's abundance of fossils testifies to a time of lushness and plenty.

During its lost aeons, Australia had passed through several phases of cooler, drier climates, but by 15 million years ago most of the continent was lush and warm. Rain fell almost every day, and much of the interior was under water.

There was a huge inland sea, and large lakes fed by wide, slow rivers. The waters teemed with giant crocodiles and freshwater dolphins, turtles and lungfish, and platypuses somewhat larger than

Opposite

An Australian scene as it might have been in the Pliocene Age, 4.5 million years ago: rainforests were being replaced by drier woodlands, and the giant browsing marsupials were giving way to grazing kangaroos, such as the banded *Troposodon* in the background. There may even have been carnivorous kangaroos — the propleopines. The shape of some fossil teeth suggests the foreground scene — though the idea of killer kangaroos remains controversial.

The last known wild thylacine (*Thylacinus cypocephalus*) was captured in 1933 and died in 1936. This is an artist's recreation of the marsupial 'wolf' in its last refuge, the forests of Tasmania. Miocene Australia harboured a great variety of these carnivores.

Palorchestes azael which belonged to the order Diprotodonta was the size of a bull, had massive forearms equipped with razor-sharp claws about 12 cm long, a longish trunk, and may have used a long, curling tongue in feeding.

the modern species. In the shallows flamingos waded, their bills sweeping the water for fish and crustaceans. Roaming the forests were large, flightless birds, forerunners of cassowaries and emus. The forest was home to a great variety of possum- and cuscus-like animals, and among them prowled marsupial carnivores, including a fierce hunter called *Wakaleo*.

On the forest floor tiny, primitive proto-potoroos ate insects, fallen fruits and the green tips of low shrubs. From among these rabbit-sized creatures would arise Australia's most characteristic animals, the kangaroos and wallabies. But at that time the ancestral kangaroos were only minor players: the stage was dominated by a large and varied group of diprotodonts, which share a common ancestry with wombats.

They were lumbering beasts, mostly browsers, and developed some strange forms with prehensile lips to seize and manoeuvre the plants on which they fed. There were even several species of tapir-like marsupials, with well-developed trunks. Among the most bizarre was *Palorchestes*: as well as a pendulous trunk, it had enormous narrow and curving claws, incisor teeth like those of kangaroos, a long tongue and a heavy tail.

The varied company of animals that flourished in the lush forests of Miocene Australia 15 million years ago meant an abundance of food for a range of flesh-eaters. As well as marsupial lions such as *Wakaleo*, there were wolf-like thylacines — and there may even have been carnivorous kangaroos, the propleopines, whose teeth were more like those of flesh-eaters than herbivores.

One species of marsupial wolf survived in Tasmania into modern times; and though sometimes called a tiger for the camouflage stripes across its back, its teeth and the shape of its head and forequarters are much more wolf-like. Unlike wolves, however, thylacines were apparently solitary hunters, wearing their prey down in dogged pursuit. Sometimes two would combine to make a kill, then share the proceeds.

Together with the other marsupial hunters, the quolls, thylacines are thought to be descended from a primitive dasyurid. They were remarkably similar to some of the South American borhyaenids; indeed, so great was the similarity that thylacines and borhyaenids were at one time thought to be closely related. In fact, each probably evolved independently and underwent similar adaptations to meet similar challenges in a phenomenon called convergence.

Thylacines tended to eat only certain parts of their prey, and what they left of a carcass was enough to sustain another group of flesh-eaters that specialised in feeding on carrion. Of that specialised group, the Tasmanian Devil, *Sarcophilus harrisii*, is the last survivor. Its unearthly howls and hellhound appearance have earned the devil its name, but it is far more a scavenger than a night stalker: its powerful jaws can crush the largest bones, and little remains of a carcass after a group of devils has finished with it. Although, like most nocturnal animals, they are solitary beasts, a large carcass — a kangaroo, say, or a horse or cow — attracts up to ten or so animals. Growling and screaming at each other, jaws agape, the devils squabble through their communal meal without ever actually coming to blows. Now restricted to the island of Tasmania, the devil was once widespread across the continent.

The devil's line arose at the beginning of the end of the good times; the great revolution in the nature of Australia. The climatic changes set in train when Australia's separation from Gondwana created new ocean, wind and pressure patterns began to catch up with the new continent around 15 million years ago. The rain-bearing winds that had penetrated to its heart fell away, the forests the rains had sustained began to vanish . . . and most of their animals with them. But as the movement of the continental plates led to climatic change, so created refuges for some of the forests, and for some of the animals that lived in them.

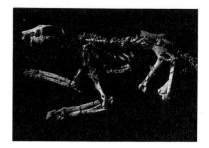

The thylacine's skeleton reveals its marsupial nature in the structure of the hindlegs. It had a stiff gait, could not run very fast, and wore its prey down with dogged pursuit.

A Living Museum

Around the same time, Australia's northward journey — which had been quite rapid, at around six centimetres a year — slowed as it encountered the massive continental plate that carried Asia and, on its edge, a chain of islands. That leading edge (part of which now forms the northern part of Papua New Guinea) collided with the leading edge of the Australian plate, which is now the southern half of Papua New Guinea. The edges crumpled upward and the Papua New Guinea highlands were born.

While the rest of what was still Greater Australia — continental Australia, Papua New Guinea and Tasmania all joined in one landmass — was drying out, the uplift of the mountains pushed remnants of the once universal forests into rain-generating, wetter altitudes, so preserving them. In one sense, to walk up a mountain in Papua New Guinea is to walk back in time.

The steep, densely forested slopes and hidden valleys of the highlands have given rise to their own patterns of life. It takes a spectacular song and dance to attract a mate in the forest gloom, and the pressures of selection have endowed the birds of paradise with a breathtaking range of colourful plumage, often accompanied by remarkable song. Each species is restricted to a defined range of altitude, so making the birds of paradise collectively the loveliest altimeter on earth.

Underlying the spectacular new colours of the Papua New Guinea highlands is a picture of ancient Australia; some of the

Riversleigh fossils return to life here. How rich the ancient Australian forests were can still be measured in these highland refuges. They harbour most of Papua New Guinea's 50 or so species of marsupials, while Australia — nine times larger — has only two and a half times that number; 130. The richest diversity of marsupial life is found in the lower montane forests, between 1000 and 3100 metres. Southern beech and oak-laurel are the dominant tree communities, and with their shrub understoreys they provide the forest animals with food and shelter at a number of levels, from the ground to the canopy.

The highest canopy level is occupied by the phalangers — the possums and cuscuses. Well-developed prehensile tails, large and strong claws and a slow, deliberate way of moving have equipped them well for their lives aloft, making the phalangers the marsupial equivalent of monkeys, sloths and squirrels.

Although they live on the same level of the forest, they avoid competition with different diets. The very tops of the trees are the province of the black and white striped possum (*Dactylopsila trivirgata*), which feeds on a variety of upperstorey insects, fruits,

The highlands of Papua New Guinea and the forests of the northernmost tip of Australia are home to many marsupials such as the spotted cuscus (*Phalanger maculatus*), once common across the continent in lusher times. The cuscus is a slow, methodical climber, that feeds mostly on fruit, flowers and leaves.

leaves, nestlings and small birds. Another possum of the treetops, the feather-tailed *Distoechurus pennatus*, feeds solely on fruits and flowers, and there is a group of ringtails that feeds only on leaves.

The middle zone of the forest is occupied by animals that climb up and down the treetrunks, commuting between the forest floor and the canopy: other species of striped possum that feed on insects, and a tiny relative, the New Guinea pygmy possum, that eats plant matter as well as insects.

Lower still, in that layer of the forest made up of the bushes and shrubs of the understorey and the tangle of fallen trees, range the dasyurids — fierce mouse-sized insect hunters such as *Antechinus*, the red-cheeked *Sminthopsis* and the larger quoll-like *Satanellus*, the New Guinea marsupial cat.

The ground floor belongs to the bandicoots, and like their cousins, the possums in the treetops, many millennia of selection have separated the various species, each in its own niche. They may cover the same ground looking for food, but there is no direct competition between them. Differences can be seen in their feet: the giant bandicoot (*Peroryctes broadbenti*), for example, has hindfeet

Ranging between the forest floor and the canopy, the strikingly marked striped possum (*Dactylopsila trivirgata*) searches tree trunks, limbs and fallen rotten logs, tapping the wood for the hollow sound that betrays the presence of woodboring grubs which it then skewers with the sharp claw of the elongated fourth finger.

A male bird of paradise (*Paradisaea raggiana*) in full display. This group of spectacular birds evolved in the isolation of the Australian rainforests. They are most diverse in the highlands of Papua New Guinea where each range of altitude has its own distinct species.

adapted for leaping, while the striped bandicoot (*Peroryctes longicauda*) has hindfeet adapted for running. The variation reflects different hunting techniques, and therefore different prey. Differences can also be detected in the shapes of their heads: the brindled bandicoot (*Isoodon macrourus*) has slightly shorter and stouter jaws and a broader head than other members of its family, which gives it a more powerful bite — and therefore the ability to tackle larger prey.

The bandicoots share the forest floor with monotremes of a kind that have long disappeared in Australia: long-beaked echidnas (*Zaglossus bruijni*). They are larger than the Australian echidna, have fewer and shorter spines, longer fur and a long snout to search the leaf litter for the succulent worms on which they feed.

The echidna, the bandicoots, the dasyurids and the possums, together with the forests in which they live, preserve a part of Australia as it was 15 million years ago. While some families show minor adaptations, they remain little changed in their essential features from the ancestral marsupials that roamed Miocene Australia. But there is one marsupial group that took a unique evolutionary path in New Guinea's highland forests.

Among the early, primitive kangaroos browsing the shrubs and low branches and digging for fungi and insect larvae in the forest floor, were some that began to specialise on leaves and that gradually made the transition back to the arboreal life of their remote possum ancestors. They became the tree kangaroos. Their hindfeet became shorter and broader, with cushioned soles to prevent slipping; their forepaws grew larger and more powerful to provide a better grip on the branches, and their tails lengthened to become a rudder and prop when climbing.

Tree kangaroos are, nevertheless, still clumsy climbers and as they make their careful way through the tree tops, they look very much what they are — animals that once had their feet firmly planted on the ground.

Rise of the Kangaroos

In a sense, the forests of Papua New Guinea are a living museum. While the rise of the highlands preserved some of the elements from Australia's golden age of marsupials, the vast, flat continent to the south was gradually being overtaken by aridity. The broad rivers of the centre began to carry less water, and finally ceased to flow altogether. The lakes dried up, the flamingos and the freshwater dolphins vanished, and the rainforests gave way to a drier woodland and grass plains.

The forests of Papua New Guinea remain the stronghold for
several species of tree kangaroos — animals once common
throughout Australia when it was still covered by forest. This
group of Goodfellow's tree kangaroos (*Dendrolagus goodfellowi*)
spends as much time on the ground as aloft, feeding mostly
on leaves. The tree kangaroos probably evolved from a
primitive, ground-dwelling browsing stock that gradually
readapted to an arboreal life.

An eastern grey joey surveys
the world. Females don't let
their young out of the pouch till
they've checked the
surroundings for danger.

That change — from browse plants to grasses — set the scene
for a rapid expansion of the kangaroo family, which had until then
been a relatively minor component of Australia's animal life.

As the forests opened out into woodland, grasses spread in the
clearings. Some of the forest wallabies developed more complicated guts and their teeth changed to cope with tougher tissue. As
well as browsing on the leaves and shoots of trees and shrubs, they
added the coarser grasses to their diets, moving into the open a
little more, but always retreating to the woodland for shelter.

The red-necked wallabies (*Macropus rufogriseus*) that inhabit the
eucalypt woodlands of the east coast fit that early transitional pattern. Although still basically solitary and nocturnal animals, extending their feeding repertoire from selective browsing among
the understorey shrubs to cropping grasses in the clearings meant
they could afford to become a little more sociable: less selective
feeding meant it was not as important for the animals to stay out of
each other's way.

As the forests receded, some wallaby groups took refuge on
rocky outcrops and heights. Isolated there, the rock wallabies
evolved rapidly into a range of species, though with remarkably
similar adaptations to fit them for life on the steep slopes. The
soles of their feet are studded to give them a secure grip, and their
long, rather rigid tails serve as balancing poles as they leap about
their rocky strongholds with speed, grace and agility.

Ten species can be found today, and they are among the most
beautiful of all the macropods. Their colours and patterns are striking, from the black-footed rock wallaby of central and western Australia, with white-striped cheeks and flanks and a black stripe down
its back to the brushtails of the southeast, with pale-grey and black
stripes and the yellow-footed rock wallabies of the Flinders
Ranges, with white-marked cheeks and tails ringed with yellow and
brown.

Their distinctive decorations camouflage them among the
shades and shadow-plays of the rocks. They are a favourite target
for wedgetailed eagles; young wallabies, playing or basking in the
sun, are especially vulnerable to the eagles' hunting strategy. A
pair of eagles often hunts together, working in tandem. They come
out of the sun; one stuns the victim and knocks it off balance, then
the second swoops in to pick up the dazed wallaby in its powerful
talons, or to send it tumbling down the rock face.

Avoiding predators shaped the way the kangaroos reorganised
their lives, and the way they moved as the forests retreated and the
open woodlands and grass plains extended. Their ancestors had a
simple technique for avoiding danger: they were small enough to
hide in the forest undergrowth and, should a predator discover
them, an explosive leap with their hindlegs enabled them to make

a quick escape. But as the kangaroos moved to take advantage of the new grasses, the coarser food they discovered led to selection for larger size: the larger an animal is, the more grass it can process, and the more value it gets from a meal.

Larger size, open grassland and greater sociability promoted by grazing, meant that hiding from predators was no longer possible. Flight became the best strategy and, since flight works best with an effective early warning system, the greater togetherness promoted by grazing became an advantage, with more eyes to detect danger.

There were physical changes, too, as the kangaroos evolved from forest browsers to animals that mixed browsing and grazing in the clearings, to exclusive grazers in open grasslands. As well as more sophisticated teeth and guts to grind and process the coarser foods and extract their nutrients, the need for sustained and rapid motion saw the hindfeet become longer and narrower, the hindlegs longer and more powerful, and the tail longer and stronger, to act both as a balance while bounding and as a prop while moving slowly or sitting. That line can still be traced, from the red-necked wallabies that live at the interface between forest and

The large plains kangaroos such as the red kangaroos (*Macropus rufus*) are the culmination of a long line of marsupial evolution that began with a tiny insectivore in the Gondwanan forests 100 million years ago. Their powerful hindlegs act as springs, enabling them to travel long distances while using relatively little energy.

clearing, through the larger agile wallabies that live in larger groups in open woodland in northern Australia, to the large kangaroos of the open plains and woodlands.

The transition from solitude in the forests to group living on the plains also meant the development of more complex social systems. Animals living together need some sort of order, and in most mammal societies, that order tends to be based on male dominance. Dominance in turn is based on size: larger males tend to 'win' the females and to perpetuate their genes. So the more sociable animals are, the more male-to-male competition there is — and the greater the size difference between male and female.

This sexual dimorphism holds true for kangaroos and wallabies: solitary male and female forest-dwelling rat-kangaroos are the same size; red-necked wallaby males are only a little larger than females. The difference is more marked among agile wallabies, and in the large grazers, such as eastern grey kangaroos, the male is three to four times the size of the female.

Kangaroos keep cool by licking their forearms: the skin is almost bare of hair there, and the blood vessels run close to the surface. The evaporating moisture allows excess body heat to evaporate — one of the ways in which these large marsupials have adapted to life on Australia's hot, dry plains.

The difference is not just weight for weight: male kangaroos do not have antlers or horns, so their forearms, shoulders and chests have become more muscular and powerful. The hindfeet, with their great ripping claws, can become awesome weapons. An eastern grey buck rearing up to its full height is an impressive sight — which, of course, is what it is meant to be for other males.

Size and powerful physique are primarily items of display. Rivals usually recognise and defer to obvious superiority, and the resident male can continue undisturbed with what, after feeding, is his main activity: checking the sexual readiness of his consorts.

Female kangaroos are sexually receptive for only a few hours, so the male must be ready to seize his opportunity. He moves from doe to doe, sniffing her cloacal and pouch area. Sometimes, however, a challenger of comparable size seeks to move in, and the resident male has to confront the intruder. The males take each other's measure with a kind of four-legged strut, circling each other to display their size. As a symbolic threat, the defender rips clumps of grass from the ground and rubs them against his chest.

Should that not persuade the intruder to abandon his challenge, the ritual display escalates into a confrontation. The bucks stand toe to toe and paw at each other's arms, chest, neck and face, with their heads thrown back and chins up. It looks a little like a cross between boxing and wrestling: each tries to grapple with the other, and to throw his opponent off balance.

Still neither gives in, and their most powerful weapons swing into action. The defender leans back on his tail and lets fly with both hindfeet, thudding his claws into the challenger's belly. But the aim is still to put to flight rather than maim or kill — for the direction of the claws is forward rather than raking downward, which might disembowel. For several minutes the combatants trade their bruising blows until suddenly, the challenger turns tail and flees.

Unlike other kangaroos, which mate soon after the females have given birth, many eastern grey females come into oestrus (become sexually receptive) around the time the joey they are carrying puts its head out of the pouch for the first time. The fertilised egg that results from her mating develops to a bundle of cells called a blastocyst, but remains dormant until a few weeks before the joey leaves the pouch. The embryo then grows quickly, and a month later the newborn is making its way into the newly vacated pouch. It means almost continuous reproduction: at any one time the eastern grey doe can have an embryo waiting dormant in her womb and a joey growing in her pouch, or a larger young at foot. After about five months of suckling inside the pouch, the joey faces a second birth — into the outside world.

It is probably the young's size that tells the doe to move away from the rest of the group, to hunch low, relax her pouch muscles

A female eastern grey kangaroo and her joey. The young kangaroos begin sampling the grass while still in the pouch: they gradually make the transition from the safety and milk of the pouch, to the independence of grazing.

and let the joey tumble out. The first excursion is likely to be a brief one. After watching her young totter about unsteadily for a few minutes, the female makes a series of soft calls, rather like clicks, and the joey returns to its mother. She grooms it, licking its fur and scratching its head, then helps it to climb back inside.

The next few months alternate between pouch and freedom — milk and grass. Gradually, the periods outside the pouch grow longer, but the young kangaroo continues to return for an occasional drink of milk until, eventually, it is wholly independent. By that stage, another joey may well be growing in the pouch.

Eastern grey society tends to revolve around the females and their young, for while the young male kangaroos form their own subgroups and disperse after a time, the female young remain in their mother's home range, eventually to draw the attention of the mob's roaming males.

By the time the young are too large for the pouch, they are well enough developed to keep up with their mother's flight from danger. The signal for flight often comes from a female, warning her young with a quick stamp of her hindfeet. Her alarm warns the rest of the group as well, and the flight becomes communal.

The hopping locomotion that began as a useful way of getting around the cluttered forest floors and springing out of the way of predators evolved into an elegant and efficient way of moving across the plains, whether escaping from danger or moving to new pastures. As the open woodlands and grasslands spread, so the large kangaroos extended their dominion across the continent, the endpoint of a unique line of evolution that began with a tiny, mouse-sized animal chasing insects around the Gondwanan forests 100 million years ago.

Along the way, isolated on a drifting, changing continent, the marsupials developed and refined their own successful solutions to the universal challenges of survival. Some of the changes that were happening on land were mirrored in the surrounding seas. There, too, the continent's gradual drift into isolation gave new shape to its plant and animal communities, and remade the nature of underwater Australia.

CHAPTER TWO

SEAS UNDER CAPRICORN

Corals grow in marvellous variety of shapes and patterns.
A number of species have come to be called brain corals, for
their obvious similarity to the human organ which made
the comparison.

*T*he sea has always been a major force in the shaping of Australia. Margins between land and sea have often been blurred: where waves now roll has been dry land many times, and deep in the heart of the continent, shells of early marine life are embedded in desert rock. And while the seas shaped the land, they were themselves transformed in the process. Australia came to be encircled by a chain of distinct marine habitats (each with a counterpart somewhere in the world, but unique as the garland of diversity that now embraces the continent), from the storm-tossed kelp forests of southern waters to the marvels of the coral reefs.

The creation of underwater Australia began when the continent sheared off from Gondwana and set out on its long voyage north to the tropic of Capricorn, 45 million years ago. Tracing Australia's marine evolution means going back to its starting point.

Standing on a southern beach in winter, just where the voyage began is unmistakable. The gales that drive the white-topped waves come howling in from the far south. They have their genesis in the blizzards of Antarctica — the only part of Gondwana to remain, more or less, in its original position.

The cold and heavy air of the Antarctic ice sheet roars down its steep coastal slopes with ferocious velocity. It cools the waters and, when winter comes, turns them into ice. The interaction of cold air and water produces one of the key factors in the weather systems of the southern world: the circumpolar current. As it revolves around the continent, this massive current keeps warmer northern waters at bay, holding Antarctica in a perpetual icy embrace. The cold air associated with the current spirals outward to flow into low-pressure regions created by the rising of warm air further north. The result is a procession of highs and lows marching across the southern oceans to rule the climate of much of Australia.

The circumpolar current formed about thirty million years ago, when the connection between Antarctica and South America was broken. With the last land obstacle removed, the oceans had unrestricted passage around Antarctica and the circumpolar current was born. The effects were dramatic. With the current now preventing the approach of warmer tropical waters, the polar environment cooled rapidly. Ice sheets formed first as caps on the highest mountain ranges, then grew and eventually joined. The forests of Gondwana were exterminated — buried under ice as much as 3000 metres thick in some places — together with the reptiles and early mammals they harboured.

Antarctica is now the coldest place on earth, with winter temperatures of around minus 60 degrees Celsius to minus 88.3 degrees Celsius, far colder than the Arctic, which is ocean surrounded by warmth-generating land, while Antarctica is a continent surrounded by oceans. Yet even in this white desert, some life clings on: primitive plants such as lichens, mosses and liverworts in the shelter of rocks. These tiny plant communities support a few kinds of insects, Antarctica's only permanent land animals.

The absence of mammal predators and the rich food supplies offshore make the Antarctic coasts a haven for huge seabird rookeries. The most characteristic are the penguins, birds that evolved in Gondwana around forty million years ago and that gave rise to several species adapted to Antarctic regions. The most highly adapted is the emperor penguin (*Aptenodytes forsteri*), the only one of the Antarctic's seven species that remains on land through the long winter night to brood its eggs and raise its young. At 1.2 metres in height, the emperors are the giants of their kind. After spending the summer months feeding in the sea, they come ashore to court and breed, gathering in rookeries that can number up to 10,000 birds. The birds establish their rookeries on ice often 100 kilometres from the open sea, and they march there in a remarkable procession — thousands of birds in single file, most of them walking, some sliding on their bellies and propelling themselves with their feet and flippers.

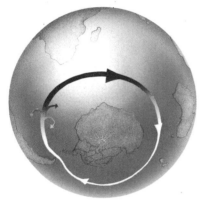

The circumpolar current — created when Antarctica was left isolated by the break-up of the supercontinent of Gondwana — is one of the key factors in the weather systems that govern the southern hemisphere, including Australia.

When the summer sun returns to the Antarctic and breaks up
the ice, there is a burst of plant and animal growth,
generating a wealth of nutrients carried north by deep
currents to sustain the marvellous diversity of marine life in
Australia's southern seas.

Emperor penguins (*Aptenodytes forsteri*) incubate their eggs and shield their chicks from the bitter cold by carrying them on their broad feet. They are the largest and most highly adapted of all the penguins. Dense plumage combines with an underlayer of woolly down to keep out the cold winds and water, and a thick layer of fat provides insulation between the skin and the muscles.

The female lays a single egg, and the male incubates it — not in a nest of stones, as other penguins do, but carrying it on his broad feet, covered with a fold of abdominal skin. The females return to the sea to feed, while the males fast. Huddled together in their thousands, buffeted by ceaseless blizzards, they stand guard until the chick hatches. It is then that their mates return from the sea, each calling to find her partner among an endless crowd of identical birds. The female takes control of the chick and the male goes to the sea to feed after a fast that may have lasted 115 days. The parents then alternate, one looking after the growing chick while the other makes the long round trip to the sea to feed.

A Summer Feast

The seas around Antarctica are as rich in life as the land is barren. Marine Gondwana had been part of a fairly uniform world in which temperatures, conditions and, therefore, plant and animal communities hardly varied. But as water temperatures dropped and shifting currents brought changes in salinity, Antarctica's became a separate and isolated marine environment. Most of Gondwana's marine animals could not survive in the new conditions, but some were able to adapt and others migrated upward from the ocean depths, which had always been cold. Antarctic waters provide very stable living conditions: temperatures vary little, and there are few disturbances. The heavy sea ice prevents turbulence and there are no rivers to reduce salinity with their runoff.

As with all life on earth it is the sun's energy that sustains Antarctica's marine communities, and because it is only available for a few months, it is an especially precious commodity. When the sun makes its reappearance after the long winter's night, the seas become busy with new growth and life. The slight warming of the surface waters carries them offshore, and cold waters well up from the deep. They bring with them mineral nutrients that, together with the sunlight, fuel the growth of vast blooms of tiny algae, the phytoplankton on which all other marine life depends. The water's winter clarity gives way to summer's cloudy soup.

Much of the wealth generated at this time eventually finds its way to Australian waters, to underwrite marine life there. Minute crustaceans — copepods and amphipods, which graze on the algae in the polar seas — in turn become food for larger animals that time their reproduction so their eggs hatch when the algae are in full bloom. The copepods, amphipods and other invertebrates that make up the dominant life forms are well suited to survive in the freezing waters, for their body fluids have the same salt concentration as the surrounding water.

One of the few fishes that can cope with the cold is the ice fish; a pale, whitish, almost translucent animal. Its paleness comes from the absence of haemoglobin in its blood: instead, it has a kind of organic antifreeze that stops it becoming literally a fish of ice. It lives close to the sea floor, and to conserve energy moves only to feed. Feeding is kept to a minimum by having a large mouth that can engulf great quantities of prey with a single lunge.

Because the annual cycles of summer feast and winter famine tend to favour animals that conserve energy and can survive on very little, the most characteristic animals of the marine Antarctic are the bottom-dwelling filter feeders; the sponges and anemones. They look like plants but are in fact animals — among the earliest (and most successful) life forms on earth.

More or less fixed in position, sponges and anemones rely on the movement of the water to bring their food within reach. Sponges draw water through pores in their outer walls, and pump it through a complex system of canals and chambers to filter out food particles and oxygen. Sea anemones have tentacles with stinging cells to catch and paralyse their tiny prey and to bring it to their 'mouths'. Because food is plentiful only during the short summer, the sponges and anemones grow very slowly . . . but because Antarctica's is a very stable environment, they grow for a long time. Sponges in particular can grow to an enormous size over hundreds of years, with many individuals reaching a diameter of 2 metres and more. They become themselves a miniature environment, providing living space for a host of smaller creatures, such as crustaceans and worms, that get their food from the sponge's waste or that take pickings from the water before it is drawn inside the host's body.

Other animals, too, are nourished by the planktonic soup. Several species of sea stars make their colourful way through the bottom waters, feeding on the minute plants and microscopic animals, eggs and larvae that together make up the plankton. There are also holothurians, or sea cucumbers — brightly patterned animals that look like short, fat tubes, and that move slowly along the sea floor on a series of suckered feet. Food tentacles surround the holothurian's mouth, pinching large amounts of sediment from the bottom; food particles are filtered out and the waste discharged from the animal's other end.

Summer brings food, but it also brings danger. Icebergs break away from winter's grip and begin to move. With only their tips above water, their huge bulk scours the shallow sea floor, wreaking wholesale destruction among its inhabitants. The cracking ice is an invitation to visitors from another element, for the rich soup of summer is crucial to the survival of other Antarctic animals, too. The emperor penguins long ago gave up flying through the air for flying through the water, diving to as much as 265 metres in search of fish, squid and crustaceans. The males, freed from their long fasts while they were incubating their eggs, now must replenish their stores of fat to see them through the coming winter.

Clouds of Krill

The most important part of the penguins' diet is a crustacean: a tiny, shrimplike creature, transparent and almost invisible. En masse it is called krill — a Norwegian word that means whale food, and that was first applied to the stomach contents of baleen whales caught in Arctic waters. The name has come to refer to eighty or so species of swarming shrimps, but it usually means the largest and most abundant form, the Antarctic krill *Euphausia superba*, which grows to 6 centimetres. In vast clouds and uncountable millions, they drift through the Antarctic seas: one swarm measured by scientists covered a surface area of 450 square kilometres, was more than 200 metres deep, and contained krill estimated to weigh 2.1 million tonnes. Not surprisingly, krill is the most important source of protein in Antarctic waters, and supports all larger and higher life forms from penguins to whales.

Krill existence is tuned to the regular annual cycle of summer feast and winter famine. When the pack ice melts and retreats to the continental shoreline, the krill gather in great swarms to feed on the phytoplankton blooming in the increasing light. The krill also breed at this time, to replenish the numbers that fall victim to age or predation. With so many mouths around, the eggs run the risk of being eaten before they hatch, so they are designed to sink, reaching depths of up to 2000 metres by the time they hatch into young larvae. The larvae then begin the long swim back to the surface; by the time they reach it, currents have swept them far away. Toward the end of summer, the supplies of phytoplankton on which the krill feed begin to peter out, the swarms disperse and krill life enters another remarkable stage. To cope with the coming winter shortage of food, krill enter a stage of reverse growth, shedding body mass and reverting to a juvenile-like form. Pared down to shadows of their former selves, they go into the long winter night to await the return of the sun, food and regrowth.

Mingling with the summer swarms of krill are millions of other crustaceans, larval fishes, molluscs, jellyfish and arrow-worms, enriching the 'soup' that makes Antarctic waters four times richer than those of other oceans. There is so much planktonic food that one kind of seal, *Lobodon carcinophaga* — misleadingly called the crabeater — specialises in feeding on krill and has evolved special cusps on its teeth to filter them from the water.

Marine Mammals

Mammals vanished from the land when Antarctica was overtaken by ice, but their marine descendants continued to flourish and diversify. Selection for various kinds of food, water temperatures and depths has produced seven or so species of seals, each with its own niche. Fur seals fish in relatively warmer waters, the huge elephant seals chase their preferred prey of squid in the open seas, and Weddell seals are adapted to live under the permanent ice.

Weddell seals (*Leptonychotes weddelli*) are equipped with protruding incisors, strong teeth to rasp away the ice that builds around their breathing holes, and large, forward-facing eyes with a tapetum or reflective layer behind the retina to improve their vision in dim light below the ice. They also have a vocal system of trills and squeaks that may help them to locate food on their hunting dives, to depths of as much as 600 metres.

Fish, krill and squid are the main foods for most of the seals, but the fiercest hunter of them all, the leopard seal, also takes penguins. Sleek and fast, with a faintly spotted silver-grey coat that makes it hard to spot amid the foam-flecked ripples, the leopard seal patrols the waters near the penguin colonies, catching the birds when they come in from feeding. A swift lunge and snap with its formidable teeth kills the bird instantly with a bite to the neck. Then, its jaws still gripping the penguin by the neck, the seal neatly skins the body by flicking it vigorously from side to side.

At the end of the food chain sustained by the krill is the orca (*Orcinus orca*), a spectacular animal patterned in black and white, that hunts in groups of up to thirty or forty, feeding on penguins, porpoises and seals. Orcas even rear up on ice floes to scare seals into the water — and the protein that began as krill makes its last transformation. Other whales are direct consumers, in such bulk that they have become the largest creatures on earth. The great baleen whales probably evolved to take advantage of the enormous food supply presented by the krill swarms. The humpbacks, the minkes, fins and the blue whales (at 30 metres and 100 tonnes the largest of all) arrive in the Antarctic on their summer migrations when the krill swarms are reaching their peak.

Like the seals, the first whales evolved from land mammals that took to the seas 60 million years ago. It was not a sudden plunge; more a cautious dipping of the mammalian toe, begun when some tapirlike animals became swamp dwellers, graduated to estuaries as they adapted to aquatic life, and finally moved out to sea.

The modern baleen whales made their appearance about fifteen million years ago, when the circumpolar current had begun producing its gigantic swarms of krill for them to feed on. Instead of teeth, baleen whales grow a sieve of springy, fibrous whalebone 'plates' that hang from the roof of the mouth. Their frayed edges form a filter with a texture like coarse matting: as they move through the water, the whales take in huge volumes of seawater and krill, then press out the water, leaving the krill and other plankton caught in the filter, to be swept down the throat by the tongue. Such an enormous intake of food helps the whales generate the energy they need to maintain their body temperature in the icy waters, and builds up the layers of blubber under the skin that provide buoyancy, efficient insulation, and food reserves for the northerly migration to breed in warmer waters.

Late summer's shortening days are the signal for the first departures. The humpbacks are the first to go. Some of the other species — the minke and fin whales — feed further south, closer to the permanent ice, and sometimes find themselves trapped when they depart too late and the autumn freeze comes early.

Just when or how the whale migrations began remains a tantalising subject for speculation. Until 30 to 25 million years ago, the waters around Antarctica were still warm, and it is possible the whale species of the time stayed there year-round, both to feed and to breed. When the polar seas began to turn cold with the cli-

matic effects of the growing icecaps, the whales may have swum north in search of the warmer waters they needed for their new-born calves, returning each year for the food they remembered. As the continents drifted further the journeys became longer, until breeding and feeding grounds were thousands of kilometres apart.

Each population of whales has its own traditional wintering place: some travel to the waters off Patagonia, on the southern tip of South America, some to New Zealand, some to South Africa and some to Australia. How the whales find their way from the Antarctic to Australia's temperate and subtropical seas far to the north to breed is a matter of conjecture. They may navigate by the sun and stars, for there are no currents to help them, or they may employ a geomagnetic sense that allows them to follow specific underwater 'highways' from one place to another.

Cold, Rich Waters

While the cold Antarctic waters flow north, they do so at enormous depths, sinking beneath the more temperate waters of the southern ocean where the two converge. The Antarctic convergence, created by the onflowing effects of the circumpolar current,

The short Antarctic summer ends: plates of 'pancake' ice form and join as the seas freeze over. The fierce winds generated by the cold air sliding down the Antarctic plateau make the region a weather factory, driving the current and wind systems that rule the climate for much of the southern hemisphere, including Australia.

Albatrosses range the cold southern oceans, spending most of their lives on the wing. The yellow-nosed albatross (*Diomedea chlororhynchos*) is one of the smaller of these ocean wanderers, with a wingspan of just over two metres. It feeds in Australia's southern waters, and in summer moves to islands on the edge of the subantarctic zone to breed.

A frond of kelp, the characteristic plant that grows in submarine forests off the coast of southern Australia, and within whose shelter live a range of intriguing creatures. The fronds are shaped to catch sunlight and efficiently extract nutrients from the water — nutrients that have been ferried by currents all the way from the Antarctic.

marks the northernmost boundary of the nutrient-rich polar seas. The interaction of the polar and temperate waters creates an upwelling effect that brings sediments and nutrients from the bottom, and it is these zones that produce some of the richest concentrations of plankton.

Huge numbers of sea birds gather to dip into the feast, and the whales too lay up some last supplies before heading north, across surface waters that are the deserts of the ocean. Little life exists in them, for there are virtually no nutrients to sustain it. Deep down, however, beyond the reach of light, the currents drive the rich, cool waters slowly north, and some of them eventually reach southern Australia. There, the slope of the continental shelf brings them to the surface, to enrich the local waters and sustain the permanent inhabitants — and many seasonal visitors as well.

Submarine Forests

The presence of sea birds, both as regular annual visitors and as all-year-round inhabitants, in enormous numbers is a sign of the richness of the southern Australian waters. Just how rich becomes marvellously apparent below the surface, where animal and plant life proliferates in a seemingly infinite variety of form and pattern. The richness and diversity springs from the Antarctic; as the deep, cool waters carried north from the polar seas by bottom currents encounter Australia's continental shelf, they rise with their wealth of minerals and other nutrients. In some places on the shelf (mainly around the Tasmanian and Victorian coasts), at depths where sunlight penetrates, they give growth to vast forests of giant kelp, *Macrocystis*. In a dim green twilight shot through with shafts of sunlight, intricately linked communities of animals and other plants find food and shelter.

The kelp forests had their origins in marine Gondwana: similar communities survive in the coastal waters of South America and southern Africa, which once were joined with Australia in the ancestral supercontinent. When Australia began her journey north, she took her marine life with her, and the original kelp communities that spanned the northern, western and eastern shores of what was then virtually a peninsula of Gondwana gradually colonised the new southern shores that formed as Australia broke away.

The life in the new continent's northern waters would change as it was carried within the influence of warmer tropical currents, but the seas off the southern shores preserved much of the original marine Gondwana, in which the kelp forests and their inhabitants were important elements. The kelp itself is a marvel of efficient design. Because it draws nutrients directly from the water it needs no roots, so it anchors itself to the sea floor with a limpet-like attach-

Bull kelp (*Macrocystis* spp.) sways in the powerful surge of the seas pounding the eastern Tasmanian coast. The thick, fleshy fronds grow to 15 metres long, and they are anchored to the sea floor by a strong, sucker-like growth called a holdfast. The turbulence helps the leaves to extract minerals and life-giving gases from the water.

ment, the holdfast. As the plant grows, float-like appendages — pneumatocysts, filled with air — lift the stems up to 30 metres towards the surface, to gain the most sunlight. The leaf surfaces are corrugated, so that the water's turbulent action as it moves over them enables the leaves to extract nutrients with great efficiency — so great that at up to 30 centimetres a day, *Macrocystis* is the fastest growing plant in the world.

Such enormous productivity sustains all other life in the forest, though mostly indirectly, for surprisingly there are few animals that can graze the tough kelp. One that does is the sea urchin. It chews through the stipe; the part that connects the stem, leaves and fronds to the holdfast. For other animals, kelp only becomes available as food when fronds die or are ripped off by wave action near the surface. Decomposition then makes it available to the many filter feeders that live among the leaves and stems of the kelp canopy, including a variety of tubeworms and minute forms of the coral-like bryozoans that have attached themselves to the kelp and that wait for the water to bring detritus and other floating food particles within reach of their tentacles.

The bryozoans become food for sea spiders and for sea slugs — nudibranchs — which in turn are preyed on by larger animals, such as prawns and small fishes. These, too, join the chain of eating and being eaten when they become prey for schools of mackerel and pike flashing through the kelp canopy.

The need to eat and the need to avoid being eaten have produced ingenious strategies among the inhabitants of the kelp. Several species of angler fish use parts of their bodies as lures to attract their prey. The tasselled angler, which lies in wait amid the fronds, has one of its dorsal fin spines modified into a rod from which dangles a worm-shaped appendage. Worms are favourite food items for small fishes such as gobies — and when one takes the bait, the angler engulfs it in a flurry of movement.

Deception also makes effective defence, and the kelp and seaweed habitats with their interplays of shadows and patterns have given rise to some striking mimicry and camouflage. The shape and pattern of the sea horse makes it difficult to detect as it floats among the weeds or reeds, anchored by its curled tail, its upright body surmounted by a head like a tiny horse's. But a keen predatory eye might still spot it, and the weedy sea dragon, a close relative of the sea horse, has made itself even harder to see with leaflike outgrowths from the spines on its head and body.

This line of camouflage has been taken to a remarkable extreme by another member of the family, the leafy sea dragon, which inhabits the edges of kelp communities off South Australia. Its body has been transformed into the precise likeness of a torn-off piece of kelp, a tattered bunch of patches and shreds. The camouflage works both ways; if predators cannot see it, its own prey cannot, and as it floats among the seaweed it so much resembles it sucks up myscids — tiny, prawnlike crustaceans — with rapid lunges of its long, narrow snout.

When leafy sea dragons are born — like seahorses, hatched from pouches on their father's body — their weedy disguise is already well formed, and they begin searching out their prey of tiny crustaceans almost immediately. They are about 34 mm long at birth; adults measure about 30 cm.

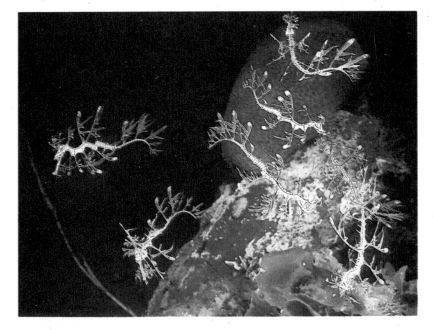

Male Pregnancies

Next to staying alive oneself, ensuring life for the next generation is the most important driving force in the kelp societies. With so many hungry mouths about, the eggs laid by the inhabitants of the kelp forests would quickly become food for others, were they not given some protection.

Among sea horses and sea dragons, that protection takes the form of a kind of male pregnancy. When a female sea horse is about to lay her eggs, a male pays court by circling her, displaying the pouch on his belly and inflating it to an enormous size. If she is impressed, she manoeuvres herself over him and deposits her eggs — usually between one and two hundred — into the pouch, where his sperm fertilises them. As he receives the eggs, the male performs a curious, twisting dance to ensure the sperm covers all the eggs and to stick them securely to the sides of the pouch.

After four to five weeks the eggs are ready to hatch, and the male gives rather violent birth by expelling his brood with a series

Leafy sea dragons (*Phycodurus eques*) belong to the same family as sea horses, and have evolved into one of the most bizarre examples of camouflage to be found in nature. They live amongst seaweed and kelp and resemble a floating piece of torn-off weed.

Among the most intriguing of the creatures that inhabit the kelp forests of Australia's southern waters are the seahorses. Males incubate the eggs in a pouch on their belly, and this male *Hippocampus abdominalis* is courting a female by inflating his pouch into a white balloon, to induce her to choose it for her eggs.

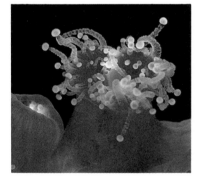

Aptly named, the jewel anemone (*Corynactis australis*) extends its delicate, deadly tentacles into the currents of Australia's temperate waters. Like corals — and belonging to the same class — anemones are animals, carnivores with tentacles to trap any microscopic creatures swept within reach. The tentacles fire barbed darts that paralyse the prey, then draw it to the polyp's mouth.

of forceful contractions. Perfectly formed, the miniature sea horses make their way to the surface, to attach themselves to floating weeds and to begin feeding on zooplankton.

Brooding the eggs is a male task among leafy sea dragons, too, though instead of carrying them in one large pouch, the dragon provides the eggs with individual capsules, which form soon after the female lays the eggs on to the male's tail. When the hatchlings emerge, their father's tail is for a time festooned with a hundred or more tiny replicas: then, with a strong wriggle, the young dragons break free and float away, like tiny wisps of seaweed. To tide them over the first few crucial days, a yolk sac provides them with food while their snouts complete the development for which there was insufficient room in the egg.

The floor of the kelp forest provides living space for a range of animals. The kelp holdfasts shelter amphipods, which move out to feed on the red algae that grow in the giant kelp's shade. In neighbouring deeper water, kelp gives way to a luxuriant, varicoloured garden — but it is a garden of animals, for there is not enough light for plants to grow. Colonies of tiny polyps cluster together to form whips, fans and plumes in reds and yellows. Bryozoans grow in a variety of shapes, and sponges, gorgonians and anemones beckon in more sheltered places.

Fish flash through the garden in bright hues — the red and blue of bullseyes and jackass morwong, the silver of boarfish, the pink of sea perch. In shallower water, the colourful flying gurnard patrols the edges of the kelp forest. A rocky ledge becomes the setting for a many-tentacled tryst as two octopuses flash their blue rings at one another. At first it is an arm's-length encounter, then, with a swift lunge, the male has the female locked in his eight-armed embrace. She struggles, but is soon subdued. In a coupling that can last two hours, the male spermatophore passes slowly along a channel in one especially adapted tentacle, which then searches out the female's oviduct and transfers the sperm directly.

Despite its small size (20 cm from one outstretched arm tip to the other) this is one of the most venomous of all sea creatures — the blue-ringed octopus (*Hapalochlaena maculosa*). When disturbed, it expands and contracts pigment sacs in the skin to produce the characteristic, irridescent blue circles that warn other animals of its venom.

Within a month of the mating, the male is dead, but the female lives on to devote all her energies to the care of her eggs. She lays them in long strings, which she forms into grapelike clusters. Unlike other kinds of octopuses, the blue-ringed does not then place them in an empty shell or rock depression, there to guard them, but holds the clusters within her body's embrace. Hardly moving and not eating, she nurses the eggs for the 90 days they take to hatch. On occasion, she strokes and manipulates the egg clusters gently with her tentacles to clean them of parasites and keep up the circulation of oxygen. Soon after the eggs hatch, she too dies.

When the young octopuses emerge into their world of kelp, they are still equipped (like the young leafy sea-dragons and several other marine animals) with a yolk sac to supply them with food while they learn about being an octopus. They are soon feeding on dead crabs, and hunting live ones within a month. To protect itself against predation, the young octopus can fire an inky kind of smokescreen, but as it grows older, the intensifying blue of the characteristic rings on its tentacles act as a warning sign — 'beware: I am poisonous'. The blue-ringed octopus is among the most venomous of marine animals: its poison can kill crabs and fish much larger than itself in 30 seconds, and also acts as a digestant, softening the tissues for the octopus to extract by suction.

Currents of Chance

When it is still vulnerable, the baby octopus may well fall prey to some of the giant crustaceans that prowl the sea floor by night. Crayfish (*Jasus novaehollandiae*), grow to nearly a metre in length, and are voracious feeders on almost anything that moves, and much that does not. As well as young octopuses, their pincers grab whatever comes within reach: small fish, crabs, molluscs and abalone. They are scavengers, too, cleaning up the dead and decaying animal and plant tissue that accumulates on the bottom. In especially food-rich places they cluster in groups of a hundred or more; and crayfish that feed together breed together. Coupling is a fairly rudimentary affair, (though a cautious one — crayfish have been known to eat each other). After some signalling with palps and pincers to appease the female and to deter her from cannibalism, the male places his sperm packet on the female's underside to fertilise her eggs, which can number half a million.

Such a great mass of eggs represents a very different reproductive strategy from that of the sea horses, sea dragons and the octopus. Their way involves relatively few eggs and much care, until the offspring hatch at an advanced stage of development. The crayfish produce many eggs and give them little care. When they hatch, their buoyancy carries them to the surface, where currents sweep them beyond the reach of the kelp predators, out to the less populated open ocean. Hatching begins a long journey that many begin but few complete: it is not unusual for a female to release 100 million eggs in her lifetime, just to replace herself and one mate.

The West Australian rock lobster shows that good timing is also important. In spring and early summer, large females gather in deep water at the edge of the continental shelf. Each female carries up to half a million developing eggs, which hatch into tiny leaflike larvae called phyllosomas, on her abdomen.

The phyllosomas are attracted to light, and swim toward the surface. By day, they hover at a depth of around 100 metres; at night, falling light levels draw them nearer the surface and into the wind-driven currents that flow away from the coast at night. The seasonal currents take the phyllosomas far out into the Indian Ocean if they can get across a main stream flowing south — the Leeuwin Current (the Leeuwin develops to the northwest of Australia, sweeps down the western edge of the continental shelf, turns west around South Australia and finally disappears south of Tasmania). To complete their lifecycles successfully, the rock lobster larvae have to cross the Leeuwin twice — on their outward journey and again on their return passage, almost a year later. For a few months of the year the Leeuwin weakens, and cross-currents are strong enough to carry the larvae through it. On their outward journey, the trade winds carry the larvae 500 to 1000 kilometres into the eastern Indian Ocean.

As they mature, they become less tolerant of light and descend further from the surface. This vertical migration brings them into a subsurface current which carries them back toward Western Australia. When they reach the continental shelf, they undergo the last larval metamorphosis into a puerulus, a form specialised for swimming the last stage of the journey across the continental shelf. At last, the miniature lobsters settle on the nearshore reefs, perhaps within sight of the place where their mothers set out a year earlier.

For every 10,000 larvae that hatched and began the journey, only three or four pueruli make it back. In some years the success rate is higher than in others: years when the numbers of returning larvae are especially low coincide with the El Niño phenomenon off the South American coast — a rise in water temperature caused by the southern oscillation, an atmospheric anomaly over the Pacific Ocean (and one that is also responsible for the cycles of drought and flood in Australia). If the southern oscillation causes the Leeuwin Current to keep flowing strongly instead of weakening for a time, most of the lobster larvae will be swept away, to vanish in the Southern Ocean.

For the southern crayfish larvae, the most dangerous parts of the voyage, both on the way out and on the way back, are their journeys through the crowded waters of the kelp forests. As tiny larvae, they add to the planktonic soup that feeds so many animals: the soup is the beginning of a food chain that leads to successively larger fish, and culminates in the sleek grey shapes of the fur seals that come hunting through the kelp. As well as fish, they feed on squid . . . and occasionally one will swoop to the sea floor to snatch up a large crayfish.

Fur seals can see very well under water, and in dimmer places may use something like echolocation to find prey. The seals are powerful, agile swimmers, and they need to be, for moving between their onshore basking places and the relatively placid depths of the string kelp and the surrounding waters, they have to pass through the turbulence of the inshore shallows, where the ocean swells that have rolled uninterrupted from the Antarctic finally break on the slopes and reefs of rock.

Rites of Reproduction

Weaving between the fronds and riding the surges along the rock channels, the seals surf shoreward on the breaking swells and haul themselves on to the pebbled beach. If they are young males and it is breeding time, they have to be careful about where they land; older, dominant bulls have established territories on most of the terrain and defend them fiercely. The real estate reflects the hierarchy: the top bulls, called beachmasters, have claimed the desirable waterfront property, leaving sites further inland to be fought over by the animals further down the ladder of size and success. The aim of each bull is to father as many pups as possible, and their territories are the key to breeding success. Unlike some seals, such as elephant seals, fur seal bulls do not have harems. Instead, the cows move around the colony, and as they enter the various territories, they mate with the resident bulls. Because the sites nearer the water carry the heaviest traffic the larger, stronger bulls pass on their genes more often.

Mating and birth are closely synchronised, and the cycle begins in late spring when the females give birth to a single pup. Within a week she comes into oestrus and is ready to conceive again. For the next eight months, she alternates between feeding at sea and suckling her pup. And even in the most crowded colonies, where several hundred animals may be massed flipper to flipper, mother and offspring find one another unerringly with call and odour. Once the young seal is old enough, its mother takes it to the water for its first swimming and hunting lessons. It is a risky time for both, for many young and inexperienced animals become targets for the large sharks that prowl these waters.

The largest is the great white shark, or white pointer, whose 6 metre length and heavy musculature demand a constant supply of

An Australian fur seal (*Arctocephalus pusillus*) gives birth. The pup is still enclosed in the foetal membranes, and the cow helps to free her newborn so it can draw its first breath. As many as 4000 seals gather in breeding colonies scattered around the southern coast, to give birth and mate. Mother and pup stay together for a week, then she comes into season again, mates, and returns to the sea to feed — coming back regularly to suckle her young. Call and odour enable her to locate her offspring amid the teeming multitude.

food. Seals form a large part of the great white shark's diet so while the pups roam and train, their mothers have to be watchful. Some are taken, and large gashes in flanks and flippers testify that other encounters were close indeed.

Seals are afforded a measure of protection at their most vulnerable stage simply by remaining together, presenting a confusing number of targets to predators. The same strategy of safety in numbers finds one of its most spectacular expressions along another part of the southern coast. At about the same time the seal pups are taking to the water for their first swim, the sandy bottom of a sheltered bay seems alive with moving carpets of thousands of spider crabs. Ther shells are soft and rubbery; they have recently moulted and are in the process of growing a new outer skeleton, and such a feast inevitably attracts predators. Stingrays sweep in to take as many crabs as possible, but with such vast numbers the law of averages favours the crabs.

Australia's southern waters become centres for many other animal gatherings throughout the year. In early winter the southern right whales (*Balaena glacialis australis*) begin to arrive, sleek and fat from summer months of feeding on the Antarctic plankton, across 3000 kilometres of ocean to a stretch of coast only 20 or so kilometres long. One evening the sun sets on an empty sea; at sunrise the next day the whales are simply there, their vast black shapes materialising in the early light just beyond the surf line. They are among the largest of whales — around 18 metres long, weighing 60 tonnes or so.

The females, who mated in these waters in the previous year, arrive first; for it is their time to give birth. Because a whale's birth takes place under water it has been seen only rarely (and then only fleetingly), but it appears that the calf, which already weighs 7 tonnes or more, is born tail first. Its mother, often helped by other females, nudges the calf to the surface, where exposure to the air causes its blowhole to open. The calf takes its first breath — and must be able to fend for itself from that first gulp.

A southern right whale is born with open eyes, alert senses, and enough muscular coordination to follow its mother immediately. The newborn calf takes its first feed within minutes; to enable it to reach her nipples, now protruding from her mammary slits, the mother turns on her side and as her baby drinks, she often uses one of her flippers to help support it. It is more a pumping than a suckling, for the mother uses muscular pressure to force out the milk. The milk is rich, with a fat content of more than 40 per cent (human milk has a fat content of 2 to 4 per cent) and abundant: a southern right whale can produce 200 litres or more of milk a day. The calf will double its birth weight in the first few weeks.

Little penguins (*Eudyptula minor*) — also called fairy penguins — recall Australia's one-time connection with the Antarctic. The smallest members of the family, they are the only ones to breed in Australia. The largest colonies are on Gabo Island, St Helens Island and Phillip Island. They wait till dark before coming ashore to roost, gathering in groups before making their way through the surf, across the beach and into burrows or crevices in the cliffs or sand dunes.

The bond between mother whale and calf is close, affectionate and playful. For tireless hours, the calf plays around its mother, sliding off her flukes, wriggling up on her back to cover her blowhole with its tail and butting into her flank when it wants another drink. Occasionally the cow will roll on to her back and embrace her boisterous infant with her flippers, as if trying to calm it down.

Mother and calf spend two or three years together, and it is not until the young whale becomes independent that the female is ready to mate again. If a bull becomes too attentive before she is ready, she simply makes herself inaccessible by swimming upside down, sometimes with her tail and genital slit out of the water. Courtship is an elaborate and drawn-out affair among the great whales. Because there are no physical indications of readiness to mate (nor, as far as is known, any sexual odour), sounds and behaviour have to carry the appropriate signals. Their body language is eloquent, too: as a sign of his ardour, the courting male will dash into deeper water to perform a series of spectacular breaches, throwing his body three-quarters of the way out of the water and slamming back to the surface with a resounding clap. Then he swims back to the object of his suit and, if she is receptive, a long

With a mighty heave of its vast bulk, a southern right whale (*Balaena glacialis australis*) rises from the water off the Victorian coast near Warrnambool. This spectacular behaviour is called breaching, and forms part of the mating rituals of these great marine mammals. The southern right whales spend the summer feeding on plankton in the rich seas of the Antarctic Convergence, and some populations come to these Australian waters in winter to mate, give birth, and rear their young.

and gentle foreplay follows — partners roll and rub their bodies over and against one another, nibbling and nuzzling, stroking and caressing with their fins and flukes.

The rituals of sex and procreation dominate much of the whales' lives, and their complexity indicates a high degree of intelligence and social organisation; indeed, play is so much a part of cetacean life that having a whale of a time is an apt description. One of their favourite toys is a great storm — to lesser mortals something to be feared and avoided, but to the great whales a boisterous playmate. Raising their immense flukes they sail downwind, then swim back and repeat the game, again and again.

The Turbulent Shores

The storms that bring the whales such enjoyment have carved spectacular coasts along Australia's southern margins. These are among the wildest coasts in the world, exposed to the full force of swells that march unimpeded all the way from the turbulence of the Antarctic convergence. Wave action wears away the rock, sculpts bridges and blowholes and carves sheer-walled islets from headlands. Centimetre by centimetre, the cliffs give ground and retreat under the onslaught. Boulders are pulverised into sand and carried by waves and currents to more sheltered places, to form long stretches of beach backed by sand dunes.

In many places lakes and lagoons have formed behind the dunes. On occasion, storms and high water combine to open them to the sea, and they become nurseries for many marine fishes and prawns; the salt lake waters, fertilised by drainage from the land, are a rich source of food. Some fishes — tailor, bream and salmon — form schools and flash through the surf to feed on crabs, worms and other organisms stirred up by the ceaseless action of water across the sand. Some schools come into the surf to spawn; females release their eggs, the males their sperm, and the turbulence of the water brings them together as fertilised eggs.

The surge of waves, tides and currents gouges deep channels and gutters in the continental shelf, and some become the haunts of sand tiger or grey nurse sharks (*Eugomphodus taurus*). With a barely perceptible motion of their tails, they hold themselves steady against the currents or swim in rhythmic figures of eight, and in these gutters and channels they gather to mate in rituals that combine grace and savagery in equal measure.

Males battle for access to females and, though the bouts are ritualised, the wounds inflicted are nevertheless real enough, as scars on most sharks testify. Rivals circle each other, their backs arched and their pectoral fins pointing down. If neither backs away, the combatants lunge at each other; it is rarely a fight to the death, since the less experienced — which usually means the younger — male beats a retreat before too much damage is done, leaving the victor to mate. Aggression is also a part of mating, and female sharks carry scars around their dorsal and pectoral fins.

The instincts that guide procreation also drive the sharks to seek protection for their young, and the females of several species gather in selected areas to give birth. In one place off the southern coast of New South Wales, the birth zone is only a few hundred metres offshore, in shallow water just outside the surf zone. Almost overnight, several hundred sharks — mostly copper sharks (bronze whalers) and the curiously shaped hammerheads — are slowly cruising the shallows.

Many sharks produce not eggs, as most fish do, but live young in a refinement of the egg-laying technique. The eggs hatch inside the protection of their mothers' bodies, and the embryos are nourished by yolk, not the maternal bloodstream. The young are on their own from the moment they are born, and many fall prey to other sharks. Those that survive have plentiful food, for the currents that provided the cue for their mothers to migrate to the nurseries also bring together huge numbers of other marine animals.

The east coast currents are part of a flow carrying warmer tropical waters south, and where they meet the cooler temperate waters vast eddies form, like three-dimensional islands of seawater. Nutrients carried by the cooler waters concentrate around the edges of these gyres, creating rich oases that attract schools of bluefin tuna, kingfish and trevally.

Highways of the Ocean

Currents rule all life in Australia's seas. The island continent's voyage across the southern oceans has been a major influence in the way the world's waters move around the globe: the break from Gondwana, which helped create the circumpolar current and so changed the world's weather, was the first major event of that influence. The next was produced by the collision of the continental plate carrying Australia with that carrying Asia. As the landmasses moved closer together, they began to constrict the flow of warm water that circles the globe at the equator.

With the uplift of many islands, including those of Indonesia's Banda arc and the forging of Papua New Guinea, the equatorial current's westward passage was all but closed off. Some of its warm, tropical waters were diverted to flow down Australia's east coast, and changes in water circulations to the northwest gave birth to the Leeuwin Current, which flows down the west coast.

The effects on the continent's marine environments were twofold: first, the birth of so many new islands combined with chang-

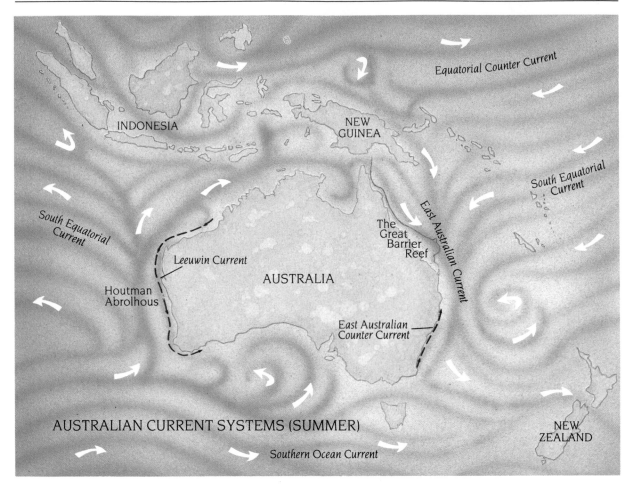

INDONESIA

NEW GUINEA

Equatorial Counter Current

South Equatorial Current

South Equatorial Current

Leeuwin Current

AUSTRALIA

The Great Barrier Reef

East Australian Current

Houtman Abrolhos

East Australian Counter Current

AUSTRALIAN CURRENT SYSTEMS (SUMMER)

NEW ZEALAND

Southern Ocean Current

A complex and interlocking pattern of currents encircles Australia, and determines the singular nature of its marine environment: predominantly tropical in the north and temperate in the south and transition zones where elements of the two mingle. These transition zones occur in the Houtman Abrolhos island group on the west coast and south of the Great Barrier Reef on the east coast.

ing seas to create many new habitats in which new forms of marine life could evolve; second, the tropical currents flowing south on each side of the continent carried much of that new diversity to colonise the continent's waters — especially those of the more favourable northeastern coast.

The effects of the new currents flowed through to the southern waters and set off changes in circulation patterns there. Australia came to be surrounded by a complex, ever-shifting mesh of currents, counter-currents, eddies and gyres, interwoven with tidal movements and localised swirls. Together, these major and minor flows determine the shape of Australia's marine life. They bring food, disperse young and serve as highways for migrations. By distributing waters of varying temperatures, salt contents and nutrient concentrations around the continental shelf, they create a mosaic of habitats that make Australia's marine environment the richest and most diverse in the world. It is home to 3500 kinds of fishes alone — almost a third of all the world's species.

The reason for that great diversity is not only that Australia has almost every possible type of habitat — from the cold southern waters to the warm tropical seas of the north — but also that each often overlaps with the next. It is the zones of transition, combining different sets of living conditions, that produce the greatest range of adaptations and therefore life forms among plants and animals. On the large scale, the most significant of these transitional zones are where the temperate south meets the tropical north. The currents set up by Australia's move into tropical waters allow two marine worlds to mingle.

The encounter is most spectacular halfway up the west coast, in the Abrolhos Islands. Clouds of seabirds signal the richness of the island waters. There is enough food to sustain breeding birds in their millions: several species of terns and gulls as well as shearwaters, cormorants and red-tailed tropic birds nest on the islands and hunt in the surrounding waters. Below the surface are kelp forests and other algae typical of southern temperate waters, together with their inhabitants. But there are also coral communities characteristic of subtropical waters.

The distinction between the two worlds expresses itself not only in the different species that inhabit each, but also in the behaviour of animals they have in common. Cowries, for example, sea snails common to all the seas, change their breeding behaviour from north to south. The female broods her clutch of egg-filled capsules beneath her large, muscular foot. In the mild northern waters of the pantropical marine zone that joins the top half of Australia to the rest of the marine world, the eggs hatch at the larval stage. Conditions are benign and there is plenty of food to help them grow, but there are great risks — the smaller the prey, the more hungry mouths it will fit. Cowries in the south brood their eggs until the baby cowries emerge as fully developed young snails that have already outgrown many of the predators of southern waters.

There is a similar transition zone on the east coast, though the change is more gradual, blurred by the effects of the east Australian current that carries tropical organisms further south. One clear marker is the annual winter gathering of the humpback whales (*Megaptera novaeangliae*). Like the southern right whales, they feed on plankton in Antarctica's summers of plenty, and migrate to Australian waters to breed. But the humpbacks travel further, for they prefer the warmer subtropical waters that maintain an average temperature of around 25 degrees.

Their journey from Antarctica takes about three weeks, travelling at a steady 4 to 5 knots, night and day. The migration follows the same pattern each year: mothers with recently weaned yearlings travel north first, followed by immature males and females, then mature bulls and cows, and lastly females in late pregnancy: the females have to feed longest to ensure adequate milk supplies for their newborn calves. Humpback (from the way the whale arches its back as it is about to dive) is an ungainly name for a graceful animal. The humpbacks are slightly smaller than the right whales — on average about 15 metres long, and weighing 50 tonnes. Their bodies are dark above, and distinctively marked in white underneath. The markings vary from individual to individual, and may well help the whales recognise one another.

The whales communicate with each other by sound — to human ears, among the most enchanting songs in nature. Once it was thought humpbacks sang to keep together on their journeys, but in fact they do not sing much while they travel; it is not until they approach their breeding areas that the chorus begins.

Each group has its own song, with individual variations, and the composition changes over the years. Much mystery still surrounds the singers and their songs: whales do not have vocal chords, and the precise mechanism through which they produce their distinctive scales of clicks, moans and whistles of varying pitch is not clearly understood. Nor is the purpose the singing serves, but as it reaches its crescendo in the breeding grounds after journeys of relative silence, much of it probably has to do with mating rituals.

Courtship among these elegant giants looks like a boisterous game, but is in fact ritualised aggression. Battles often begin when other bulls jostle for position with one escorting a lone female or a cow and calf. Unlike right whales, humpback cows come into oestrus again soon after birth, so the male that is closest to her has the best chance of mating. In the meantime, he tries to head off other bulls seeking to interlope.

Bulls competing for access to a female race along the surface at breakneck speed, then dive and come up in a series of spectacular breaches, throwing themselves out of the water, performing a half twist in midair and landing on their backs with a resounding splash. To make themselves look even larger, bulls lunge through the surface, their throat pleats engorged with water and air. Rivals also charge each other, butting their chins or flailing with their flukes. On occasion, the impact sends the two soaring out of the water, locked together in what looks so like an embrace it used to be mistaken for copulation. Just how humpbacks do mate is not known exactly, but is probably similar to the mode of the right whales: female on the surface and male beneath, belly to belly.

Toward the end of winter, the humpbacks begin to leave their shallow, sheltered breeding waters to move south again — recently impregnated females, bulls and cows with new calves.

Tropical Invasions

As the continent's top quarter drifted above the tropic of Capricorn into the tropics, new lifeforms colonised its northern waters, mingling, competing and coexisting with assemblies carried on the voyage from the south. The voyage was accompanied by many rises and falls in the levels of the oceans, governed by the growth and contraction of the Antarctic ice cap.

Because Australia is such a flat continent, huge areas were inundated whenever the seas rose. Plants on the flat coastal margins, already adapted to submersion by the daily tides, gradually evolved to cope with a completely aquatic existence. Unlike the primitive seaweeds that have always been marine plants, the new sea grasses still set flowers, and have roots and protected seeds, as they did on land.

Vast submarine meadows ripple in the shallow waters and, as meadows do on land, they attract grazing animals. As Australia's northward drift carried its coastal meadows into the tropical waters of the Indo-Pacific, they came to be grazed by the sea cows of that region, the dugongs. Like whales, dugongs are descended from land animals that returned to the sea, and share a common (though distant) ancestry with elephants.

Australia's flat, shallow northern shores have seen the sea invade and retreat many times, and grasses have evolved to meet the challenge of growing and flowering underwater, making submarine meadows where dugongs (*Dugong dugon*) come to graze. Like whales, their ancestry lies among terrestrial animals — possibly the group that also gave rise to elephants. The dugong is now the only living herbivorous mammal that is completely marine.

The tangle of mangrove roots and seedlings makes a rich environment for many forms of life: sea fishes use these areas as nurseries for their larvae; the trapped mud provides food for molluscs and crabs. When mangrove seedlings first become established, they face the additional challenge of having their leaves submerged with each high tide.

Dugongs feed mainly on sea grasses and have a special liking for the more delicate and nutritious kinds, which they search out with sensory bristles on the upper lip. The lip itself is a versatile tool that digs out clumps of grass, roots and all, and conveys them to the mouth. Herds of a hundred or more dugongs graze together in leisurely fashion, moving across the meadows like a company of lumbering lawnmowers.

The tropical currents carried other invaders, too. On the blurred margins between land and sea, mangroves took root — strange trees that tolerate salt water and that can grow in mud devoid of oxygen. Mangrove is a general description, covering some twenty-six Australian species of trees and shrubs.

The origins of Australia's tidal forests are not clear: some mangroves almost certainly travelled with the continent's coastal margins from Gondwana, while others took root after drifting in on the tropical currents: Australia shares many of its mangroves with those of other tropical regions. As the continent was invaded by shallow seas several times during its long journey north, different groups of plants evolved independent ways of coping with life on the fluid margins. What all have in common are adaptations to a stressful environment in which tides and coastal currents make for constantly changing physical, chemical and biological conditions.

There are two constant problems — getting rid of excess salt, and getting enough oxygen. Mangroves have three ways of dealing with salt, and most employ at least two of them: salt filters in their roots, salt storage in leaves that are later shed, and glands that excrete the salt to be washed away.

To anchor themselves in the mud, mangroves have shallow but widely spread root systems, and there are various designs to enable the roots to obtain the oxygen the mud lacks. Some are raised from the tidal mudflats on stilts, exposed to the air when the tide is out; others have breathing roots that project from the mud like periscopes. Yet others have knobbly or blade-like protrusions. The aerial roots have spongy, gas-filled tissues and pores in their outer layers. While the roots are submerged the gas pressure drops as the tree uses up its stored oxygen; then, when the tide recedes and the roots are exposed again, fresh air is sucked in through the pores.

Reproduction in such an environment also poses special challenges. Normal seeds might simply wash away on the ebb tide before they have a chance to take root. Some mangroves solve this problem by having the seeds begin their development while still attached to the parent plant. The seedlings grow a long, dagger-like root which, when the parent finally releases them, plunges into the mud to give the seedling a firm hold. Other seeds float while

The blurred margins between land and sea have been colonised by mangroves, a group of about 26 species of plants belonging to 14 different families that independently evolved to cope with growing in salty mud, devoid of oxygen. Raising the roots above the mud enables mangroves to take oxygen directly from the air when the tide is out.

they mature, and the buoyant shells dissolve when the roots are developed enough to give them a grip on the mud.

It is the characteristic tangle of mature and growing mangroves that makes these tidal forests such a vital link in the life of the sea. Roots and stems weave into nets that trap sediments and nutrient-rich organic matter carried by rivers to the tidal flats. The nutrients are taken up by the mangroves and eventually recycled in the form of leaf litter, which then becomes the basis for a rich and diverse array of life forms. Bacteria and fungi colonise and break down the litter, making it available to small animals such as amphipods and prawns, which in turn become meals for others.

Life in the mangroves is dictated by the tides. When the tide is out, legions of crabs emerge to forage on the mudflats. Mudskippers are active, too — fish that walk on their fins over the exposed mud, carrying their own water supply in their gill chambers. They are aggressive predators and their prey includes crabs as well as worms and molluscs. When the tide returns, the mud foragers retreat into holes, move toward the shore or — like some of the molluscs — climb up the mangroves above the tide. The aquatic shift takes over — fishes, shrimps, prawns and jellyfish in search of food.

Both the food and the shelter provided by the mangrove forests make them important nurseries for many fishes, including mullet and barramundi. Both spawn at sea, but the larvae make their way back to the mangroves for the early phases of their growth.

Providing nurseries for many marine animals is one important contribution that the tidal forests make to the life of the sea. An even greater effect is that of the massive filtering system created by the mangroves and their animal communities. By trapping muddy sediments carried down by rivers and by processing nutrients into soluble forms, they keep the shallow offshore waters relatively clear for corals to flourish.

Coral Castles

Corals belong to the same groups as anemones and jellyfish — just above sponges on the evolutionary scale, and just below various wormlike groups. They are not plants, but animals — many thousands of individual animals, called polyps, growing together to form a colony. Each polyp is essentially a cylinder with a ring of tentacles at the top, surrounding an opening that serves as both mouth and anus. Food is processed, by cells in the cylinder's outer layer, into the basic building material that binds the colony together: limestone. Polyps need shallow, clear water because sunlight provides the energy for manufacturing the limestone; the clearer the water, the more limestone produced. Close inshore,

where the water is still relatively turbid, corals tend to grow in iso-lated colonies. As the water becomes clearer further from land, polyps can produce more limestone — enough, eventually, to form massive barrier reefs.

The ancestors of today's reefs probably first colonised Australia's northern waters about eighteen million years ago, as the continent moved into current systems that originated in the coral-rich regions of the Indo-Pacific.

There had been coral reefs in Australian waters before, but in a much remoter past. Though formed of an earlier and different type of coral called rugose, which became extinct 200 million years ago, the reefs were strikingly similar in appearance to modern reefs built out of the later scleractinian corals.

The modern corals that succeeded the rugose forms probably evolved in the warm and shallow waters of a vast and ancient ocean called the Tethys Sea, which separated the northern and southern landmasses. It closed as the landmasses moved together, and the evolving corals were pushed gradually eastwards into what is now the western Pacific, when at the same time Australia's northward drift was taking it into those same regions.

The Great Barrier Reef is one of the most enchanting places on earth, crowded with an almost infinite variety of life — a kaleidoscope of colour and movement held in dynamic balance by the universal urges of survival and reproduction.

An almost continuous and interlocking chain of coral reefs, running up the northeast coast of Australia for 2300 kilometres, makes the Great Barrier Reef the largest living structure on earth. Corals began to colonise Australia's northern waters when its long voyage from Gondwana took its northern half into tropical latitudes.

Probably the first shoreline to become festooned with coral reefs was the coast of present-day Papua New Guinea. From there they spread to Australia's northeast coast, gradually migrating further south as the waters warmed up. By two million years ago, the southernmost foundations of the Great Barrier Reef had been established.

In the millennia that followed, when the seas rose the reefs rose with them to keep within reach of the sun. When the seas fell, the reefs died and their skeletons stood as limestone ramparts in the coastal plains to become the foundations for the next generations of coral when the waters returned again.

The latest growth began perhaps only 8000 years ago, when the seas reached their present levels, and created the greatest reef complex on earth.

The Great Barrier Reef runs for 2300 kilometres along the continental shelf of northeastern Australia, so distinctive it can be seen from the moon. It generally follows the contours of the shelf, closest to the mainland in the north where the shelf is relatively narrow, furthest away in the south where the shelf broadens out. An aerial view best conveys the reef's magnitude, and the variety of sizes and shapes of the more than 2000 separate reef systems that form more or less interlocking chains of coral.

Yet this enormous living structure, which itself supports the greatest variety of life on earth, is sustained by waters that are virtual deserts. By the time they reach Australia the tropical currents have lost most of their nutrients, but they are rich in another substance: calcium carbonate, the raw material corals convert into

The outer edge of the reef takes the brunt of the breaking seas. As a result, corals grow in squat, solid shapes. The surge of the waves and tides pumps fresh supplies of water through the reef, ferrying in cargoes of calcium carbonate that corals convert into limestone — the basic material that binds the entire edifice together.

their living rock. So it is where the reef first meets the ocean, on the outer edge of the continental shelf, that the coral is at its most diverse and grows most rapidly, for it is these corals that have first access to the calcium carbonate. Most of the 350 species of coral that make up the Great Barrier Reef are found on this turbulent frontal zone, just below the ceaseless crash of the breaking waves.

    To extract the calcium carbonate from the water at a sufficient rate to outstrip the sea's eroding and dissolving powers requires much energy. Corals get that energy from their association with minute, single-celled plants called zooxanthellae. The zooxanthellae live inside the coral tissue, and use sunlight to manufacture carbon dioxide and water into carbohydrates and oxygen for use by the coral polyps. They themselves live on the coral's metabolic wastes, such as phosphates and nitrates. It is a finely balanced relationship between plant and animal, with each depending on the other — the plant for shelter and nitrogen, the coral for growth. That interdependence is the basis for all life on the reef, and makes sunlight the single most important ingredient.

Sunlight is a crucial ingredient in the life of corals: tiny plants inside the polyp tissue convert it into energy for growth. Many of the shapes have evolved to give as many polyps as much exposure to the sun as possible: a garden fashioned in limestone, blooming with a myriad polyps.

Opposite

Many of the creatures that live on the coral reef rely on the tides and currents for their reproduction. This giant clam (*Tridacna gigas*) shoots a cloud of sperm into the water — later it will release eggs — and the movement of water will mix and match them with those of other clams. Eventually a tiny larva will settle to begin its long growth — to a weight of as much as 260 kilograms. A clam opens to the sun during the day, and minute algae in its lips convert the sun's energy into some of its food requirements: other food comes from plankton, filtered from the water passing through its mantle.

Battle for the Sun

There are various strategies aimed at securing a place in the sun. Some corals grow fast to overshadow their competitors, such as several *Acropora* species, which grow in the shape of flat-topped tables at what for corals is a breakneck speed of 10 centimetres a year. Others, such as the staghorn corals, grow complex branching structures designed to give each group of polyps the maximum possible exposure to the sun.

There is more direct competition, too, and many corals attack one another. Some put out filaments to digest the tissues of their neighbours; some grow long tentacles with poison-laden tips that sweep the nearby water and sting any encroaching colonies; and others exude lethal chemicals into the water. With all that fierce competition, it is remarkable that so many different species that have the same requirements manage to coexist: it may be that the reef's astounding diversity is maintained by a regime of disturbance that prevents the development of a more uniform community. For coral reefs, which used to be thought of as benign and stable environments, can in fact be violent places where any competitive advantage one species may be establishing may be wiped out by the destructive force of a cyclone, or the chance loss of a new generation of recruits.

Sunlight is the primary force for growth on the reef, and for holding it together. The profusion of coral on the reef's outer wall ends abruptly where the surf zone begins. The ramparts that with-

The need to hide from predators — and to stalk prey unseen — has given rise to bizarre body shapes and camouflage among the inhabitants of the reef. This lionfish (*Scorpaenidae* spp.), with its striking array of fins and stripes — it is also called the butterfly cod — emerges at night to hunt smaller fish. The spines are coated with a venomous mucus.

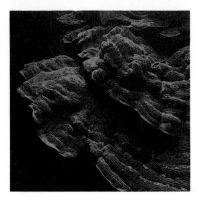

As well as need for sunlight, stresses from waves and currents add to the array of the corals' architectural responses, producing shapes as lush and complex as the folds of a flamenco dancer's skirt.

stand the waves on the reef crest are built of limestone secreted not by corals, but by millions of tiny, primitive plants called coralline algae. Being plants, they use sunlight directly to convert seawater into rock. The algae form ridges and spurs that effectively deflect and absorb the force of the waves.

The breakwaters built by the coralline algae create shelter for reef areas behind the crest. Instead of surging waves, it is the daily tides and their associated currents that become the important water movement. The ocean waters may be virtual deserts, but they do contain some nutrients, and the whole of the barrier reef system revolves around making that little go a long way. The tides play a crucial part: they transport fresh supplies of ocean water with their content of oxygen, calcium carbonate and minute amounts of nutrients. Currents set up by the winds and tidal movements distribute the supplies around the individual reefs.

The almost infinite complexity and variety of life that exists in and around the reef is built on a tightly interlocked series of recycling mechanisms that makes for a virtually self-sufficient economy. Among the important early links in the chain are thin, almost invisible films of microscopic blue-green algae that grow on almost every surface of the reef structures. The tiny plants absorb nitrogen from the water and convert it to nitrate: bacteria break down the algae, releasing the nitrate to supplement the meagre supplies of this important nutrient washed in from the ocean. The waters also bring particulate material — living and dead — that sustains guilds of filter-feeders and plankton-eaters.

The suspension feeders are the largest group of animals on the reef, diverse both in their form and in the manner in which they trap their food. Among them are the corals themselves, though the planktonic soup supplies only a small part of their requirements, the bulk of which are met by their symbiotic relationship with the zooxanthellae living in their tissues.

Most corals do their feeding in the dark. Like an instantaneous bloom of millions of flowers, the coral polyps open their bouquets of tentacles soon after nightfall. Sooner or later one of the myriad copepods and amphipods swims into a tentacle, where it is immobilised by stinging cells and ensnared by others before being swallowed. Night feeding reduces the chances of the polyps themselves being predated upon, but an even more important reason may be that keeping the tentacles withdrawn during the day increases the area of coral exposed to the sunlight, so vital to the zooxanthellae on which the coral relies for most of its energy.

In slightly deeper water, gorgonians spread their fans across the currents, and sea whips wave. They, too, are corals, but their skeletons are made of a tough, flexible skin coloured yellow to deep orange, scattered with polyps like tiny white flowers. Fans

Some corals, called gorgonians, grow in elegant, feathery fan
shapes, at right angles to the current for the polyps to trap
food when they extend at night. A crinoid, or feather star,
has attached itself near the top of this fiery red specimen:
when darkness comes, it too spreads its feathery arms to
catch whatever the currents bring the gorgonian's way.
Within the crowded world of the coral reef, no opportunity is
left unexploited.

grow at right angles to the current and when the polyps are extended their tentacles almost touch, making an efficient plankton net. The strength of the water flow determines the size of the mesh — larger in slow currents, smaller in strong currents to provide greater rigidity. Some are sculpted by the currents, changing their pattern as they grow to respond to subtle variations of food availability and of water pressure. And everywhere, sea anemones — from which the coral groups evolved — sweep their long, delicate tentacles through the water, ready to paralyse any small creature.

Death and Birth of a Reef

When daylight returns, the hard corals withdraw their tentacles: the flowers close, and the zooxanthellae resume their task of converting sunlight into the energy the corals need to produce the limestone that is the foundation for the entire reef system. For the reef to survive, limestone needs to be produced at a faster rate than the various agents of destruction can operate. And there are many of these: some fishes feed exclusively on coral polyps, somehow immune to the stinging protection of the tentacles. One species of parrotfish has a powerful beaklike mouth to bite off pieces of coral rock, digesting the animal and plant matter within and excreting the rest in rains of coral sand. In some areas, fish are reckoned to -consume a third of the annual growth of coral.

Another voracious predator on coral is a species of sea star, the Crown of Thorns, which feeds by turning its stomach inside out, wrapping it around a coral colony and sucking the life from it. Periodic outbreaks of Crown of Thorns can devastate entire reefs: the outbreaks seem to be linked with disturbances of the reef's inshore waters, where the Crown of Thorns breeds. An increase in turbidity, such as that caused by unusually large runoff of eroded soils from the coastal forests, seems to favour the survival of the sea star larvae. It is likely that one of the most recent species to arrive in the region — humans — may be a factor in these disturbances, increasing the frequency and severity of outbreaks. The Crown of Thorns and other attackers can do much damage, but it is probably the enemy within that wreaks the most destruction. Several kinds of mussels, worms and sponges bore deep inside the coral, destroying it with acid secretions that dissolve the limestone.

Some corals do not need outside agents such as storms to clone daughter colonies. They pinch off small sections, which then drop to the reef floor and begin growing, or they send out runners to establish a new colony in a vacant spot nearby. But this asexual style of reproduction has one disadvantage. By propagating copies of a parent cell, asexual reproduction does not allow for rapid

Eating and being eaten is a major driving force on the reef, as in all living systems. A giant triton (*Charonia tritonis*) has latched on to a Crown of Thorns starfish (*Acanthaster planci*), which itself is eating a coral. The triton is one of the Crown of Thorns' few predators: it slices the starfish open with a radula — a cutting organ that works a little like a bandsaw — and sucks out the soft tissue. A small butterfly fish (*Chaetodon* sp.) hovers on the sidelines, to snatch up any spilt fragments.

Left

Holothurians, or sea cucumbers, are sausage-shaped animals, with a leathery, flexible body; a mouth surrounded by feeding tentacles at one end, and an anus at the other. Like this *Pentacta anceps*, they often suggest a vase filled with delicate flowers. The tentacles are coated with a sticky mucus to catch plankton swept within reach by the currents.

change, while organisms that exchange and recombine genes in sexual reproduction evolve faster and are less likely to become extinct during times of environmental change.

Corals are just one of many groups to alternate between both methods, producing clonal copies for local dispersal and sexually produced larvae that drift to more distant locations. Being stationary animals, corals cannot go in search of partners, and they have evolved a way of using the currents as go-betweens — a strategy that ranks among the most marvellous displays in all of nature. Once a year, on just a few spring nights, after a full moon, when the sea temperatures have undergone a rapid rise, when there is a neap tide and the water is at its stillest, the Great Barrier Reef gives birth. In a remarkable mass spawning, up and down the length of the reef, the corals fill the lagoons with multi-coloured clouds of spawn.

Like many of the creatures that live within their shelter, corals use water as a go-between for their own reproduction, in a mass spawning that ranks amongst the most spectacular displays in all of nature. Sperm and eggs, wrapped together in tiny, often brightly-coloured bundles, are drawn through the polyp's mouths and released simultaneously one warm spring night.

Tide and temperature provide the cue for the almost simultaneous culmination of individual processes that began many months before. Within the uncountable millions of polyps, sex cells had ripened to form eggs first, and sperm later. Most polyps have both female and male organs; in some corals, the sexes are separate and each colony is either male or female. The warming waters of spring stimulate the eggs and sperm to develop rapidly. The eggs become coloured according to species — most often pink, red or orange, with some purples, blues and greens — and the sperm develop tails. In the days before the spawning, the hermaphrodite polyps wrap their sperm and eggs into bundles less than half a millimetre in diameter. The unisexual polyps make ready their male or female gametes.

Most corals are hermaphroditic — they release both male and female gametes. Some are single sex, and release either eggs or, like this mushroom coral (*Fungia fungites*), sperm.

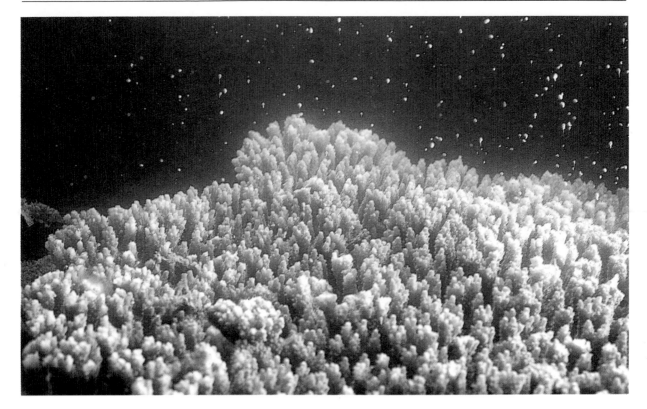

As the time approaches, they draw the bundles near their mouths and slowly begin to squeeze them out. Over hundreds of kilometres, the reefs are festooned with brightly coloured bundles. As at some silent signal, the bundles are released — sometimes in one mass ejaculation by an entire colony, sometimes in bursts by individual groups. Colonies hundreds of kilometres apart are synchronised so closely that they release their egg and sperm packages within a few hours of one another. The moonlit coral seas swirl with colour as the clouds of spawn float to the surface.

There the packages dissolve and the eggs and sperm are set free. The minute sperm, propelling themselves with their tails, find their way to eggs of their own species and burrow inside. Within minutes the fertilised egg divides and divides again, and develops into a larva. The coral larvae — only around one and a half millimetres long — swim off with minute hair-like paddles. Some species stay on or near the surface for only a few hours, others for weeks or months. Somehow — probably by chemical means — the larvae sense when they are near a suitable place to settle, make their way down and cement themselves in a vacant spot with the first of their limestone secretions — tiny grains of rock that will eventually grow into great and complex edifices.

For a few hours, the coral seas swirl with blizzards of brightly-coloured balloons, filled with sex cells. The bundles rise to the surface, where they break up: the sperm and eggs mingle with others of their own species, larvae form, and within days or weeks settle on the sea floor to begin another generation of coral growth.

The Marvellous Variety

Tide and temperature provide the cue for the corals' mass ejaculation. The strategy evolved to counter the hordes of hungry mouths that inhabit the reef: single emissions would be devoured quickly, but the sheer volume of a mass spawning soon saturates the predators, and ensures that sufficient eggs and sperm reach the surface to achieve procreation. These are *Acropora* species, of the staghorn and plate varieties.

At the heart of reef growth is the polyp's ability to produce large numbers of exact copies of itself that remain connected to each other, to form one colony. A common method of budding is for the circular ring of tentacles around the mouth to become oval, and for the mouth to move to one end. A second mouth develops at the other end; beneath it, the polyp's body is also dividing. Then the oval tentacle ring splits and two complete polyps are formed — which then repeat the process. There are many variations on this basic theme: three mouths may form in a triangle, for example, or in line. The way each species of coral buds determines the pattern of its limestone secretions, which are then further sculpted into cups, ridges and spikes by the rate and manner of their deposit. Each species has its own blueprint, and the variations are endless.

The result is a range of living structures that for diversity of form, colour and texture has no rivals in the natural world. There are 1000 species of coral in the world, and a third of them are found on the Great Barrier Reef alone.

By the time Australia's north drifted into tropical waters around fifteen million years ago, coral life was already immensely diverse, and it seems Australia inherited that diversity: almost all the species occur elsewhere, and only a few are endemic. Although there has probably been insufficient time since Australia acquired its coral reefs for much evolution into distinct species to occur, fluctuations in sea level have continued to isolate and recombine communities, which helped produce local variations to add to the almost infinite array of coral life.

Next to the coral itself, the diversity is most visible among the fishes, of which there are around two thousand species.

What at first glance seems a chaos of colour is in fact a tightly organised and finely partitioned society, in which each group of fishes has its place: many are shaped and patterned to fit that place and no other. As well as the specialists, there are species whose requirements do overlap; in a stable environment competition might lead to a reduction in diversity, but on the reef other forces usually intervene and diversity is maintained. The imperative that holds the reef communities in a kind of dynamic balance is survival — the need to eat, to avoid being eaten, and to reproduce.

As many as 200 species of fish may make their home on any one reef. Part of the reason for the enormous diversity is the great range of habitats: varying depths, degrees of clarity, temperature, calmness and types of food add up to a set of living conditions whose permutations are almost endless. Size is one measurement of diversity: fishes range from 10 millimetre gobies weighing less than a gram, to 5 metre tiger sharks that weigh around a tonne, and every other size in between. The smaller the fish the greater is their number, both in species and in individuals. Higher on the scale the number of both species and individuals becomes smaller — like a pyramid, with the big predators at the top.

Behaviour and physical adaptations are the other dimensions of reef diversity. Competition for food and space has produced many specialisations. Some take physical shape, like the snout of the butterfly fish (*Forcipiger*); a long tube with a tiny mouth at its end, designed to probe cracks and holes for the tiny crustaceans other fish cannot reach. There is a wrasse called a slingjaw for its remarkable extendable mouthparts, which it throws forward to engulf some small animal that thought it was safely out of range.

There are specialisations in behaviour, and in the way various fishes organise their lives. Many of the smaller fishes feed on algae, and they establish territories they defend fiercely — especially against members of their own species, which have the same needs for food and space. Territorial herbivores not only graze the algae within their territories, but also actively 'farm' their holdings: weeding out the larger, tougher algae and disposing of them to provide more growing space for the smaller, more nutritious plants they prefer.

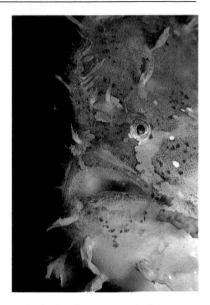

Only the bright eye reveals this to be a living animal — it is an angler fish, perfectly camouflaged within a patch of *Sargassum* weed while it waits to snap up smaller fish that come within reach.

Everywhere the eye turns, it meets a spectacular sight — on the large scale as well as the small. The Sacoglossan seaslug (*Cyerce nigricans*) wears a coat of brightly-coloured leaves — they contain glands that exude noxious secretions when the animal is attacked. It 'grazes' the seaweeds that grow profusely on the reefs.

Many reef creatures form partnerships for mutual benefit: one of the most remarkable is the cleaning service performed by some species of wrasse on larger fish. The 'customers' hang still in the water, while the wrasses remove parasites from their bodies, inside the gills — even inside the mouth. The wrasses get their 'fee' from the nourishment provided by the parasites they clean off.

Some species, such as the blue and gold angelfish, use territorial defence to control a group of mates. Four to seven form a group that establishes a joint territory on some algae-covered patch of reef. There is usually one male in the family, and while the females graze the algae and produce eggs, he patrols the territorial borders to stop encroachments by neighbouring families.

Should the patriarch die, the largest female changes sex, becoming a male and taking over the breeding and patrolling duties. The borders of each group's territory may be invisible, but they are real enough to neighbouring males and the patriarch must be prepared to fight trespassers.

Some members of the wrasse family have developed averting potential aggression into a fine art. They provide a cleaning service, eating the parasites that grow on the skin of larger fish. Wrasses station themselves at prominent places that become cleaning stations for a range of fishes, from parrotfish to sweetlips and moray eels. The cleaners, identifiable by their distinctive blue on white stripe, advertise by performing a gyrating, dancing swim. Customers respond by suspending their normal predatory instincts and hanging almost in a trance, mouths and gills open, while the cleaner wrasses work — often swimming inside the mouths of larger fishes to find the parasites.

Even more remarkable than the cleaner wrasses is a fraudulent variation on the theme. A small blenny fish has evolved to look exactly like the cleaners, and even performs a similar swimming dance. The disguise fools the waiting customers — until, instead of delicately picking off parasites as the true cleaners do, the false cleaner takes a quick bite from a fin or gill.

Partnerships for Survival

Associating with other animals is a common way of surviving on the reef. Pilot fish enjoy free transport by riding the bow wave at the head of a shark, though a slow, sick or injured pilot fish will soon be eaten by its host. Remoras have dorsal fins modified into a sucker, which attaches to the body of a shark, marlin or whale: while some remoras eat parasites, others feed on scraps from their host's own meals.

Clownfish seek protection with another kind of animal altogether. They live within the shelter of the anemones' poisonous tentacles, darting out to feed on plankton and returning to their host's embrace should a predator come close. The clownfish are not immune to the stinging cells in the tentacles — they protect themselves by covering themselves with the anemone's mucus — and the anemone will not sting what it senses to be part of itself. What the anemones get out of the relationship is not clear,

Anemone fishes (*Amphiprion* spp.) sheltering within the
stinging tentacles of an anemone, while themselves
remaining unharmed. The fishes gain their protection by
covering themselves in a mucus secreted by the anemone,
which will then not sting what it senses to be part of itself. It
is a measure of the reef's diversity that there are 29 species of
anemone fishes, involved in more or less close partnerships
with 13 different species of anemone.

though there are reports that their guests defend them from predators such as butterfly fishes.

The partnership between some gobies and shrimps is more clearly a reciprocal affair. Pairs of them set up home in the sandy floor between patches of reef, where the shrimps do the work of actually excavating and maintaining the burrows, while the gobies with their keener eyesight dart out for food and keep watch. Should danger loom, the goby signals the shrimp with a flick of its tail, and fish and crustacean vanish into their common burrow.

Camouflage is a good tactic for catching food as well as for protection. Scorpion fish are festooned with flaps of skin of different colours to look like a rock draped in algae. They lie absolutely motionless until a potential meal comes within reach, when they strike with a speed that defies the eye. A close relative, the stonefish, half buries itself and merges with the coral sand to lie in ambush. Should it be detected by a larger fish looking for a meal, its needle-sharp dorsal spines — each equipped with a pair of poison glands — are effective deterrents.

One drawback of the camouflage and ambush technique is that it does rely on prey coming within reach. A possibly surer, and certainly quicker, way is to become mobile while remaining camouflaged — a refinement perfected by the trumpetfish, a queer elongated animal that moulds itself to the shape of a large grazer such as the parrotfish, and travels with it. Smaller fry perceive the parrot as harmless; when it is within range, the trumpeter darts out from its unwitting host's cover to snap up a meal. Another way to stay mobile and hidden at the same time is to change camouflage pattern with the terrain. Spangled emperors change from a plain greyish hue to a dappled pattern as they move out from cover into open water rippling with shadows.

The Language of Colour

Important though it is, camouflage is but one of the purposes served by colour and pattern. Most reef fishes, in fact, advertise their presence boldly. The reason lies in the complex and diverse nature of reef society. With such a great number of species, there is a correspondingly great need for an efficient signal system: in the clear waters of the reef, colour and pattern are the most effective way to communicate, for most fishes have extremely good colour vision. With such a density of species, many of them with similar shapes and living in similar places, it is important not to waste energy trying to mate with the wrong kind, and bold colours help males and females of one species recognise one another; it seems the importance of finding the right mate outweighs the risks involved in advertising to predators.

Not all corals build reefs: some, like this *Heliofungia*, grow as solitary, free-living organisms. They closely resemble anemones, and have similar tentacles. A shrimp has found shelter within them — it feeds on fragments caught on the sticky mucus.

Many fish have territories to defend, and it saves energy if they can recognise whether or not an intruder is of the same species and, therefore, whether or not it is a threat. Within species, too, there are variations in markings that help individuals recognise each other. Males and females are often coloured differently, and among many fishes (especially the diverse smaller species such as the damsels, angels, gobies and butterflies) colours become brighter during breeding time to reduce the risk of mistaken identity and to help coordinate the mating ritual.

Accurately identifying sex is especially important among fish that change gender. Sex change is a normal part of the life cycle of many species, and they may have three different colour patterns — females, males and those that are in the process of changing from one to the other.

Changing sex enables an individual to produce more offspring. Among blue and gold angel fish, for example, larger males can control territory and breeding rights more successfully than small ones because they are stronger fighters. So for young fish growing up it makes more sense being female and producing offspring, rather than being an unproductive male. Once the female reaches a competitive size, it is worth her while changing sex at the first opportunity, such as when the dominant male dies. For the ultimate advantage of becoming one of the ruling males is that they mate with all the females in the harem, and so produce the most offspring. Ensuring the offspring's survival is the next step to reproductive success. Fishes are most vulnerable when they are in egg or larval form. There are two basic ways to prevent offspring being eaten. Generally, smaller fishes are demersal spawners — they produce relatively fewer eggs, lay them on some suitable site, and increase their chances by giving them some degree of protection. Larger fishes tend to be pelagic spawners — they release a great many eggs directly into the water: the odds are that some will survive. Within the two kinds of strategy, there are almost as many variations as there are species of fishes.

Ruled by the Tides

The time is dawn, a day or two after the full moon, an hour or two before the highest tide of the month. The place is just inside the outer edge of the reef, in a channel where the outgoing current will be strongest. Now the water is still, and as the early light grows stronger and penetrates more deeply, indistinct shapes begin to materialise into parrotfish. They have gathered here from all over the reef — many have come tens of kilometres, alone or in small groups, answering the signals of moon and tides and guided by a kind of tribal memory. Hundreds of fish hang in the water, waiting for the tide to turn.

The gathering has attracted the reef's big predators — a tiger shark cruises by, and trevallies and barracudas prowl the periphery. At any other time, the mere sight of such hunters would send the parrotfish scattering, but now procreation is more important than individual survival. The assembled fish suspend their normal wariness and enter an almost trancelike state to accomplish their goal: to release their spawn on the outgoing tide, and to have it carried safely to sea.

To prepare for that moment, the males establish temporary, three-dimensional territories. Ignoring the predators, the parrotfish have attention only for their own kind. The tide has turned, the currents begin to flow and movement quickens. Small groups of subordinate males and females roam between the courtship territories. When a group ventures on to a particular patch, the resident male chases off the subordinates and courts one of the females with a circling, bobbing swim. When she signals her acceptance with a rising movement of her body, the male moves next to her and together they make a sudden dash several metres up into the water column. Other males and females follow — the females release their eggs, the males their sperm, and instantly the group descends again, leaving behind clouds of spawn, like puffs of smoke, that mingle and fertilise and float away.

The wealth of spawn makes a feast for schools of small fishes, but they are soon sated and most of the eggs are carried beyond their reach by the strongly flowing tide.

The parrotfishes' spawning is but one of many: every tide in summer carries uncountable masses of eggs out to sea, and the larvae of those that have hatched within the reef. Sheer numbers are the key to success, for even away from the reef, there is risk. Parrotfish eggs hatch about twenty-five hours after spawning, long enough for them to be carried well away from the hungry mouths on the reef . . . but into open water, where there may be little food. Many will simply starve once the initial supply provided by their yolk sac has run out. Some may find refuge — and minute fragments of food — among the tentacles of jellyfish. Drifting patches of seaweed also provide shelter and food, though fellow passengers may include crustaceans and fishes with a taste for larvae.

Spawning is a numbers game; the odds are that enough fish larvae will survive to be carried back to the reef to replenish their kind. Sometimes chance favours one species: it has spawned on the right current at the right time, and its larvae have had more food, less predation, or both. Great numbers have survived the ocean journey, and for a time that species will dominate its patch of reef: next season it may be the turn of another group.

Underlying the patterns of change among their occupants, the reef systems themselves are always in a state of flux. When the young parrotfish mature, their strong, shearing beaks will become one of the many elements in that process. Grazing algae, they bite off large chunks of the coral skeleton on which it grows. Massive bony plates in their throats grind the algae and rock into a sandy paste: the food is absorbed and the sand is voided, adding to sediments generated by the other eroding and decaying mechanisms at work on the reef.

Sands of Birth

Waves and currents mould the coral sand and in places heap it up, eventually to emerge above the water as coral cays. Waves refracting around the cays release more loads of sediment, and keep the cays growing. Cyclones may scatter them, but most last long enough for seeds to arrive, floating on the waves or carried by birds, and sprout vegetation to bind the sand together. Rainwater accumulates in the ground, the soil grows richer to support larger plants — and so, out of the reef and delivered by the currents, an island is born. Such islands become resting and breeding places for the large numbers of birds that find their food in the reefwaters.

Some also become beachheads for a remarkable annual invasion that begins somewhere in the tropical seas 2000 or more kilometres away. Early in summer, green turtles (*Chelonia Mydas*) — massive animals a metre across and weighing around a quarter of a tonne — begin to appear in the approaches to the islands. Most are females, heavy with eggs that are still to be fertilised.

Many gather in a single area of shallow water, resting on the sandy floor to recuperate from their long voyage and to prepare for the labour that will follow. They are bothered neither by the surgeonfishes that graze the algae growing on their shells, nor by the sharks cruising within striking distance. And for some reason the male turtles intent on copulation do not molest the females while they remain in their rest area. Once they leave, however, the males move in quickly and mount almost immediately if the female is receptive. If she is not she simply swims away; if he pursues she signals her refusal by hanging vertically in the water and biting him if he approaches too close. Copulation may last six hours, during which time competitors may try to dislodge a successful male. There are far fewer males than females (sometimes only one for every 40), but so strong is their reproductive urge that eventually even the most reluctant female has been impregnated.

As the light fades, the female turtles begin to move ashore, the grace and power of their movement in water giving way to an awkward lumber as they emerge into the element of their remote, ter-

Having evaded a gauntlet of predators — from rufous night herons on the beach to ghost crabs and reef sharks in the inshore waters — a newly hatched green turtle (*Chelonia mydas*) makes its way into the open ocean. Many risks lie ahead, and of the hundreds of thousands that hatched in this season, few will reach maturity. Females will be about 40 years old before they are sexually mature, and only then will they return to the coral beach of their birth to bury their own clutches of eggs.

After a hard night's labour of digging nests in the coral sand of Raine Island, in the far north of the reef, and laying clutches of 50 to 150 eggs, the green turtles (*Chelonia mydas*) return to the sea. Some seasons see as many as 10,000 come ashore in a single night.

restrial ancestry. Green turtles took to life in the sea 100 million years ago, but return to land to lay their eggs.

It takes many hours of hard work for the huge body to drag itself beyond the high water mark and to dig into the coral sand. In a summer of peak numbers, as many as 10,000 turtles come ashore on one island beach every night, and nesting space is at a premium. Each turtle's urge concerns its own offspring only, and some dig where other clutches have already been buried, destroying many eggs and early hatchlings in the process. Every available site on the beach is soon occupied and sprays of sand rise and fall as the turtles scoop out their nests.

They lay their eggs deep enough so that temperature and moisture will be constant, but not so deep that the eventual hatchlings will suffocate as they dig their way out. Each nest contains around a hundred eggs, and some turtles will repeat the process three or four times over the next few weeks. With 10,000 adults laying eggs each night, several million baby turtles will be awaiting birth by the time the season ends. The work of digging the nest, laying the eggs and covering them over again takes all night, and the eastern sky is already lightening when the turtles begin their slow trek back to the sea.

The eggs they left behind take six to seven weeks to develop, and in common with other reptiles such as crocodiles, temperature inside the nest determines the sex of the hatchlings: lower temperatures produce mostly males, higher temperatures females, and at 30 degrees the mix is about even.

Hatching reaches a peak in late summer, and the sands are astir night and day with the struggles of hatchlings making for the surface and the sea. Their inbuilt sense of direction points them at the sea — but to get there they have to evade a series of predators; mostly crabs at night, and in daylight birds as well. The reef herons are voracious predators, for their own breeding cycle is synchronised with the turtle hatching and baby turtles are the main source of food for the chicks in the nests that crowd the shrubland behind the turtle rookeries. When the surviving hatchlings finally reach the water they are still far from safe, for reef sharks and other predatory fishes move in for their feast. With such heavy predation it is surprising that any hatchlings manage to survive at all — yet one estimate puts the proportion of hatchlings that succeed in reaching the open ocean as high as 80 per cent.

It will be 40 years before they return, for it takes green turtles that long to reach breeding age. Where they go in that time, no-one knows. They simply disappear into the vastness of the oceans. But eventually, one early summer day, some will arrive in the waters of the reef and the cycle will begin again.

The Barrier Reef as it exists today is only about eight thousand years old — the latest phase in a cycle of growth, decay and consolidation that began when Australia's northward journey carried her northeast coast into the coral-rich waters of the Indo-Pacific ocean 18 million years ago.

Australia's break from Gondwana and her voyage changed the patterns of tides and currents, accelerated the rise and fall of the seas and the fluctuations of climate, and shaped her unique assembly of marine environments, culminating finally in the thousands of living systems that make up the great reef.

The only habitats that compare in variety and complexity are the rainforests that rise on the horizon along much of its length. If the reef is the culmination of evolutionary forces at work in Australia's seas, rainforests mark the beginning of a parallel evolution on the continent itself; from their diversity emerged Australia's characteristic heaths and woodlands, and their animal inhabitants. They began the making of the bush.

CHAPTER THREE

THE MAKING OF THE BUSH

The unique ability of Australian plants to regenerate after fire
has been a major ingredient in shaping the characteristic
forests and woodlands.

Australia's rainforests run in a thin, broken line down its eastern edge. They occupy only few refuges now, but for most of Australia's history they covered the larger part of the continent, from tropical jungle in the north to the cool, temperate forests of the south.

Immensely ancient, they are of common stock with rainforests elsewhere in the world. Yet they gave rise to plants and animals found nowhere else — so different early naturalists thought they were the product of a separate creation.

In fact, the making of the Australian bush and the elements that give it its distinctive flavour began, like terrestrial life elsewhere, in the primeval rainforests. That there still are remnants of that original vegetation is one of nature's ironies, for their survival is due in part to the same event that led to the demise of rainforest as the continent's dominant plant community.

When Australia broke away from Gondwana to become a separate continent, an uplift along what is now the eastern edge formed the basis for the Great Dividing Range. At the same time climatic changes were set in train that would cause the new continent to dry out and the vast rainforests to contract. But the Great Dividing Range catches enough rain to water the eastern strip and to preserve a few patches.

Although it is called a range, the Divide falls somewhat short of true mountains. In places at its northern end, it is only a few hundred metres above sea level: even at its highest point of 2400 metres in the southeast, it would be dwarfed by the lowest peaks of the Himalayas or the Andes. Unlike those dramatically serrated mountain ranges, the Divide is more a high plateau unfolding in a series of rounded, weathered rises.

The areas of Australia where different types of vegetation dominate. Rainfall and soil type govern the distribution; from forest in the higher-rainfall areas nearer the coast, to more open woodland further inland, and the hardy acacias and spinifex in the central regions.

But in a land of flat plains, even a modest rise assumes towering proportions, and the Divide's influence on the nature of Australia is great indeed. It is just high enough to send the winds that come in off the southern ocean into cooler altitudes, forcing them to release their cargos of moisture as rain, and in winter in the higher southern parts, as snow. When the winds continue to the vast hinterland to the west they are almost always dry, so the Divide stands as a barrier between the fertile eastern coastal strip and the barren plains to the west. To the east, the rivers run steep and fast and always have water. Only a few flow to the west, and droughts frequently see them disappear in chains of diminishing pools.

The high country in winter is the surprising face of Australia.

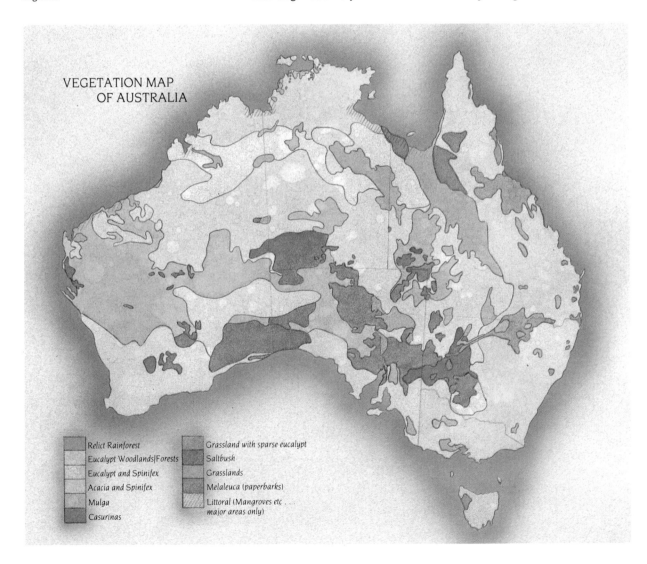

VEGETATION MAP
OF AUSTRALIA

Relict Rainforest
Eucalypt Woodlands/Forests
Eucalypt and Spinifex
Acacia and Spinifex
Mulga
Casurinas

Grassland with sparse eucalypt
Saltbush
Grasslands
Melaleuca (paperbarks)
Littoral (Mangroves etc . . .
major areas only)

Snow comes as a surprise in arid Australia. Yet in the highlands of the Great Dividing Range, it covers the ground for much of the winter at altitudes above 1700 metres. Wombats (*Vombatus ursinus*) live in burrows, shielded from the cold, and find enough grasses and roots in snow-free patches to keep them well fed.

Snow seems an incongruous setting for gum trees, wombats and cockatoos usually associated with the dry bush. But in all except the very highest places — above 1700 metres — snow is a short-lived presence of only a few weeks, and plants and animals do not need to make great adjustments to survive. Wombats live in holes that insulate them from the cold, and when the snow reaches down into the forests where they live, they still find enough plant material in snow-free patches around the bases of shrubs and trees. The gang gang cockatoos — lovely grey birds whose males have fiery red-plumed heads — breed in the upland forests in summer, and move higher to feed on the seeds of the snow gums well into winter before migrating to the lowland and returning in spring, often when the snow still covers the ground.

Snow gums, with their pale and dappled trunks, form the characteristic woodlands of the alpine country. They are mainly of one species, *Eucalyptus pauciflora*, with some *Eucalyptus nictophila*. They are the only trees that grow above the snow line, and the progressively more severe conditions and the shorter growing season at increasing altitudes are reflected in their stature: the greater the altitude, the smaller the trees and the shorter their leaves. But their fruits grow larger, for in the tougher conditions at greater heights the seeds need more of the food supply the fruit provides to have a chance to germinate and establish themselves. It is the snow gums' fruit that attracts the gang gang cockatoos and the occasional flock of rosellas into the higher altitudes.

The roof of Australia carries a diversity of plant life greater than is found in most places on the continent. And because winter comes much earlier — and spring much later — than elsewhere, there is only a short time to set flowers and seeds. With the flowering, insects breed and the result is a brief but abundant supply of food for birds. The abundance draws streams of visitors from the lowlands; the gang gangs are joined by flame robins, crimson rosellas, crescent honeyeaters, wattle birds and the occasional flock of yellow-tailed black cockatoos. The seeds and insects are also food for the small mammals that make their homes in some of the plant communities. Among them is the only marsupial that lives exclusively above the snow line. Other species, such as the wombats, two species of antechinus and the bush rat are equally at home in lower altitude forests and grasslands, but the mountain pygmy possum (*Burramys parvus*) lives only in the high country.

Burramys belongs to an ancient strain and probably represents an accurate living portrait of Australia's marsupial ancestors. It was known only from fossils until 1966, when one was found living in a ski hut. It is not surprising that it took so long to be discovered, for its preferred habitat occurs in only very few places. It is restricted to scree slopes formed during the last ice age, and over which grows a unique heathland of mountain plum pine, *Podocarpus lawrencei*. The mountain plum pine, a conifer, is the oldest living plant on mainland Australia and grows in a variety of forms, depending on the depth of the scree and the nature of the soil.

The mountain pygmy possum lives a virtually subterranean existence in the tunnels and crevices beneath and between the jumble of rock. It feeds on the summer abundance of seeds and insects and like a squirrel puts away a store of seeds to last it through the lean times of winter. The winter covering of snow insulates its subterranean world from the icy conditions above, and its dense fur also helps to ward off the cold.

Should conditions become particularly severe, the mouse-sized possum can go into torpor for periods of over a week — sometimes so deeply that it seems barely alive. Its body temperature drops to a mere 6 degrees and its metabolic rate to as low as a hundredth of its normal active level.

Burramys has organised its reproduction to make the most efficient use of its resources. Even a few metres of altitude can produce different combinations of plants and growth rates, and therefore shelter and food supplies. Females have the energy-intensive task of rearing young: they need more food, and it needs to be within easy reach. Males, unencumbered, can afford to spend more

The mountain pygmy possum (*Burramys parvus*) is the only Australian mammal that lives exclusively in alpine and subalpine regions. It has dense fur to protect it against the cold, and in especially severe conditions goes into torpor to conserve energy.

energy ranging more widely in their search for food. So for most of the year the possums live segregated lives — the females in the denser, more food-rich areas at the top of the slopes, the males in the less productive terrain downslope.

When the snow melts in spring, the male pygmy possums migrate up the slopes to seek out the females, who have spent most of their winter holed up in nests beneath the snow, living on their summer-stored caches of seed. After fathering the next generation, the males return to the lower slopes, leaving their mates to care for the young.

Litters usually number four, with roughly equal numbers of each sex. When they grow too large for the pouch, the mother leaves them in the nest while she goes out to forage, returning to suckle them. By midsummer the young are independent: the sons move downslope to join their fathers, some daughters establish their own small territories in their mothers' country, and the rest move to new terrain.

Ancestral Forests

The lush, humid environment of the rainforest teems with life: it has been estimated that between two and four million different organsims (most of them microscopic) make up the complex cycles of growth and decay. Many of the plants and animals that now give Australia such a distinctive character emerged from these primeval nurseries.

The Divide generates enough rain to keep rainforest growing in favourable pockets along the eastern coast. The type of forest varies according to soils, altitude, rain and temperatures.

Furthest south, in Tasmania, are the cool and sombre stands of southern beech, their shaggy trunks clothed in mosses and lichens. Mingled with the beeches are ancient pines, and below them grow ferns and tall, palmlike plants. There are patches of temperate rainforest on the southern mainland and, like those of Tasmania, they are simple communities of relatively few plant species.

To the north, as the climate changes to subtropical the character of the rainforests alters, too. Plants grow in greater variety, and their leaves tend to be larger and softer.

The forests are at their most luxuriant and diverse furthest north, in the tropics. There, a mean annual temperature of around 23 degrees combines with deep red basalt soils and an average

annual rainfall of 4 metres to produce close to the optimum conditions for rainforest to flourish. Altitude provides its variations:
from the cloudforest atop the Divide, perpetually dripping with
moisture, to the upland and lowland forests that in places reach to
the margins of the sea.

In appearance, tropical rainforest does not vary much around
the world. Travel over the canopy between the Divide and the sea
could be a journey over forest in Africa, South America or Malaysia.
The pattern is that of classic rainforest: the crowns of the trees in-
terlock to make a dense weave of vegetation, with here and there a
giant emergent tree thrusting its crown high above its neighbours.

Inside the canopy, too, there is at first little to say that this is
Australia. Then the sounds register — or, rather, their relative absence. There is no screech and chatter of monkeys, no roar of tiger
or jaguar, just the wind in the trees and the occasional call of birds.
A closer look shows that while the plant communities might appear
similar to those of other forests, there are differences that mark
them as distinctly Australian. An intriguing pattern emerges.
Australia's rainforests indeed share many plants with those of the
Indo-Malayan region to the north — birds and floating rafts of vegetation ferried them when Australia's northward journey brought it
close to Asia. But they also contain a unique element.

The northern, most stable parts of the forests harbour many of
the world's most ancient flowering plants. Of the 19 recognised
families of primitive angiosperms, 13 occur in the Queensland
rainforests, many represented by species found nowhere else.
They include what is perhaps the most primitive form of flowering
plant still living: a type of very primitive magnolia, *Austrobaileya
scandens*, whose pollen closely resembles the oldest known fossil
pollens from a flowering plant dated at 120 million years ago. That
was soon after the flowering plants first arose in Gondwanaland,
and their survival in such densities in the Queensland forests
suggests that the Australian division of the ancestral continent was
— if not the cradle of flowering plants — apparently one of the nurseries for their early and rapid radiation and certainly a continu-
ously stable sanctuary for their survival.

It has been estimated that between two and four million different life forms inhabit rainforests — at least half the total number on
earth. Many survive in Australia's rainforest refuges. Plants make
up its most visible component, and there are around 1200 species
of trees and other higher plants. Half a hectare of forest may contain a hundred different kinds of trees, yet the diversity is not immediately apparent, for the forces shaping the trees have given
them much the same features: smooth bark to shed the rain, tall,
slender trunks to reach the light and large, soft green leaves for
efficient photosynthesis.

Fungi form an important link in the life of the forests, helping to break down the wood of fallen trees and branches. Typical is the jelly fungus (*Tremella* sp.), part of the process which returns valuable nutrients swiftly to the soil.

A smell like that of rotting flesh attracts flies to this 'stinking' fungus (*Aseroe* sp.) which grows in temperate forest. The flies collect the fungal spores, and distribute them, so helping the fungus to reproduce.

Right
Among the rainforest's many agents of decay are these delicate miniature toadstools (*Mycena viscid cruenta*).

Reaching for the Light

With dense crowds of plants all trying to reach the light and to avoid being overshadowed, the tendency has been for plants to select for rapid growth through highly efficient root systems that can take up nutrients as soon as they become available through decay. The forests may be immensely fertile, but most of their mineral and organic riches are locked within the living system.

Most of the rainforest's two to four million species of living organisms are microscopically sized agents of decay, going about their work within the hidden world of the forest floor. Dead leaves and fallen trees and branches are invaded almost as soon as they come to rest in the litter. Bacteria consume the sugars and fungi spread veils of mould over the dead wood, dissolving the cellulose with special enzymes. Once the outer layers are softened, many kinds of beetles and their larvae burrow into and feed on the rotting wood to hasten the breakdown.

The decomposers themselves become food for other animals. There is a lizard that lives only in the tunnels that form inside decaying wood, feeding on the animals that make the tunnels. The *Strangesta* snail is a voracious carnivore, hunting soft-bodied detritus feeders with daggerlike teeth. Sometimes the snails themselves are recycled by one of the few birds in the world known to use objects as tools, the noisy pitta (*Pitta versicolor*), which uses a stone to smash open the snail's shell. The predators help speed the process, too: they rip open rotting logs in their search for insects, and jungle fowl turn over the litter with their claws. Millipedes and centipedes, amphipods and peripatus, earthworms and mites, and finally legions of microscopic soil organisms combine in their activities to turn the forest litter into humus.

Rain plays a crucial part in the final stages of the process. Falling regularly for most of the year, it keeps moisture percolating through the decomposing litter to dissolve the nutrients being released and to make them instantly available to the shallow roots of the forest plants. Nutrients supply one need, but to use them for growth and reproduction, the plants need the sun. The struggle to reach the life-giving light has weeded out the less successful plants, and those that survive are not so much competitive as complementary: selective pressures have sorted them into a more or less orderly pattern in which each plant species has an opportunity to enjoy a place in the sun.

The pattern begins while the agents of decay are still at work on a dead and fallen tree. The gap it has left in the canopy allows sunlight to penetrate to the forest floor, and stimulates a burst of growth. Seedlings of the eugenia and laurel families, which can tolerate very low light levels (but which have been growing very slowly as a result) now leap toward the canopy: within two or three years they will grow as much as they did in the previous twenty.

Other species employ a different strategy. Seeds of trees such as the sarsaparilla and the stinging trees have been lying dormant in the soil, sometimes for many years, waiting for the warm touch of sunlight to germinate. Once that touch comes, the seedlings grow so fast they overtake the eugenias and laurels: the stinging trees soon reach their maximum height of 5 metres or so, and have time to produce several crops of fruit before the other trees pass them and block out the light once more. While the trees build solid wooden supports to raise their crowns to the light, other plants take a quicker route. Climbing vines, with slender, flexible stems, use the support of other trees to hoist themselves to the light. Soon they festoon the clearing with a tangle of looping and twisting lianes.

After a few years the clearing has become a dense thicket of trees and other plants in various stages of growth. Then there is a thinning out. Fast growing but short-lived trees such as the sarsaparilla die. Of the early starters, some are overshadowed, and fall behind in the climb to the canopy. Eventually — possibly after a century or more — only one or two trees of the many that began the race spread their crowns in the forest canopy and close the gap. Equilibrium has been restored, but somewhere another giant is toppling, and the forest's cycle of decay and regrowth continues.

There are about twenty-six species of pittas in the world, of which three live in Australia. The noisy pitta (*Pitta versicolor*) lives mostly on the forest floor, turning over leaves and litter in search of insects, worms and other small animals. Snails are favoured food, and to crack the shell, the pitta holds the snail in its bill and smashes it on a stone or piece of wood. To protect them from flying fragments, its eyes are covered with a special membrane, much like safety goggles.

One of the characteristic trees of the rainforest, the strangler fig (*Ficus destruens*). Its seeds germinate high up in another tree, then send down roots which eventually strangle the host. Figs are thought to be among the plants that invaded Australia from the rainforests of Indo-Malaysia, to mingle with the original community that travelled with the continent from Gondwana.

Interwoven with this basic pattern are many others. Some plants — figs are a good example — often take a short cut to the canopy at the expense of others. A bird drops a fig seed high up in the canopy: it lodges in the fork of a tree and, in time, germinates. Obtaining its initial nutrients from the organic matter that has collected in the tree fork, the seedling soon sends its roots down along the branches and trunk of its host to find the forest floor. Other roots come down through the air, and within a few years the host tree is enmeshed in a rapidly thickening tangle, while overhead the strangler fig's crown overshadows its own. Cut off from light and food, the host dies and rots away inside the strangler's embrace. Now strong enough to stand on its own, the fig continues to grow to become one of the tallest trees in the canopy.

Other plants use existing trees to raise themselves near the light, usually without harming them. Ferns, mosses and orchids, which are usually ground-dwelling plants, have developed forms that allow them to live a self-contained life high in the canopy, using the networks of trunks and branches for support alone. In these forms they are called epiphytes. Wind-borne spores settle on

the bark, and find enough moisture and nutrients to put out clinging roots and leaves that eventually form funnels and saucer
shapes to collect rainwater and leaf debris for the fern to feed on.
Once established, the ferns ensure the survival of their kind by releasing vast quantities of spores into the wind, counting on at least
some finding a favourable spot to produce another fern.

It is important for rainforest plants to broadcast their spores
and seeds as widely as possible, to give their species a good chance
of survival. When the seeds are simply dropped, many are caught in
the canopy's web and perish, and those that reach the ground
often fall prey to animals, have their growth in the soil prevented
by chemical defences of their own parents' roots, or simply have to
wait too long for sufficient light

Winged Couriers

There are many potential carriers of seed in the rainforest, from
wind to animals — especially birds. But if the wind is free, birds are
not. They need a payment for their services: payment the trees provide by wrapping their seeds in a package of succulent flesh. In
some cases the package promises more than it delivers: only a thin
coating of flesh covers the large and unpalatable seed.

Birds must therefore eat large numbers of fruits to get a meal. It
is only the flesh that is digested: the seeds pass more or less rapidly
through the digestive system. Some, such as fig seeds, are coated
in a sticky substance that glues them to the branch on which the
bird is perched, there eventually to germinate. Other seeds are
voided on to the forest floor, together with a small supply of fertiliser. Seeds that have passed through the chemical processes of an
animal's gut, in a way that is not yet clearly understood, have a better chance of germinating and growing strongly.

With most of the rainforest trees producing fleshy fruits, they
avoid flooding the market by not all fruiting at the same time. Even
trees of the same species sometimes fruit at different times in different parts of the forest. The result is a movable feast as crops
ripen around the forest; an almost continuous abundance of food
for many forest animals.

For the fruit-eating birds, collecting their daily meals requires
relatively little time and energy and leaves correspondingly more
to spend on reproduction. Two groups of Australian rainforest
birds have channelled the males' reproductive energies into spectacular and intricate displays.

Male birds of paradise have evolved dazzling plumage and
vocal displays designed to tell any female that comes within range
that the owner is a well-fed and healthy bird, a possessor of
favoured genes that in turn will favour her offspring. The greatest

diversity of birds of paradise is in the rainforests of Papua New Guinea, once a continuation of Australia's forests. Most striking of the Australian species (and characteristic of birds of paradise in general) is Victoria's riflebird. Not the female, however, for she like others of the family is a dull creature: it is the male that needs to impress, and the Victoria does so with a plumage that combines a subtle, velvet black with iridescent green markings. In the breeding season he establishes a display territory in the forest canopy, perches on a clearly visible vantage point and displays his charms. Wings raised, body pivoting and swaying, green-tipped body plumes fanned out in a circle and tail cocked forward, he tries to lure a passing female into his territory.

Display is central, too, to the reproductive life of another group of forest birds unique to Australia and Papua New Guinea; the bowerbirds. They share a common ancestor with the birds of paradise, but instead of using the natural backdrop of the canopy for their display, the male bowerbirds construct their own arenas on the forest floor.

On a slope of mountain forest, the golden bowerbird piles up twigs and sticks around two saplings about a metre apart, glues them with saliva and adorns them with mosses, lichen, green and white flowers and fruit. The twin towers are bridged by a branch on which the gardener displays. He guards and tends his bower for much of the year, repairing and refurbishing the towers and adding to the decorations. In the breeding season, he perches in the trees above the bowers, calling like a spruiker advertising his wares. When a female comes in sight he flies down to his display perch to perform his courtship song and dance, hopping from side to side and fanning his tail, sometimes hanging off the branch like a highwire acrobat, flapping his wings to highlight his bright, golden-yellow plumage.

There seems to be an inverse ratio between plumage and bowers: the more modest the courtship plumage and display, the more elaborate the bowers. In contrast with the ostentatious glitter of the golden bowerbird, the satin bowerbird is arrayed all in sober black, with a satin sheen of purple and blue. The subtly elegant hues complement the graceful symmetry of its bower, an avenue formed by two walls of woven sticks that it paints with chewed vegetable matter, daubing it on directly with its bill; or using the chewed end of a twig held in its beak for a brush. The bird clears areas at each end of the avenue, there to display mostly blue decorations: flowers, feathers and berries.

The aim of all this effort is to persuade a passing female to enter the avenue and to copulate with its owner. The bowers advertise that the males have much time to spend on them, which in turn means they must have access to much food. And so a well-

The spectacular display of a male Victoria's riflebird (*Ptiloris victoriae*), a member of a group akin to the birds of paradise. In the breeding season, males establish display territories in which they dominate all vantage points. They perch on a thick stump in the crown of a tree, sweep their wings upwards till the tips meet, and sway the body in an elegant rhythmic dance.

THE MAKING OF THE BUSH

Bowerbirds are a uniquely Australasian group that evolved in the isolation of the forests of what are now Australia and Papua New Guinea. The regent bowerbird (*Sericulus chrysocephalus*) has brilliant plumage, but a relatively modest bower: a simple avenue of upright twigs, adorned with snail shells, berries and pebbles. The bower serves as an arena for the male's display; the objective is to woo as many females as possible in a season.

constructed and maintained bower fulfils the same role as the plumage that adorns the birds of paradise: it is visible proof that the owner is endowed with genes that favour survival.

Although the basic design is probably incorporated in the bowerbird's genetic blueprint, much of the actual building, decoration and maintenance seem to involve learned skills. The problem is that owners guard their bowers jealously, and drive away any other males that come too close.

The solution is an elegant one: immature males look like females for their first seven years. In the grey-green and brown plumage of adult females, young males spy on older, successful males and learn their skills. As their colouring changes to that of mature males, the young cocks practise on communal sub-bowers — rudimentary constructions that belong to no bird in particular, and that give young males a chance to complete their apprenticeship free of harassment by their elders.

The isolation of the Australasian rainforests has given rise to several unique groups of birds, among them the megapodes, which serve a life sentence of hard labour ensuring their procreation. The brush turkey (*Alectura lathami*) builds a mound of vegetation and buries its eggs inside, using the wamrth of the decaying plant matter as a natural incubator. The mounds are added-to over successive seasons — typically, they measure 4 metres in diameter, and a metre high, but many grow to much greater size. The birds spend much time and effort raking and rearranging the top layers, to keep the temperature inside at an even 33 degrees.

Scratching a Living

The evolutionary line that produced the elaborate courtship arrays and displays of the birds of paradise and the bowerbirds emerged only in the Australian and Papua New Guinea rainforests isolated with the break-up of Gondwanaland. Those isolated forests probably gave rise to another unique Australasian group of birds, with reproductive strategies as remarkable in their way as those of bowers and plumes. They are the mound-builders, also known as the megapodes; the big-footed ones.

The mound-builders probably evolved from a group of ground-nesting birds. Dense mats of decaying vegetation on the floors of the early rainforests generated warmth, and selection favoured birds whose nests made the best use of that natural advantage. Nests became enclosed, then grew into mounds that became larger and more complex as the technique evolved.

Closest to the ancestral stock among living mound-builders is probably the brush turkey, which inhabits both tropical and subtropical rainforests. Black feathered, with a naked red neck and head and bright yellow wattles, the male brush turkey's strong build and powerful, large feet equip him well for his life of hard labour, building and defending his pile of soil and vegetation until it is ready to incubate his mate's eggs.

The brush turkey's mound is impressive, but a smaller relative builds an even larger structure. Orange-footed scrub fowls, which live in the hotter coastal forests, share the labour between the sexes. Males and females pair for life and spend it in prodigious toil. Their large, orange feet — even more specialised tools than those of the brush turkey — rake together soil and plant matter into a mound that over several seasons can reach a height of 2 or 3 metres and measure 6 or 7 metres across.

Their management of the incubator is a stage more sophisticated, too. At the beginning of the breeding season, the scrub fowl pair digs out the top of the mound, refilling it with fresh material. As it decays, they sink a series of test shafts to check the temperature with their heat-sensitive bills. At first, the decaying process produces intense, steaming heat, and it is not until the temperature inside the mound settles to between 29 and 35 degrees that the female lays her eggs.

She does so over a period of several days, digging a separate hole for each egg. The vegetation decaying inside the mound releases a steady warmth to incubate the eggs; when the young fowl hatch they are fully developed, and dig their own way out. They are independent from that moment on, and possibly never encounter the parents that invested so much effort in giving them life.

Scrub fowl, like the brush turkey, are birds of the forest floor.

They scratch their living from the decaying litter, which contains a wealth of invertebrate life. When they are not gathering material for their mounds, they systematically rake through the litter, leaving not a patch unturned in their search for food.

Given the amount of food that is available at ground level in the rainforest, it is surprising there are not more marsupials taking advantage of it. It could be that most of the ground level niches are already being successfully exploited by other animals: fruits and seeds at ground level form a big part of the diet of ground-dwelling birds such as the scrub fowl and the brush turkey. The next layer, the fruits and nuts growing on the understorey shrubs, is harvested efficiently by cassowaries, large flightless birds that live on in a form very like that of their Gondwanan ancestors.

Cassowaries harvest food from individual territories, which they defend against intruders. Usually a display of fluffed feathers and a low, rumbling call is enough to have the trespasser turn tail, but sometimes — especially among males guarding their chicks — encounters are more aggressive. Their powerful feet are armed with large spikes, and when cassowaries fight they charge each other, kicking with both feet at once. Nevertheless, bouts are usually brief and little damage is done before the loser flees. Despite their bulk, cassowaries move quietly and easily through what is sometimes tangled undergrowth, their heads protected with a kind of horny helmet.

The canopy is the realm of the possums — ringtails, brushtails and the largest members of the group, the cuscuses. Possums evolved in rainforests, and the earliest species still live there. Probably the most primitive ancestral form still living is the green ringtail possum (*Pseudocheirus archeri*), the green tinge of whose fur is produced by an unusual combination of black, white and yellow pigments in the hairs.

The green ringtails partly fill the role primates do in rainforests on other continents. The three-dimensional world of the treetops has produced similar features in two very distinct groups of animals: eyes pointing forward, which leads to stereoscopic vision; opposable thumbs on hands and feet to provide a sure grip on branches and vines; and in some species, a prehensile tail that acts as a fifth limb.

There are some striking examples of convergent evolution among the possums and primates. The striped possum of the Queensland rainforests and the prosimian primate, the aye-aye (*Daubentonia madagascarensis*) of Madagascar, both feed on insects they extract from crevices in tree bark with the nail of their elongated fourth fingers. Another Australian rainforest dweller is so like another prosimian that it has been called the lemuroid possum (*Hemibelideus lemuroides*). Monkey-like, the lemuroid ringtail

The damp forest floor provides ideal living conditions for frogs. Some extraordinary reproductive techniques have evolved among Australian species. *Rheobatrachus* spp. brood their eggs in the stomach, turning off the digestive juices so the eggs will not be harmed. When the eggs hatch, the young frogs make their way into the world through their parent's mouth.

*The marsupial frog (*Assa darlingtoni*) earned its common name with an extraordinary adaptation: the males help their eggs hatch; the larvae wriggle onto their father's flanks, and push their way into pouches that have formed there, to complete their development.*

Cassowaries (*Casuarius casuarius*) are large, flightless birds of an ancient lineage, whose ancestors almost certainly travelled with Australia on its voyage into isolation from Gondwana. They are now restricted to the rainforests of far north Queensland, and New Guinea. The horné 'helmet' may have evolved as a head protection for their wanderings through the sometimes tangled forest. Cassowaries eat fallen fruits — so helping plants disperse their seeds — as well as fungi, snails and even dead birds.

possum swings through the tree tops, leaping 2 or 3 metres from the tip of one branch to another.

Cuscuses (of which there are two species in the northern rainforests and more in Papua New Guinea) also resemble primates; especially the spotted cuscus, which was often mistaken for a monkey by early observers. It is a superficial resemblance, however; the cuscus is more like a sloth or a slow loris (a primitive, slow-moving primate) in the ponderous way it moves.

The possums that live in the Australian rainforests are little changed from their forebears. Perhaps because there are relatively few species, there is a greater overlap between where they live and what they eat than there is in the more sharply partitioned world of eutherian-dominated forests.

Apart from the tree kangaroo and a few rodents and bats that arrived much later, the possums are the only mammals in the rainforest canopy. Most are primarily herbivores, though they eat insects and grubs as well. The cuscuses and brushtail possums are the more generalised feeders, eating a mixture of leaves as well as buds and fruits. The ringtails are a little more specialised: leaves form the major part of their diet and — like most leaf-eaters — their colons harbour bacteria that break down cellulose. But the ringtails also eat their faecal pellets so their food is passed through the gut twice, enabling them to obtain the greatest possible value from their food.

Odd one out among the group is the striped possum, with its primary diet of insects and grubs. That elongated fourth finger makes it especially adept at probing cracks in bark and hollows in rotting wood, and it is likely the striped possum, like the aye-aye, detects the hollow spaces tunnelled by wood-boring insects and their larvae by tapping with its feet along trunks and logs.

Basically an arboreal animal, the striped possum is equally at home on the forest floor. The Herbert River ringtails live in the understorey and secondary regrowth of their now very restricted range, at altitudes of more than 300 metres. The green ringtails are more widely distributed, but also live only in the higher altitude forests and occupy the lower parts of the canopy, where they eat their preferred food, the leaves of fig trees. To move from one tree to another, they descend to the ground and make their way across the forest floor: but for the lemuroid possums, which occupy the highest levels of the forest, climbing down to the ground may take too much time and energy, and leaping from one tree or branch to another is a more direct route. Their fore- and hindlimbs stretch out, and it is easy to see how folds of skin between the fore- and hindlimbs might evolve into specialised membranes, to turn leaping into gliding. A likely impetus for that development would be the need to cover longer distances.

This rare and striking white form of the lemuroid ringtail possum (*Hemibelideus lemuroides*) lives in only one small area of upland rainforest in northeast Queensland, at an altitude above 1100 metres, among a population of more usual dark-coloured individuals. Lemuroids are leaf-eaters but rather than move between trees across the ground, they leap from one crown to another.

Retreat of the Rainforests

The impetus came with the changes that began to overtake Australia around thirty million years ago, changes that led to the contraction of rainforests and their displacement by more open communities. The changes were the result of events associated with the continent's northward journey. The separation from Gondwana had allowed ocean currents to circulate completely around Antarctica, and therefore a progressive lowering of temperatures there, and a consequent change in world weather patterns, eventually produced an increasingly cool and dry climate over most of Australia.

Of course, it was not a regular, steady process; there were many oscillations along the way, with expansions during wetter intervals followed by further contractions during drier times. But the oscillations increased in frequency and amplitude, culminating in the ice ages, and the overall trend was to a diminishing of the ancestral forests. It was largely only in northeastern Queensland that conditions remained warm and wet enough to allow the survival of Gondwana's tropical forest.

At the height of the last ice age, around eighteen thousand years ago, much of the remainder had also retreated, but the rainforests persisted in pockets on higher rainfall sites, such as mountain summits and wet valleys. When the ice age ended around ten thousand years ago, those pockets provided the genesis for a recolonisation of the surrounding areas, and the rainforests came to occupy the areas they do today — or, at least, the sites they did on the eve of European settlement. The subtropical rainforests to the south and, further south, the temperate rainforests dominated by *Nothofagus*, contracted into refuge areas: but their total area represented less than 1 per cent of the continent's surface.

The retreat of the rainforests happened in periods ranging from several thousand to a few hundred thousand years — more rapidly on exposed plains, more slowly in sheltered and moister valleys. And while they were decimated as communities, the rainforests contained some families of plants that could adapt to the new conditions and give rise to new types of floral communities.

For while the rainforests were generally luxuriant places, there were areas where conditions were relatively more stressful and that made efficient nurseries for hardy plants. In upland areas, high rainfall had leached and eroded the soil, plants had to compete for scarce nutrients, grew more slowly and were smaller. Because shallow soils contain less water, the leaves became smaller to reduce moisture loss. And because the plants were more exposed, they evolved strategies to cope with more intense radiation: lighter

The forest canopy is the realm of the possums. The green ringtail possum (*Pseudocheirus archeri*) lives in dense, upland rainforest. It's a silent, solitary animal, feeding almost exclusively on leaves, for preference those of fig trees. The female has two teats in the pouch, but usually gives birth to a single young.

coloured leaves and leaf surfaces angled away from the sun.

Low lying, waterlogged areas, of which there were many at the margins of rainforests, also set challenges for plant survival. Paradoxically, waterlogging stops plants absorbing moisture, and they developed similar features to those of their relatives in higher, drier areas: many became smaller and developed tougher leaves. These slightly less favoured patches became breeding grounds for the hard-leaved plants — the sclerophyll flora — that would come to dominate the new, arid Australia, among them casuarinas, acacias and, above all, the eucalypts.

The First Eucalypts

The precise ancestry of Australia's most characteristic plant is still a mystery. Part of the problem is that the fossil record for the eucalypts only goes back to the Oligocene epoch, a relatively recent 35 million years ago. It seems, however, that while eucalypts have always been regarded as belonging to a single group, they may have descended from a number of different rainforest ancestors — possibly as many as nine.

All trace of those ancestors has disappeared, but a few plants thought to be closely related still grow in some places in the rainforest. One was only recently identified — like all eucalypts, it is a member of the ancient Myrtaceae family. It has been placed in a presently unnamed genus of its own, but it has a close affinity to another rainforest tree with features that are thought to point to a eucalypt ancestry, *Eucalyptopsis* (or *Allosyncarpia*).

Neither the new genus nor *Eucalyptopsis* look in the least like the typical modern eucalypts, for their leaves are fleshy, broad and held horizontally and they have large, dense canopies. One similarity with some kinds of eucalpyts is its rough, fibrous bark, but the real clue is on a much smaller scale: *Eucalyptopsis* has ovules, the flower parts that become seeds after fertilisation, very similar to those of eucalypts.

The proto-eucalypts and the other, hardier trees, such as casuarinas, probably arose from among the plants that specialised in colonising the margins of the rainforest; areas of less nutritious soils and water stress. In the increasingly frequent drier interludes that came with the climatic change overtaking Australia, it was these trees — already well versed in coping with disturbances or tougher conditions — that were equipped to survive, and they formed the nucleus of the new plant communities that displaced the rainforests.

The eucalypts formed but one element of the new dry sclerophyll communities, which in the earlier stages also included she-oaks (*Casuarina*) and native pines (*Callitris*). But the increasingly

Gliding evolved independently in three groups of Australian possums, a development probably stimulated by the gradual displacement of the denser rainforests by more open forests and woodlands as Australia became drier. The squirrel glider (*Petaurus norfolcensis*) is now a rare species that inhabits the dry sclerophyll forests and woodlands of eastern Australia.

Right

Gliding evolved among leaping possums: folds of skin between the fore- and hindlimbs gradually developed into supple membranes. Typically, gliders launch themselves from a high vantage point, and volplane for distances of up to 100 metres. Just before reaching the target tree, the sugar glider (*Petaurus breviceps*) 'stalls', and lands on the trunk on all fours.

dry conditions brought with them a greater incidence of fire: there were more thunderstorms, and more dry fuel for fires to feed on. Eucalypts, with a broader range of mechanisms to survive fire, radiated and diversified to become the dominant vegetation: more than five hundred species now grow in settings that range from the bleak alpine heights of the mountain pygmy possum's home to the deserts' rivers of sand. In the swings back to wetter spells that punctuated the gradual drying-out of the continent, rainforests were not always able to recolonise many of their former preserves and the eucalypts secured a firmer hold.

One of the most striking aspects of Australia's forests is the sharp dividing line between rainforests and the eucalypt forests that abut them. Rainforests stand as islands in the eucalypt seas. There is no transition: the dim rainforest ends abruptly and the open, lighter eucalypt woods begin. It is in these more open surroundings that gliding would prove an efficient means of getting about. Possums that could adapt to the new conditions would find new living opportunities.

Among the ancestors of today's lemuroid possums, selective pressures favoured those with slightly larger areas of stretched skin to help them leap further, eventually producing a possum that was

Possums are usually only active at night and spend the days in nests or tree hollows. A sugar glider (*Petaurus breviceps*) grooms its fur using the syndactyl toe (a fusion of the second and third toes) of the hindfoot — a feature peculiar to marsupials. Sugar gliders are very social animals: seven adults and their young may share the leaf-lined tree hollow.

an accomplished master of flight — the greater glider (*Petauroides volans*). The greater glider's domain, like that of the lemuroids in the rainforest, is the top of the tree canopy, where it feeds on eucalypt leaves, buds and shoots.

As the forests changed, so did the foods that could be found within them, and other possum groups produced their own gliding versions to take advantage of the new opportunities. In drier, more open forests, eucalypts produce smaller, drier fruits that make poor food, but provide sugary substances in various forms. Insects that suck the trees' sap secrete a sugar-rich liquid called honeydew; manna, another kind of sweet balm, collects around the wounds caused by insects; and there is the sugary sap itself inside some eucalypts. Some possums took up gliding to harvest these rich but patchily distributed food sources.

The yellow-bellied, or fluffy, glider (*Petaurus australis*) has become adept at tapping the eucalypt sap. It takes other food as well, and in fact derives most of its nourishment from insects, but tree sap is a favourite food. Glider society revolves around the precious food trees. In wetter northern eucalypt forests, yellow-bellied gliders live in groups of up to six animals, each group with a home range that contains twelve or so trees used for sap and which it defends vigorously against intruders. A typical group consists of a dominant male, three females ranked in order of seniority, and usually two juveniles outranked by all the others.

Soon after nightfall, group members emerge from one of their communal dens — tree hollows lined with young leafgrowth — in which they have spent the day, and glide in a series of silent swoops to one of the sap trees. At the last moment, each angles its body sharply upward and lands on the bark on all fours, securing its foothold with sharp claws. With equally sharp teeth, it slices a v-shaped incision in a suitable spot on the bark, and waits for the sap to gather. For the next few hours, spreadeagled on the bark and head often pointing downward, it will feed, licking up the sap as it oozes from the wound.

The sap excisions made by the yellow-bellied gliders are often visited by other gliding possums; the smaller sugar glider (*Petaurus breviceps*) and the tiny feathertail (*Acrobates pygmaeus*). But while tree sap is a handy food source for them, it is an occasional extra rather than a staple. The feathertail's small meals come mostly from nectar, pollen, honeydew and the smaller insects. And the sugar gliders — midway between the feathertails and the fluffies in size — as well as harvesting sweet supplies of nectar, manna and honeydew, have access to another kind of food the other gliding possums cannot stomach: the gum of the acacias that form part of the understorey in many of the eucalypt forests.

One of the rarest of the possums, Leadbeater's possum (*Gymnobelideus leadbeateri*), lives only in the mountain ash forests of Victoria's central highlands, and it appears that they flourish only at a certain stage of the forests' regrowth after fire. Like the sugar gliders to which they are closely related and to which they bear a striking similarity, Leadbeater's possums are social animals, and share a communal nest of shredded bark in the hollow centre of a mountain ash.

Sugar gliders have an enlarged caecum (a part of the hindgut) that enables them to process otherwise indigestible resins. But while all these saps and juices are a good source of energy-rich sugars, they need to be supplemented by protein, especially at breeding time. So in spring and early summer, the sugar gliders switch their attention to insects. They forage among the foliage of the eucalypt and acacia trees for moths, beetles, small spiders, and the larvae of butterflies.

How important insect food is in reproductive success is illustrated neatly by the case of a rare animal thought to be the sugar glider's immediate evolutionary ancestor. Leadbeater's possum (*Gymnobelideus leadbeateri*), lives only in a particular type of wet eucalypt forest in the continent's far southeastern corner; and then only in forest at a certain stage of growth, to provide both the tree hollows it lives in and the food it needs. An attractive animal, with appealing large eyes that give it such good night vision, it is very like the sugar glider except that it lacks gliding membranes.

Like the sugar glider, Leadbeater's possum feeds on manna, honeydew, eucalypt saps and acacia gum, but it also has virtually year-round access to a particularly rich source of insect food: tree crickets, which live beneath the loose bark of the forest trees. The crickets provide the Leadbeater's possums with enough protein to produce two litters a year — one in spring and another in late autumn. In sheer weight of numbers, however, Leadbeater's cannot be reckoned as successful as its gliding descendants: while all have made a successful transition from the contracting rainforests to the new eucalypt forests, the greater gliders, the sugar gliders and the yellow-bellies have made themselves at home in many types of eucalypt communities, while Leadbeater's is restricted to a small, specialised niche.

Cathedrals of Green

While the wet forests where the Leadbeater's possum lives cover a small area, they give the eucalypt its most majestic expression in trees that rise to 100 metres and more: the tallest flowering plant in the world, the mountain ash. There is a cool, green calm in these spacious woods. From a billowing layer of delicate ferns, the straight, clean trunks soar unimpeded to a lacework canopy through which the clear light filters down.

If rainforest is a window into Australia's origins, the mountain ash community is a view of the continent in transition. With the dominance of the eucalypts the theme is becoming distinctively Australian, but among the plants of the understorey, many reminders of Gondwana persist: there are tree ferns, myrtle beeches, banksias and sassafras, and the ground is covered with soft green mosses and fungi. Some of the animal inhabitants of the lower forest levels look and live much as their rainforest ancestors did. Although the drier eucalypt leaves mean there is not as much material to fuel the processes of decomposition at the rainforest's rate, insects and other invertebrates occur in sufficient abundance to provide a living for a number of small marsupial hunters.

The smaller dasyurids are little changed from the very first marsupial animals: shrew-sized, sharp-nosed, furred greyish-brown, and with sharp teeth that bite, cut and shear.

If their physical make-up lacks distinction, the strategies some have evolved are remarkable indeed. One example is the mouse-sized brown antechinus (*Antechinus stuartii*), a fierce and fearless hunter of insects and invertebrates. It is usually active only at night, but when food is short in winter, it hunts by day as well. Its chief weapon is speed: once it spots potential prey — perhaps the gleam of a wolf spider's multifaceted eyes — it pounces so fast that the victim has no chance of escape. Even the wolf spider's often fatal fangs are no defence, and it is soon being converted into energy to power the antechinus' next hunt.

Toward the end of the winter, activity among antechinus males becomes even more frantic; but the search for mates is even more important than the hunt for food. They have only one season to mate and pass on their genes. So urgent is their drive that the mating itself takes up to six hours. Males are 'programmed' to put all their effort into reproduction: they hardly eat, and expend a great deal of energy fighting to secure females. Stress hormones rise to such high levels that they suppress the animals' immune systems and cause gastric ulcers. By the end of the season, all the males are dead.

Elsewhere in the forest litter, reproduction takes a more elegant course. The superb lyrebird (*Menura superba*) traces its ances-

The brown antechinus (*Antechinus stuartii*) is a small, ferocious carnivore that fearlessly tackles almost any kind of small prey in the eucalypt woodlands of eastern Australia, but its sex life has attracted the most attention. The males live for only one season, and start fighting for females and mating when they are about 10 months old. A month later, they are all dead — their immune system destroyed by stress.

try to the rainforest: it descended from the same group that produced the bowerbirds and the birds of paradise. The densely forested and dimly lit gullies where it lives retain many rainforest ingredients, and its feeding habits are like those of the jungle fowl and brush turkeys — raking through the litter with strong claws in search of insects and worms. Like the megapodes, it builds mounds but for a very different purpose. Like the bowerbirds and birds of paradise, elaborate sexual display is central to the lyrebird's reproductive life.

Males build up to twelve mounds in their territories and in winter the mounds become stages for a series of spectacular displays. The male's purpose is to attract as many females as possible: he woos potential mates with an overture of soft singing, then ascends one of his mounds for the main performance. The rather nondescript, dowdy bird undergoes a remarkable transformation: its lyre-shaped tailfeathers fan out and bend forward, and its body vanishes in a cascade of silvery plumage. As the silver shivers and dances, the lyrebird gives forth song — its own and, in perfect mimicry, that of many other birds of the bush. Like the display, the mimicry is the product of thousands of generations of sexual selection: the more ostentatious the display and the more elaborate the song, the more females are attracted, and the most exhibitionist males mate most often.

The hens are left with the task of building nests, incubating the eggs and caring for the chicks. They are meticulous housekeepers: many other birds remove their chicks' droppings, but the lyrebird disposes of its chicks' faecal sacs in a nearby stream.

Forest Streams

Water continues to underwrite life in these wetter, open forests, and there is sufficient rainfall to sustain permanent streams that provide home and a living for a range of animals, from crustaceans to the platypus and water dragons that feed on them. *Physignathus lesueurii*, the eastern water dragon, is as much at home in the water as on land. It often basks on a log over a stream and dives in when it spots danger — or prey. The eastern water dragon shares life on the margins between forest and stream with its mammalian counterparts, the platypus, which is almost wholly aquatic, and the golden-bellied water rat (*Hydromys chrysogaster*) which, like the water dragon, spends time ashore as well.

The water rat (one of Australia's native rodents, a group that entered the continent when it moved close enough to Asia to allow immigration) has broad, partially webbed hindfeet and dense, waterproof fur that together equip it well for life in the water, where it hunts large aquatic insects, fishes and crustaceans.

The forest sustains the life in the streams on which the water rat, the platypus and the water dragon ultimately depend. Runoff carries plant litter into the water to provide food for simple organisms, which in turn become part of a complex web supporting many animals. But the more or less regular rainfall that sustains the permanent streams also means that fire rarely penetrates the mountain ash forests. When it does — before humans arrived in Australia, perhaps only once every few hundred years — the mountain ash dies, for unlike most other eucalypts it has no individual defence. But while fire kills individual trees, its heat causes the seed capsules to open, and the ashes provide nursery beds for the forest to grow again. As a result, mountain ash forests tend to be of an even age and height, and their successive stages of growth provide different sets of living conditions to support different sets of animal life. Leadbeater's possum thrives in great numbers when the growing mountain ash canopy interlaces with that of the acacias, which also regenerate after fire. The network of branches and foliage provides ideal foraging, and the burned remnants of the previous generation of mountain ash provide the possum with nesting sites. Eventually, the mountain ash soars free of the acacia understorey, the network of foliage breaks up and the numbers of Leadbeater's possum drop.

Fire is an integral part of life in the Australian bush. Many eucalypts and other plants depend on it for regeneration. Within a few weeks after a fire, the bush is veiled in green again: seeds germinate in the ash-covered ground, and the eucalypts' reserves of epicormic buds under the bark of trunks and branches have sprouted new leafgrowth.

Shaped by Fire

While fire is an infrequent, though essential visitor to the cooler, wetter heights, it is a more regular part of life in the forests and woodlands of drier regions. The features that enabled eucalypts to cope first with poor soils and then with dry spells, also proved an advantage in coping with fire.

Eucalypt leaves are loaded with flammable oils, so when fire comes it burns intensely but briefly, destroying the leaves but usually only charring the tree itself. Thick bark protects the sapwood, and immediately beneath their bark many eucalypts have an emergency reserve of leaf buds. Chemical changes in the bark, caused by fire, signal the buds to shoot quickly, and the new leaves restore the vital process of photosynthesis. Both the tree's thick bark and its ability to put out epicormic shoots probably first evolved as a response to soils poor in nutrients: the heartwood acts as a nutrient reserve, which the thick bark protects and to which the epicormic shoots have direct access. In this way trees can repair their damaged crowns quickly, rather than relying on the much slower supply from the roots.

Eucalypts are very good at making the best use of what nutrients there are in the soil: enzymes produced on their root systems, together with special fungi, increase the roots' ability to take up one of the most important of nutrients — phosphorus. And once having obtained phosphorus, the eucalypts are very efficient at recycling it. Before they let a leaf fall, for example, the trees of several species withdraw up to three-quarters of the phosphorus it contains. Their thick bark helps eucalypts conserve water, too; as do the hard leaves and the way they hang vertically, angled away from the drying heat of the sun.

Equipped with a basic survival kit, eucalypts evolved rapidly into hundreds of species, each adapted to its own suite of rainfall, temperature, topography and soil composition. It is these communities that make up the typical open woodlands and forests known as the bush — the vague region that begins somewhere just beyond the coastline, ends somewhere just before the outback and covers around a quarter of the continent. Although the species may vary from place to place, the variations are subtle and the main themes recur: slender, light-coloured trunks with wispy crowns of silvery or olive green that cast little shade give the bush its unique character of openness and light.

The lofty, misty green enclosures of the mountain ash cathedrals have given way to a brittle dryness: the trees are not as tall, and all trace of the soft rainforest plants has disappeared. The woodland and forest floors are covered by coarse grasses, and where there is understorey it is dominated by wattles, banksias and other heath-leaved shrubs that can tolerate seasonal droughts.

Fire is the common denominator, setting the rhythm of life in the bush as much as the seasons. It takes many forms, from the firestorm that blasts through the canopy to a line of low flames that flickers slowly through the dry litter and undergrowth. But even the fiercest fire rarely kills the forest: the bush may be reduced to a stand of blackened skeletons, but within weeks it is wreathed in green again and life returns. There are always some pockets left unburned, and they provide both refuges and bases from which animal life can eventually recolonise the forest. The seeds of some species can only germinate after fire, so fire helps to maintain a diversity of plants and therefore animals.

Among the first animals to move back into the new growth are the insects, for it is in the early stages of their growth that the leaves are at their softest, most succulent and nutritious. Even when the forest has returned to normal, the combined body mass of insects far outweighs the rest of the forest's animal life. Its trees and other plants — but especially its eucalypts — are under heavy and continuous attack from a vast array of suckers, nibblers, cutters and munchers. The trees defend themselves by loading their leaves with poisons, but the attackers adapt to cope with each escalation in the chemical war.

Each type of eucalypt has its own population of insect lodgers, adapted to that species and no other. Although they live together, each keeps to its own patch in time or space, attacking different parts of the plant in different ways. The most common leaf predators are the larvae and caterpillars of moths and butterflies. Companies of caterpillars move methodically across the leaves, in the case of chewers, demolishing them altogether; in the case of suckers, reducing them to a delicate brown lace of ribs and veins.

Insect predation is especially intense on eucalypts: it has been estimated that some lose up to 60 per cent of their leaves to insects. One reason for the high levels of grazing may be the eucalypts' remarkable ability to keep producing new growth. There is some return for the host trees, for insect predation is in effect a kind of pruning that conserves water and nutrients; and the accumulated insect droppings — the frass — serves to fertilise the impoverished soil around the trees.

The leaf-eaters themselves become food for other insects, which in turn fall prey to spiders and other hunters. The hunters become the hunted, too, when owls and bats take flight in the night. Strategies for attack and defence have evolved into many forms. Among spiders, techniques range from a simple, fast pounce to the creation of intricate webs. Some weaving spiders have spun exquisite refinements: one waits in ambush and casts a net of gossamer over a passing victim, another dangles and twirls a faintly luminescent globule to lure moths to a sticky end.

Life in the Bush

The forest's insects form the foundation for much of its other life. Antechinuses and dunnarts move back even before the new green has veiled the black scars of the fire. Skinks and other small reptiles too find plentiful food among the insect abundance, and become prey for hawks, kookaburras and lace monitors.

The lace monitor (*Varanus varius*) is the largest predator in the bush, filling a similar niche to that occupied on other continents by mammalian hunters such as jaguars and tigers. Among its close relatives are the world's two largest living lizards — the 3 metre-long Komodo Dragon of Indonesia and the salvatore, which lives in Papua New Guinea. Lace monitors are impressive: adults can grow to 2 metres or more. They are territorial, and grapple with sharp claws and serrated teeth, their long, powerful tails seeking leverage. Such sights are rare, however: once fixed, territorial boundaries are rarely violated.

Lace monitors are active hunters, though for only a relatively short time of each day. It has been calculated that they spend about 8 per cent of the day hunting, the rest of the time they remain

The raucous call of the laughing kookaburra (Dacelo novaeguineae) is the signature tune of the Australian bush. They are ubiquitous throughout the eucalypt forests and woodlands of eastern Australia, hunting in the classic kingfisher mode of perching motionless on a vantage point, then pouncing on the prey — usually insects and other small invertebrates, but frequently also lizards and snakes. When they've snatched a meal, they return to their perch to eat it which, in the case of a snake, takes some deft manoeuvring with the bill.

virtually motionless, their skin patterns providing perfect camouflage among the litter and leaf patterns of the woodlands. They feed on carrion as well as live prey. Despite their size and lumbering gait, they can move quickly and are proficient climbers. Their long forked tongues probe tree hollows for the birds and small mammals that nest and shelter there.

Another important hunter — certainly in terms of numbers — is the kookaburra (*Dacelo novaeguineae*), the largest kingfisher in the world. It sits motionless on a branch, its bright eyes alert for prey until, with a flash of blue, it darts to the ground. It hunts a range of animals, from insects to small snakes. The kookaburra's laughing call is the signature of the Australian bush; it also signals a social system that occurs more often among Australian birds than it does anywhere else — the phenomenon of communal breeding, in which not only the parents but other relatives, too, help care for the young. Several generations of kookaburras stay together to form extended families: older brothers, sisters and unattached uncles and aunts all help incubate the eggs, and to feed and rear the young. It may seem altruistic, but there are rewards for the helpers. They gain experience in feeding young for the time they have their own; there is safety in staying close to the parental territory; and eventually the young they have helped to feed may return the favour.

As the woodland recovers from fire it offers more food for a greater number and diversity of birds, and they become its most conspicuous inhabitants. Eucalypt woodland only covers about a quarter of the continent, yet it supports more than half its birds. Nectar and insects are the main bird foods. Thornbills and warblers forage for insects in the treetops, and tree-creepers and sitellas explore the bark of the trunks. Yellow-tailed black cockatoos (*Calyptorhynchus funereus*) hack into the trunks and branches to reach insect larvae; in some areas they hew platforms on which they perch while they slash the wood with their beaks, sometimes so vigorously that they fell slender trunks altogether.

Flocks of smaller parrots, such as the brightly coloured eastern rosellas, move through the treetops feeding on eucalypt and acacia seeds and fruits, their sharp, curved beaks well adapted to cracking the fruits' woody outer cases. Nectars and sugary saps harvested at night by some of the gliding possums, by day provide food for another large group of birds, the honeyeaters.

Another sweet harvest comes in the form of tiny shells that grow on the leaves of some eucalypts. The shells are called lerps, and they are made by the larvae of psyllid insects to protect themselves from drying out in the heat of the sun. The larva plunges a feeding tube into the leaf and sucks out the sap; what the larva does not digest goes into forming more lerp that one species of

honeyeater, the bell miner (*Manorina melanophrys*), finds irresistible. It is one of their major sources of food in spring and early summer, when the sapsuckers are at their most abundant and productive.

Groups of bell miners mark out a tree or a part of a tree as their territory, and defend it vigorously against rivals, giving loud voice in a clear, ringing call that has given them their name. It is a problem for other honeyeaters, as they are denied access to the nectar provided by the tree's blossoms; and it is a problem for the tree as well, for it needs the honeyeaters for pollination. With the bell miners protecting them, the psyllids' voracious appetite for leaf sap is unchecked — sometimes to the point where the tree dies — but the trees usually stay ahead in the race, producing leaves and sap at a slightly faster rate than they can be eaten.

Even before the woodland has recovered completely from fire, its eucalypts come under pressure from other plants as well as animals. Mistletoe, a parasitic plant that anchors itself to a tree's higher branches, and that sends root runners to probe the bark to draw life-giving sap from the host, is a common sight. But how the mistletoe reaches those high branches is at the centre of one of the most curious relationships in the bush. To disperse itself, the mistletoe relies largely on the courier services of one species of bird, which has become especially adapted for the task.

Dicaeum hirundinaceum, the mistletoe bird — the only Australian member of a widespread tropical family of flowerpeckers — has its gut arranged in such a way that the plant's berries pass directly into its intestine instead of into its stomach. They pass through the gut very quickly as a result, and only a small amount of nutrient is taken

Left

One of the colourful characters of the Australian bush: the crimson rosella (*Platycercus elegans*). Small groups wander among the tall-timbered eucalyp forests and woodlands of eastern Australia,m feeding on fruits and wide range of seeds. On a hot day, a forest stream proves irresistible.

Right

A bell miner (*Manorina melanophrys*) feeding on lerps — sugary shelters built by the larvae of psyllid insects while they suck the sap of eucalypt leaves — one of the many intriguing animal associations that have developed in the Australian bush.

A male mistletoebird (*Dicaeum hirundinaceum*) feeding its chicks on mistletoe berries. Mistletoe is a parasitic plant that grows on eucalypts, and its seeds are spread by the mistletoe bird. It feeds on the berries, which bypass the stomach and pass directly into the gut, to be only partly digested. When the bird defecates, the still-sticky berries adhere to the branch and germinate, sending roots into the bark of the eucalypt host to extract nutrients.

out. When the partially digested berry emerges, it is still sticky; and when the bird lands in another tree to defecate it does not perch across the branch, but aligns itself so that the seed, instead of falling to the ground, adheres to the branch, eventually to germinate there. So efficient is this bird-plant association that the mistletoe is an integral part of almost all forests and woodlands in Australia: the mistletoe family is an old Gondwanan one and must have been here throughout the history of Australia's vegetation. When the eucalypts emerged from their rainforest ancestry, the mistletoes came with them. There are even mistletoes that grow on other mistletoes, and mistletoes that grow on those — all taking advantage of the eucalypts' great efficiency in extracting every last morsel the meagre soils have to offer.

Mistletoes also provide the stage for another intriguing animal partnership, albeit one that does not work to their advantage. About 25 species of butterflies choose mistletoe leaves as nurseries for their eggs and as food for the emerging larvae. The infant butterflies have gargantuan appetites, and between them wreak much destruction on the leaves. Many of the species — especially in the group known collectively as the 'blues' or 'azures' — have formed an association with ants: the insect larvae provide the ants with sugary food in return for protection.

The relationship has developed to a high degree of complexity with the larvae of the Genoveva azures. Their partners — sugar ants of the *Camponotus* species — give them shelter in their own nest during the day. At night the larvae emerge from the nest, often at the base of the mistletoe host's trunk. Attended by their ant guardians, they climb the branches to feed on the mistletoe leaves. By the time they return to the nest, shortly before dawn, they may have travelled the larval equivalent of a marathon — 40 metres or so. During their foraging, the ants' presence protects them from predators such as spiders and assassin bugs.

The ants receive their reward from the larval honey glands, which secrete droplets of a solution of sugars and amino acids. Another set of special glands also keeps the relationship going, not by providing food, but by producing a substance that mimics the pheromones ants use to communicate with one another.

Night Attacks

Because they are the primary producers in an impoverished environment, processing minerals and solar energy into food that can sustain other life, the pressure on the eucalypts never slackens: by day, birds and some insects; at night, other companies of insects and plant-eating mammals. Of the original rainforest stock of possums, only those that acquired special adaptations could move into the drier, tougher eucalypt forests and woodlands.

Both brushtail and ringtail possums gave rise to species that would thrive in the dry bush that replaced rainforest. Two in particular colonised the forests and woodland so successfully that they are among the most common of Australia's marsupials.

The liver of the common brushtail possum (*Trichosurus vulpecula*) can detoxify poisonous plant matter, enabling this widespread species to feed on a wide range of vegetation, from fruits and flowers to grasses, herbs and eucalypt leaves. Its reproductive and social life are also flexible; it can breed at different times and the ratio of males to females varies according to the habitat's carrying capacity: a flexibility that enables the brushtail to respond quickly to food opportunities opening up in a forest recovering from fire.

Like most Australian animals, the brushtail is a nocturnal animal and spends its days in its den, usually in a tree hollow. Even at night, it spends half its time resting to conserve energy, for the eucalypt leaves that form the bulk of its diet are relatively low in food value. Though the brushtail is among the eucalypts' predators, its presence can also be a benefit because of its liking for mistletoe foliage, which is not as toxic, and which has a higher food

Compared to the ancestral rainforests, a few species of leaf-eating possums have managed to adapt to the tougher, more toxic foliage offered by the eucalypt woodlands. One that has, and so successfully it has become one of the most abundant and widespread of marsupials, is the common brushtail possum (*Trichosurus vulpecula*). Its liver is able to detoxify eucalypt leaves to some extent, and the brushtail supplements this abundant food with fruits and buds.

Above and right

Koalas (*Phascolarctos cinereus*) are the quintessential characters of the Australian bush: of all the marsupials, they have tied their fortunes most closely to the eucalypts. They inhabit the eucalypt woodlands and forests of eastern Australia, feeding predominantly on only a few kinds of gum leaves — 17 or so species out of a total of nearly 600 eucalypts. In the north of their range, their preferred trees include river red and forest red gum; in the southeast, grey, blue; manna and swamp gum. Eucalypt leaves contain oils and phenolic compounds that make them unpalatable, even poisonous to most mammals, but the koala's digestive system is equipped with various detoxifying mechanisms.

value. So the brushtail helps the eucalypt by cropping its parasite, which in turn has prompted some mistletoes to mimic their more toxic hosts in leaf shape, form and colour.

The other possum that has made itself at home in almost every type of eucalypt community is the common ringtail (*Pseudocheirus peregrinus*). Like the brushtail it feeds on a range of vegetation, though its preference is for young, fresh foliage of eucalypts and understorey shrubs. Its grasping tail, like a fifth limb, helps it climb out along slender branches to bring a spray of tender young leaves within reach. Unlike other possums, ringtails are not dependent on tree hollows for shelter; they can build their own nests.

Carrying the nesting material of leaves and twigs curled in their tails, they construct their dreys in a forked branch; clumps of mistletoe are favourite building sites. Their nest building skill enables the ringtails to extend their range into immature woodlands where the trees have not yet developed hollows. At breeding time, males and females nest together and — unusually among marsupials — the father may help care for the young. The usual litter size is two, and breeding is timed so the young emerge from the pouch when there is a peak flush of plant growth, flowering and fruiting. The young ringtails make their first explorations clinging to the back of either mother or father, probably learning what is good to eat by parental example.

For both brushtails and ringtails, eucalypt leaves are an important food source, and both possums have digestive systems modified to cope with the oils and toxins. But they can also eat other plant foods, and in fact need the occasional supplement — in the case of brushtails, often mistletoe.

A distant relative of the possums has moved much further down the road of specialisation, and has come to rely exclusively on eucalypt leaves for its food. That relative is the koala (*Phascolarctos cinereus*), the product of a line of evolution that began with a generalised planteater in the rainforests; an animal probably similar in form to the wombat that lives on the eucalypt woodlands, sheltering in burrows by day and feeding on grasses and herbage at night.

The ancestral koala took to the trees at about the time the eucalypts and other dry sclerophyll vegetation began to displace the rainforests. Its earthbound origins are betrayed by its backward-opening pouch — fine for a burrowing animal like the wombat, but not the most efficient of arrangements for a tree-dweller. But the koala's jaws and teeth make a very efficient mill to grind eucalypt leaves, and its digestive system, already well able to cope with coarse plant food, only needed some fine adjustments to become an efficient processor of eucalypt foliage, with a liver to filter out poisons and bacterial cultures to extract proteins.

Koalas prefer the leaves of certain types of eucalypts — red gums in the northern woodlands, grey, manna, and swamp gums in the southeast. Not surprisingly, their lives are centred on these important food trees. They are mostly solitary animals, all with their own ranges, but male ranges overlap those of females in such a way that dominant males share their domains with as many as three females. Sometimes the ranges of younger males overlap with those of one or more of the females' and at breeding time this can lead to violent confrontations if young bucks try to move in on a doe the dominant male regards as his own.

At such times koalas give the lie to their daytime image of lethargy. Hearing the wail of a female being approached, the dominant male bounds from his perch, gallops to the tree of would-be seduction and, bellowing loudly, sets about the intruder with tooth and claw, often bowling him to the ground. As a result it is the dominant males' genes that are passed on most often during the mating period — but frequently not without a struggle on the female's part. Courtship and copulation are attended by much sound and fury, and the yearling koala — the result of the previous year's bout — still clinging to its mother's back has to fend for itself while the adults do amorous arboreal battle. It is, nevertheless, good practice in the skills of keeping balance and climbing around precarious, slender branches.

Earlier in its life, when it was about to emerge from the pouch, the young koala was primed for another, even more vital part of tree life. As well as milk, it was fed a pap of soft green faeces from its mother's cloaca. The pap, which is thought to contain some of the mother's digestive microorganisms, may equip the young koala's gut with the means to process its eventual diet of leaves.

On the Margins

When the first daylight touches their treetops, the koalas find themselves a comfortable fork and prepare for sleep. At about the same time, in a woodland in the west of the continent, a pointed, whiskered nose emerges from a hollow log, and sniffs the air. After a cautious interval, a numbat makes its appearance. It is a strikingly attractive animal, with reddish-brown fur striped with white to blend into the early morning shadows. Unique among marsupials, the numbat is active only by day.

Like the koala, the numbat (*Myrmecobius fasciatus*) is the specialised outcome of a long line of evolution. But whereas the koala arose from the mainly plant-eating possum group, the numbat's ancestors branched off from mostly carnivorous dasyurids. It is distantly related to animals such as quolls and antechinuses, but like the koala, the numbat is totally reliant on one particular kind of food — in its case, termites. Its pointed nose enables it to explore crevices and cracks in rotting wood, and its tongue can extend half its body length to flicker through galleries in the wood and near the soil surface, licking up several hundred termites a second.

But specialisation did not extend to equip the numbat with powerful front claws to rip open the rock-hard mounds where the bulk of termites are concentrated. Instead, the claws are only sharp and strong enough to excavate the tunnels and galleries that extend just beneath the soil surface and into the rotting wood that litters the woodland floor. Because termites only become active in those networks when the day warms, the numbat is also forced to expose itself to daylight and its dangers.

In the semi-arid woodlands, in the marginal areas on the edges of the dry interior, frequent drought and fire have stunted the eucalypts' growth. But they survive, and regenerate, from their lignotubers, bulbous rootstocks that hold reserve supplies of food and water. They grow rather like shrubs, with multiple, gnarled and twisted stems instead of the single, more or less straight trunks of the better watered woodlands and open forests.

Among the most striking of Australia's marsupials, numbats (*Myrmecobius fasciatus*) were once common in a wide band of semi-arid country, stretching from western New South Walses, through South Australia, and across the southern half of Western Australia. Now they're restricted to small areas of eucalypt woodland in the southwest of Western Australia, where hollow logs provide them with shelter, and where there are good living opportunities for the termites they eat almost exclusively.

That arid form of growth is called mallee, and it has given the name to the vast sweep of inland Australia where it occurs. Mallee is the eucalypt at the driest extreme of its range, the outer limits of its drought tolerance. It has other limits, too. Eucalypts are very efficient at harvesting Australia's generally impoverished soils, but once essential minerals — especially phosphorus — fall below a certain level, they cannot grow. There are other plants that can, and they form that other distinctive component of the Australian bush: the heathlands. Heath lumps together banksias, grevilleas and hakeas, boronia, native pea and non-eucalypt myrtles. It grows as understorey in many types of eucalypt forest and woodland, but comes into its own on the acid soils of some coastal and mountain regions. What all heath plants have in common is their characteristic growth form of short internodes and densely crowded, small, sharp and stiff leaves: an efficient response to nutrient-poor soils.

Heath: the Miniature Forests

The glories of the Western Australian heathlands have produced a matching wealth of insects. Jewel beetles are especially glittering prizes in the competitions among plants to attract pollinators. Not only do plants like the *Eremea* spp. offer nectar, the beetles cut into their tissue to excavate brooding chambers for their larvae. This *Julodimorpha bakewelli* is the largest of Australia's jewel beetles.

Like the eucalypts, heath had its origin in the rainforests, where ancestral proteas and other heath groups still live. Among them are several kinds that evolved in low-lying, frequently waterlogged areas, and that adapted to cope with being starved of moisture and nutrients. Any plants that can handle those conditions are also equipped to survive in arid and meagre soils; and soils do not get much more meagre than those of the southwest of Western Australia — they are almost pure sand, their nutrients leached away over many millions of years.

Yet here is where the heath finds its richest expression. Part of the reason is isolation: the west of the continent has been a stable land surface for tens of millions of years, separated from the rest of Australia by sea or desert for the past five million years, and thus has produced a vast array of plant forms. And though the soils are meagre in the extreme, there have been small variations in both moisture and nutrients which, coupled with small but important differences in topography, have created a changing mosaic of conditions, each drawing forth its own plant response.

Selective pressures came from the frequent climatic swings of the past two million years, from wet and warm to cold and dry and back again. They had their greatest impact — and produced the greatest number of species — in the transition zone between the wetter southwestern corner and the arid region.

The result is one of the most diverse floral communities in the world, with 3600 species identified so far (of which 2450 occur nowhere else) and many more yet to be described. There is greater variety here even than in the rainforest: in fact, in many places the

Honeyeaters (Family Meliphagidae) are a characteristically Australian group of birds, and they are at their most diverse in the spectacular heathlands of Western Australia. Kangaroo paws are among the many plants visited by this brown honeyeater (*Lichmera indistincta*) for nectar. Typical of the family, it has a long bill to reach deep inside the flowers, which are shaped so that the bird collects a dab of pollen while it feeds, to carry to another plant.

heath resembles a miniature forest, with many plants dwarfed forms of their rainforest progenitors.

Such a wealth of plants means an abundance of flowers, and therefore of nectar and pollen for animals. The heath offers flowers for much of the year, for the summer is long and the winter short, and the plants flower in an arrangement that gives each species the maximum access to the available pollinators and a continuous food supply to the pollinators themselves. Among the most important pollinators are the honeyeaters, and the heath is one of their major strongholds. As their name implies, nectar is important food, and their long coevolution with the blossoms of the banksias and other proteas has seen them develop long, thin, slightly curved beaks to penetrate the flowers and long, extendible tongues, brush-tipped at the end, to soak up the nectar.

In turn, the birds have been a major force in the colour, shape and structure of their favoured plants' flowers — all designed to attract the honeyeaters, to give them access to nectar and to ensure they carry away pollen. Many of the honeyeaters occur elsewhere, but there are some that coevolved with the heath of the southwest and that are found only there.

Typical of the resident honeyeaters is the western spinebill (*Acanthorhynchus superciliosus*), a prettily marked bird that instead of perching on food plants, hovers like a hummingbird while it sips

A western spinebill
(*Acanthorhynchus superciliosus*) on a
banksia — plants that often
form an understorey in eucalypt
woodlands, but that come
splendidly into their own in the
dry, sandy soils of the heaths,
where eucalypts cannot grow.

nectar. The spinebills usually live in pairs and time their breeding
so the nectar flow is at its peak when their young hatch. The female
is the main nest-builder, fashioning a small cup of shreds of bark,
plant stems, and cobwebs. If it is early in the season she lays only
one egg; if later, two, possibly because there is not quite as much
food for an early hatchling as there will be later. The father protects
the nest, helps feed the chicks and proclaims his territory with regular display flights in which he rises to a height of ten metres or so,
calling loudly, then swoops down to the nest again. As the spinebill
pair gathers nectar to keep up its own energy and keep its chicks
growing, it helps its favourite food-plants reproduce and so ensure
a continuing food supply for future generations.

With such a great variety of species, plants must compete for
pollinators. Many have flowers too small for birds, and rely on a
range of winged insects to carry their pollen. Some pollination
strategies have become highly complex, arranged so a plant can
only be pollinated by one insect. The kangaroo paw, for example,
folds its flowers in such a way that it bars all but one particular kind
of bee. Once inside, the flower's tight embrace ensures the bee
cannot leave without a parcel of pollen.

There are many variations on that theme: an insect visiting a
trigger plant releases the springlike action of its stylar column,
which hits the insect with a dab of pollen. So neatly have trigger
plants arranged matters that when the same insect visits other

types of trigger plant, it emerges with dabs of pollen on different parts of its body. The receptive parts of the various plants are also structured so each plant receives the right kind of pollen.

Some heath plants offer their pollinators not only food, but nurseries for their offspring. One group of shiny, brightly coloured jewel beetles has its mouthparts adapted to suck nectar from heath flowers, and uses the plant interiors as brooding chambers for its larvae. Female beetles cut into the plant stems or seed cones with their lancetlike ovipositors and lay their eggs: the larvae are hooked into the plant's hormone system, which ensures that the same chemical signals that tell the plant to flower also trigger the larvae's emergence so there is plenty of nectar for them to tap as adults. In their short adult lives — two weeks or so — the beetles repay the plant's hospitality by carrying away its pollen.

False Pretences

One spectacular group of orchids in the heath favours seduction over entrapment — seduction under false pretences, what's more. It costs energy to produce nectar, and in the impoverished environment of the heath there is a significant advantage in attracting pollinators in a less energy-expending way. The orchid's chief pollinators are thynnid wasps, and the orchids' strategy of deception and seduction is based on the thynnids' distinctive method of reproduction.

It is only the males that can fly: the wingless females rely on the males to carry them to food plants. Early in the morning, the female digs herself out of the sand where she lives and crawls up the stem of a nearby plant. Rubbing the upper part of her body with her front legs, she releases pheromones, chemical signals that are soon detected by one of the patrolling male wasps. The male plucks the she-wasp from her perch, copulates with her on the wing, then carries her to some nearby flowers where he feeds on the nectar and regurgitates some of the food into her mouthparts. After their nuptial breakfast, he takes her home.

The orchids have keyed into the wasps' reproductive transports by mimicking the female role, releasing pheromones so similar that male wasps are fooled into landing on the orchid flowers and picking up pollen instead of a mate. Some of the orchids have taken the mimicry a step further, with parts not only smelling but looking almost identical to female wasps in both colour and shape: so real are these floral imitations that male wasps have been known to fight over them. When the male lands, grasps the female mimic and tries to carry her away, the orchid's hammerlike trigger flips him on to the plant's pollen source.

A dragon orchid (*Caladenia barbarossa*) resorts to false pretences to induce wasps into carrying its pollen. Its labellum sends out chemical signals so similar to those transmitted by female thynnid wasps that the males try to mate with the flower — and collect a parcel of pollen in the process.

This winged male thynninae wasp (*Dimorphothynnus bicolor*) still has pollen attached to his thorax from his attempted mating with an orchid. Now he is feeding on a bottlebrush (*Calothamnus quadrifidus*), carrying his wingless mate. The flightless females send out chemical signals, pheromones, for males to come and fetch them.

Right

The Albany pitcher plant (*Cephalotus follicularis*) is a remarkable example of convergent evolution. It occurs only in southwest Western Australia and belongs to an Australian group of plants that otherwise grows in conventional forms; yet it has evolved to become almost identical to 'true' pitcher plants found elsewhere. The leaves are modified into the shape of a small jug, filled with a liquid that drowns and digests insects attracted to the plant. In the impoverished heath soils, insects are an abundant alternative source of nutrition.

Mimicry to attract pollinators without paying a nectar price has evolved in various forms among other heath plants attempting to economise on the nutrient cost of reproduction. Some plants have shiny scales that look like droplets of nectar: others, which don't produce nectar, have flowers identical to those of plants that do. In a bid to attract potential pollinators not usually attracted to nectar, one of the hakeas has flowers coloured and smelling like rotting meat — and soon has them covered in blowflies.

Cutting back on nectar production — or cutting it out altogether — is one way of conserving resources. Another is to seek supplements elsewhere, and several plants have turned to trapping insects, not for pollination but for food. It is not restricted to heath lands: sundews, which catch flies in their sticky tentacles, grow in many areas of nutritionally poor soil in Australia, but the heath has produced a remarkable example of evolutionary convergence in the Albany pitcher plant.

It is not even remotely related to the large group of insectivorous pitcher plants found in other parts of the world, but is a member of a family of Australian plants that elsewhere grow in conventional forms. Yet in the isolation of the heath, selective pressures generated by a particular nutrient deficiency have produced a plant with almost identical features to those of the pitcher group: a leaf shaped like a jug, filled with sweet-smelling digestive liquid that entices ants and other insects into a fatal plunge.

Eating insects is among the more visibly dramatic of the many ways heath plants make more effective use of available nutrients. The processes are usually underground, out of sight. There, plants have set up chemical associations through their root systems; with fungi to provide phosphorus, and with bacteria to fix nitrogen. One plant has taken this to the extreme. The underground orchid (*Rhizanthella gardeneri*) lives an entirely subterranean existence: a fungus supplies the carbohydrate the rest of the plant world derives from sunlight. The orchid blooms underground, too; its flowers grow upward to just below the surface, where they are pollinated by a tiny fly that reaches them through cracks in the soil.

Obtaining food and reproduction are for plants (as for all organisms) major driving forces. Like eucalypt communities elsewhere, the heath communities of the west's sandplains convert a very meagre store of raw materials into a rich and diverse environment that offers opportunities for a large variety of animals. Most of those niches arise directly from the plants' need to reproduce — they offer (or pretend to offer) food to animals that distribute their pollen. There are almost as many strategies as there are kinds of plants: some form an association with a particular animal, others try to attract as many potential pollinators as possible.

Honey for Possums

Birds and many insects are active only by day, so there may be special opportunities for plants that can form associations with nocturnal animals as well. Many banksias (dominant plants in the heath lands) have features that attract honeyeaters by day and small marsupials at night: tightly packed flowers, strongly attached to stems to support both birds and mammals; predominantly yellow in colour, so they are visible at night as well as by day; abundant nectar and pollen; and a strong, sweet scent at night.

The association of the *Proteaceae* (of which banksias are widespread representatives) with marsupials probably goes back to the

The honey possum (*Tarsipes rostratus*) is one of the few mammals in the world adapted to feed exclusively on nectar and pollen. Like the honey-eating birds, it has a long, brush-tipped tongue to probe flowers, especially banksia blossoms, and take up the nectar. Though it's called a possum, it's only distantly related to that group, and appears to be the only survivor of a long-extinct marsupial family. Females have a well-developed pouch with four nipples, and usually carry two or three young.

ancestral rainforests of Gondwana — long before honeyeaters had evolved — and became increasingly specialised in Australia's subsequent isolation. How the association began and developed is a matter for conjecture, but some insights are offered by the marsupials that stayed with heath plants as they diversified into their own arid-adapted communities.

An early stage may well be represented by the dibbler, (*Parantechinus apicalis*) an antechinus-like animal now extremely rare but once widespread through the West Australian heath land. Like other antechinuses and dunnarts the dibbler, as large as a small rat and weighing 60 to 100 grams, mainly forages for insects, but it also has a liking for nectar. And because much of its insect prey also feeds on nectar, the odds are the dibbler often collects pollen on its fur and has it brushed off again as it moves around.

That kind of general, almost accidental, pollination becomes much less haphazard in the case of the western pygmy possum (*Cercatetus concinnus*), a tiny animal weighing only 8 to 20 grams. It still feeds on insects occasionally — much smaller insects than does the dibbler — but they are only a small portion of its diet. The abundant nectar and pollen produced by the proteas provide the pygmy possum with a regular and reliable food source: nectar for energy-rich sugars, pollen for protein. Its well-developed toe pads and prehensile tail enable it to scamper about the branches and flowers of its favoured plants, and while it eats a good share of the flowers' pollen loads, enough sticks to its fur for the possum to be an effective pollinator on its nocturnal floral rounds.

The ultimate floral specialist is the honey possum (*Tarsipes rostratus*). Although it is called a possum, it is only distantly related to that group, and belongs to a family all of its own, the Tarsipedidae. The honey possum is totally dependent on nectar and pollen and is one of the few mammals in the world that has no other source of food. Because it does not feed on insects it does not need teeth, and indeed has only a few peg-like rudiments. Instead, it uses its long, pointed snout to penetrate the tubelike flowers of the banksias and other plants, and extendible, brush-tipped tongue to take up the nectar and pollen.

Such a high degree of specialisation was only possible in Australia, because not only does the heath land offer copious amounts of nectar, it also offers them virtually all year round. The honey possums are unique among Australia's marsupials in another way, too — the females, not the males, are larger and dominant. Because food is available all year they breed all year, with a peak in spring when the nectar flow is at its most abundant, and when the plants on which they rely are most in need of pollination.

Like the koalas and the numbats in the eucalypt woodlands, the honey possums of the West Australian heath characterise the making of the Australian bush: each in its own specialised way is the outcome of a process of change and adaptation that began when Australia's ancestral rainforests were carried into isolation. Further inland, beyond the bush, that same process would transform the centre of the continent into its arid heart . . . and present the plants and animals that live there with an even greater challenge.

CHAPTER FOUR

THE SUNBURNT COUNTRY

Fierce winds accompanied the climatic changes which
produced the arid interior, and set waves of sand rolling
across the landscape. The waves are stabilised into dunes
now, and only the crests stir in the desert wind. Dunefields
dominate vast areas of the interior: on a continental scale,
they form a huge, anticlockwise arc.

On the edge of the treeless plain, the slanting light of the early sun throws
into relief a complex of hillocks and craters. Squat, powerful-looking animals are on the move in the spaces between, the early light catching their silky
grey fur. They are hairy-nosed wombats (*Lasiorhinus latifrons*), and during the
night they have grazed coarse grasses and shrubs nearby. They are on their way
home to underground shelters before the sun blankets the surface with heat.

For the young and inexperienced animals of the colony it is a risky time, for
wedgetailed eagles soar overhead. They usually feed on carrion, but sometimes
a young or sick animal makes easy meat. Now one folds its wings and dives, its
enormous talons outstretched. But the young wombat reacts just in time, hurry-
ing to the nearby burrow as fast as its short legs will carry it, and vanishes to
safety. The eagle pulls out of its dive and with a few powerful strokes of enormous wings, climbs away again.

The burrow where the young wombat has found refuge is part of a labyrinth
of tunnels and chambers excavated in the limestone sand by many generations
of wombats. Individual burrows have joined over the years to create a subterranean city. There may be many citizens here, but there is not much interaction
between them except at breeding time, and the burrow system is large enough
for individual members of the colony to keep out of each other's way. The hairy-

The southern hairy-nosed wombat (*Lasiorhinus latifrons*) lives in extensive burrow systems in the semi-arid regions of South Australia. It rarely has access to water, and converts moisture from the coarse vegetation it grazes. Despite the slow, bumbling appearance, it is capable of short sprints of up to 40 kmh to escape from danger.

nosed wombat is a relative of the common wombat of the bush, and it has taken the burrowing way of life to a highly developed stage to enable it to survive in the semi-desert. It copes with the harsh conditions mostly by avoiding them: it is so humid deep inside the tunnels that the wombats can do without drinking, and their metabolic rate is even lower than that of other marsupials — just as well, because the coarse plants on which they graze during the night are very low in food value. To conserve energy, they spend most of their time asleep in their underground city.

It is a technique that enabled the hairy-nosed wombat and its ancestors to survive the progressive drying-out of Australia that became general 15 million years ago, rolling back the mantles of forest and turning three-quarters of the continent into semi-desert. The sieve of selective forces filtered out maladapts and left only those, like the hairy-nose, whose way of life, physiology or both could be modified to buffer them against extremes of climate and unpredictable supplies of water and food. In its stolid, undramatic way, the hairy-nosed wombat symbolises the tenacity of life in the outback — that region, of the mind as much as of fact, Australians so fondly or so fearfully think of as the never-never.

The eagles have abandoned their survey of the wombat colony, and have sailed higher into the sky. It is their view that reveals the pattern of the landscape. The limestone plain that stretches west from the wombats' territory was once the floor of a shallow sea that penetrated deep into the continent. Further inland, the vast reaches of the flat, almost featureless terrain that make up so much of Australia's arid zone were the floodplains of a vast river system.

The outlines of the network are still there, skeletal traces and contours in the landscape millions of years of floods, droughts and erosion have not erased. But the rivers and plains are sand and stone, and they lead to long-dead lakes that now fill only when exceptionally heavy rains are driven far inland — perhaps only two or three times a century.

The fossil rivers still play a vital role in the life of the deserts. Deep within their sandy beds, moisture left by the sporadic deluges percolates along the ancient courses to sustain the desert plants and the animals they support.

The central regions continue to its driest extreme the trend to aridity begun in the bush; a trend that had its origins in the birth of Australia as a continent. The break-up of Gondwana, the consequent formation of circumpolar currents and the cooling of what had been warm seas led to a corresponding cooling of the air circulating above them. A sharper temperature gradient developed between the cool and warm air masses between the South Pole and the northward drifting Australian plate. This increased the flows

Little corellas (*Cacatua pastinator*), the characteristic nomadic cockatoos of inland Australia. Flocks of several thousand gather to feed on the plains, and roost in the trees lining the watercourses.

between them, intensified the high and low pressure systems circling the globe and forced their northward migration, causing them to overtake Australia more than 15 million years ago.

Australia now lies astride the atmospheric high pressure belt that circles the southern hemisphere. The high-pressure cells suck moisture from the centre and as the air flows back to the equator, it takes up moisture from the oceans. The rotation of the earth causes this now moist airflow to deflect, and to form the southeasterly trade winds that strike Australia on its east coast. As the air is pushed higher by the Great Divide it cools and loses much of its moisture: once it travels across the Divide, it is dry, and rarely produces rain. On the other side of the continent, winds passing over the cool currents from the Antarctic become warmer on contact with land, and so cannot release their moisture.

The shift to aridity produced by this pattern gathered pace around six million years ago, and intensified until 2.5 million years ago. It also produced a change from summer to winter rainfall in the south of the continent. The north continued to receive its rain mainly in summer; the centre fell between the two regimes, and received rain only in exceptional circumstances.

The general trend to aridity was complicated by another pattern of swings back to wetter climates, then a return to a régime even drier than before. These cycles last approximately 100,000 years, and correspond to global ice-ages and their warmer, wetter intervals. Today, Australia and the rest of the world are at about the midpoint of the cycle.

What causes the climatic pendulum to swing in this way is not altogether clear, but it is thought to be related to changes in the earth's angle to the sun. Our planet wobbles slightly as it circles the sun; that wobble alters the angle at which solar radiation strikes the various ocean and land surfaces, causing global temperatures to rise or fall fractionally. It takes only a slight fall to start the polar ice caps growing, resulting in a 'positive feedback' effect — ice reflects sunlight, which causes a further cooling, which produces more ice and a yet greater area to reflect sunlight . . . until half the world is covered by ice. Then there is another wobble, the earth's angle changes slightly and the pendulum begins to swing back.

Echoes of the Past

In Australia, these swings from wet to dry and back again (overlying a basic and accelerating trend to aridity) created an environmental sieve for plants and animals that, especially in the arid centre, would allow only the hardiest, best adapted species to pass through. Yet surprisingly, deep in the dry heart of the continent, some echoes of that distant, lusher past linger on. Within the eroded crags that are now the MacDonnell Ranges — once 3000 metres high, but worn down long before Australia even became a continent — are chasms where water from infrequent rains percolates through the rock layers long after the surrounding country has returned to drought. In places along the lower slopes and the valley floor there is permanent seepage: the high chasm walls keep its depths shaded from the sun for most of the day, and help maintain a microclimate that preserves elements of the ancient rainforests. Some of the world's oldest plants still grow here: several kinds of ferns (including the delicate maidenhair and the skeleton fork) and primitive cycads and palms.

The palms are species of *Livistona*, the cabbage palm group, and the small population — about seven hundred at the latest count — of the desert valley forms a species of its own. The nearest relatives are another relict group 1000 kilometres away in Western Australia. The cycads of the area, *Macrozamia*, belong to one of only a hundred or so species in the world. They are survivors from the age of gymnosperms, the plants that preceded today's dominant flowering plants.

Primitive they may be, but cycads have several features that have proved handy attributes to their long survival: an even more primitive plant, a blue-green alga, lives on their roots and provides them with food; their foliage is poisonous, which prevents it being grazed; and they produce fleshy seeds that enable them to disperse via animal transport. In the desert valleys, rock wallabies feed on the cycad fruits, digesting the flesh and voiding the seeds during their wanderings up and down the valleys. The cycads and palms provide shade for other rare plants to grow, and together with the spring-fed waters make the desert valleys attractive to animals. Dusky grass wrens run around the rock-strewn slopes, hunting insects. Brightly coloured finches and budgerigars jostle as they take a quick, nervous drink. Black-footed rock wallabies make their way down the slopes to the water. Among the more permanent residents of the water's edge, the green tree frogs recall the original rainforest inhabitants.

Dragonflies skim the pool surface and the waters themselves hold an abundance of life: fishes, including species normally found only in tropical waters, such as the rainbow fish, and a range of

The central deserts of Australia were created by millions of years of erosion, with rivers carrying the waters from the increasingly infrequent rains cutting deeper and wider through the rockshield, to provide the raw material for the plains of sand and stone.

aquatic invertebrates that feed on each other and are in turn eaten by the fishes. The pools, and the valleys that enfold them, are an incongruous discovery at the heart of a dry continent: they are made possible only through an accident of geology, which tilted and arranged the layers of rock to channel surplus rain from the surrounding area to the valleys.

The chasms and gorges themselves were carved by the mighty river systems that flowed through the centre during the time of the rainforests, gradually cutting down through layers of sandstone and limestone.

Burning Stone

Especially as the centre became more arid and the vegetation loosened its grip on the soils, erosion accelerated. Rainfall was not as frequent, but when it did come, it usually arrived as storms that produced short-lived, violent floods. Their eroding force carved the river valleys ever wider, and as they cut down through the vast shield of rock of which the desert mountains are the outliers, they exposed cliffs and pediments to the wind. In time, they produced the characteristic mesas and buttes of the central deserts — hard rock that resisted the forces of erosion while the rest of the plateau wore away around it. The primeval floods fanned the eroded rock out into plains of stone. Wind, water and time pulverised the softer rubble into sand, but the pieces that had formed the duricrust — the hardened cap of the plateau — resisted further breakdown and were polished to a hard glitter. Beneath the desert sun, it is as if the stones are burning; the gibber plains form one of the world's most desolate regions.

Yet even amid the wilderness of stone there is life, much of it uniquely adapted. Tough little plants grow in patches between the stones, and on the plants live insects: among them several species of (mostly wingless) grasshoppers, coloured rusty red to match the stones. They only become visible when they move, and it is then they are most likely to become prey for small lizards.

Lizards form the most diverse and successful vertebrate group in the arid lands, and each variation on the desert theme has its matching company of lizards. The gibber has its dragon, *Amphibolurus gibba*, which spends the hotter part of the day in a small burrow it digs into the sand beneath a stone. When it emerges to hunt insects, its grey and brown markings and its pebblelike shape serve as almost perfect camouflage.

Unless an animal is a burrower or is smaller than the stones, there is nowhere for daytime species to hide; so selective pressures have favoured the survival of animals whose colouring or markings make them less conspicuous. So the gibber bird (*Ashbyia lovensis*) is a dull yellow-brown, and when it stays still it is virtually invisible.

The gibber bird belongs to the chat family, desert birds unique to Australia. Most of the other members are brightly coloured, but the gibber bird is dressed for survival in the sombre tones of its stony habitat. Its life style is different too: it rarely flies, but instead runs, crouched low, over the stony ground. Like many other desert birds, the gibber bird has virtually eliminated the need to drink: it obtains some moisture from its insect prey and turns some of its food into water. As it runs, the bird holds its wings folded slightly away from its body, which may well keep air circulating. Gibber birds often build their nests out of stones, and protect their chicks from dehydration by shading them with their outspread wings.

When night falls and the stones cool, small mammals venture from their burrows. The fawn hopping mouse (*Notomys cerrinus*) is one of a distinctive group of native rodents. It is a tiny animal, only 10 centimetres long, yet it is capable of digging its burrow a metre deep into the stony gibber soil. Groups of up to four might share a burrow, both to conserve energy and to share the humidity. In the cool of the night, the hopping mice go foraging; mostly for seeds, but also small insects, and eating green plants to obtain moisture.

Kowaris (*Dasyuroides byrnei*) testify to the tenacity of life in the arid interior. They live in the harsh gibber deserts of southwestern Queensland and northern South Australia, sheltering in burrows during the day and emerging at night to hunt insects and small mammals, including hopping mice. Kowaris mark their home ranges and burrow sites with urine and faeces — olfactory 'keep out' signs to other individuals.

For such small animals they move remarkably quickly, bounding on their long hindlegs rather like miniature kangaroos. But their hopping gait evolved independently, partly as an energy-saving device in their barren habitat and partly as a way of escaping predators, for a fast hop can change an animal's direction instantly to throw a pursuer off its trail.

In some parts of the gibber, that pursuer can be an animal not much larger than the hopping mouse itself — a marsupial hunter called a kowari (*Dasyuroides byrnei*). Small dasyurids, such as the kowari, have survived most successfully through the climatic changes that saw the inland forests become deserts. The kowari's adaptations have centred on changes in behaviour and minor physical changes: it still looks very much like its woodland relative, the tuan, except for the light yellow to greyish fawn colouring that helps it blend into its stony surroundings.

The kowari copes with daytime heat by avoiding it — like the hopping mice in a burrow, but unlike them alone. Adult kowaris do not mix except at breeding time, and individuals mark the area around their burrows with scent to keep others away. They do so with a curious manoeuvre: pressing the head and chest against the ground, they kick themselves along with their hindlegs as if they were swimming in the sand: it is also a way of grooming the fur, a kind of sandbath.

Kowaris are efficient hunters — insects are their usual prey, but they will also take larger animals such as hopping mice if they get the chance. Their hunting style is very like that of the eutherian cats — carefully stalking their quarry, then leaping on it with a fast pounce and killing it with a bite to the neck. The mouse's hop is occasionally not fast enough, and the moisture and nutrients that have been accumulating in its flesh and bones as energy is converted into more energy for the kowari — the end of a surprisingly rich food chain for such a barrenness of stone.

Waves of Sand

The processes that create the various types of desert continue — most of them at a pace well beyond the human time scale. But when the wind blows along the gibber, the forces that shaped some of the sandy deserts can be seen at work. Between the patches of gibber are finer particles of sand; every now and then a stronger gust picks up a few grains and whirls them away: a small-scale illustration of the way the fierce, steady winds that came with the ice ages sifted and shifted the sands the rivers had carried into the vast and now dry lake systems, and fanned them out to form part of a complex of sand dunes and ridges that arcs around half the continent. It is the largest sand ridge desert of its kind in the

Inland Australia is rich in reptiles: even the most meagre of environments supports a varied company of lizards and snakes. The fierce snake (*Parademensia microlepidota*), also called the inland taipan, is extremely venomous. It patrols the sandy desert by day, hunting small mammals in their burrows.

world, and it finds its most dramatic expression in the Simpson Desert; row upon row of parallel sand dunes, some of them 120 kilometres long, spaced a regular 100 to 400 metres apart. Their height varies from around seven metres to 35 metres.

A satellite view reveals that the Simpson dunes form part of a great fan of sand ridges — over their entire span across the arid regions they gradually change, from a southeast to northwest alignment to directly east-west in the western part of the continent. This sweep matches the anticlockwise swirl of strong winds that blew across the continent during the ice ages. The direction ranged from predominantly westerly in the south, to southerlies and southeasterlies further inland and to easterlies in the central regions. It has been calculated that the winds blew steadily at more than 30 kilometres per hour for years at a time, setting the sands in motion very much like waves on the sea.

The waves stabilised gradually as the winds began to die 20,000 years ago. In places, it is only the crests that now are still stirred by the wind — vegetation, sparse though it is, seems to have anchored the rest of the dune. The characteristic deep red of the central-northern dunes is painted by iron oxide in a thin coat covering each grain of sand. Further south the sands pale to almost pure white, their colour leached by gypsum.

It seems a meagre basis for life: yet, as on the gibber plains, life there is. Its presence is more obvious than in the stony deserts, for it can be read on the sand, in hundreds of animal tracks that cross the dunes and the corridors between them. Most of the tracks were made at night: they belong to animals that retreat to shelter at first

The sand monitor, or Gould's goanna (*Varanus gouldii*), is among Australia's largest goannas — it grows to 1.6 metres — and the most ubiquitous: the only place it does not occur is in the extreme southeast. With its even more formidable relative, the perentie — which can exceed 2 metres — the sand monitor performs the role of some of the large mammalian hunters on other continents: it is a major predator on insects, birds, mammals and other reptiles, and also feeds on carrion. The forked tongue combines with a special organ, Jacobson's Organ, to detect the most minute trails of scent.

Right
A female stripe-faced dunnart (*Sminthopsis macroura*) reacting aggressively to disturbance: she is especially alert to danger because of the young clinging to her body. They are too large now for her pouch to hold them, and she carries them with her while she hunts at night.

light. Some, like the larger reptiles, search for food at dawn and dusk. The tracks are not random: there is a pattern to the dawn patrols, for the predatory goannas and snakes quarter the terrain regularly and methodically.

Following one set of large tracks, the technique becomes visible: a sand goanna is making its way across the lower reaches of the dune slope, its dragonlike head sweeping from side to side, the forked tongue flickering over the sand. Like most reptiles, the goanna has only moderate eyesight and its tongue is its chief sensor. The twin prongs combine with a paired set of nasal glands in the roof of the mouth, a sense organ (called Jacobson's Organ) unique to reptiles and which can detect both taste and smell. It picks up the most minute traces of an animal's scent, even when the quarry has dug itself into the sand and has caved in the entry.

The goanna stops in its tracks — its tongue flickers even more rapidly and with a sudden blur of movement, it digs into the sand with its powerful front claws. Its head vanishes, then reappears: clamped in its mouth is a scorpion, its tail curled back but with its venomous barb just out of reach of the goanna's armoured skin. The goanna's jaws crush or tear, they do not chew, so the scorpion is swallowed virtually whole.

The few small mammals that live in this patch of sandy desert keep well out of sight during the heat of the day. Hopping mice and

Several species of small
marsupial carnivores thrive in
the various arid habitats of
inland Australia, including
planigales — the smallest of the
marsupials, weighing as little as
6 grams. The paucident
planigale (*Planigale gilesi*) lives in
the cracks of dried-out clay
soils. It has the flattened
triangular head typical of its
group, the better to squeeze
through the miniature canyons
in search of insects and their
larvae.

dunnarts are asleep deep in their burrows, safely beyond the reach
of all but the most determined reptilian diggers.

There has been no rain to speak of for several years now, and
deep cracks have formed in the clay floors of some of the dune corridors. The cracks provide readymade shelter for planigales,
smallest of all marsupials. Their heads and bodies are flattened —
in the long-tailed planigale (*Planigale ingrami*), the skull is only 3 millimetres high — to enable them to fit down the cracks, some of
which can be 2 metres deep. It puts the planigales out of reach of
the sun — and beyond the grasp of any predators.

At sundown, the planigales emerge to explore for food.
Although they weigh only 6 to 12 grams, depending on the species,
they are skilful and ferocious hunters. They need to be, for at their
size their energy intake needs to be relatively much greater than
that of larger animals; the planigales eat their own weight in insects
each day. They do much of their hunting on the surface, even
climbing shrubs and grass stalks in search of beetles and grasshoppers. But their narrow heads also enable them to explore minute cracks and crevices in the sand and clay where other predators
cannot reach — the tiny nooks and crannies that can produce a
rich harvest of insect food.

In more sandy areas, the layer just below the surface has become the domain of perhaps the most remarkable marsupial of

Perhaps the most remarkable of all marsupials is the marsupial mole (*Notoryctes typhlops*): it has become specialised to live in the desert sand, 'swimming' through it in search of insects and their larvae, and small reptiles. It has evolved almost identical features to those of eutherian moles elsewhere in the world: it is blind, and the eyes are reduced to vestigial subcutaneous lenses, the ears have only holes, and the snout is protected by a horny shield. One feature marks it very definitely as a marsupial: the (backward opening) pouch.

them all; the marsupial mole (*Notoryctes typhlops*). It is a rare and elusive animal: it has been little studied, and its place in the marsupial family tree is far from clear. Its teeth, and the structure of its hindfoot, suggest it is related to dasyurids, but its chromosomes point to a kinship with possums and kangaroos.

Whatever its ancestry, it certainly is out on an evolutionary limb of its own — the marsupial equivalent of the moles of the eutherian world. Although descended from completely different stock, selective pressures have produced almost identical physical features and life styles. The marsupial mole spends most of its life swimming through the sand, searching out its prey — thought to consist mainly of subterranean insects and their larvae. Its forelimbs have greatly enlarged claws that plough through the sand. Its snout is protected with a horny shield, and turns the mole into a miniature bulldozer. It has no earlobes, just tiny holes hidden in its dense, golden fur; and because sight is no help in sand, its eyes have all but disappeared and it is completely blind. The mole is unmistakably a marsupial, for the females have a well-developed pouch that opens to the rear and is equipped with a pair of teats.

Such extensive physical and behavioural adaptations take an immensely long time to evolve, certainly much longer than the 15 million years since aridity is generally reckoned to have become widespread in Australia. The existence of the marsupial mole suggests there must have been at least some sandy desert in Australia perhaps as long ago as 40 million years. The other possibility is that the mole's adaptations were not so much to desert life as to the development of loose, friable soils that created a new niche to be explored. If that were so, the mole would be expected to still live in those types of areas — which it doesn't. The desert is its domain, and it probably always has been.

A Legion of Lizards

After sunset, the cooling sands begin to stir with the comings and goings of the desert's most numerous and varied group of vertebrate inhabitants, the lizards: there are 200 species in the arid regions, out of an Australian total of five hundred. A square kilometre of sand ridge desert may support as many as 40 species: an extraordinarily rich assemblage for such a harsh environment. Why there should be such a great diversity of lizards and so few mammals and birds in the continent's arid regions has been the subject of much speculation. Certainly, reptiles have become well adapted to desert life, but no more so than mammals or birds. For a time it was thought that Australian lizards fill niches occupied by other animal groups elsewhere: large, carnivorous goannas such as the perentie, for example, were seen as the Australian equivalents of mammalian predators such as the kitfox of the Kalahari. Some, like the tiny *Menetia* skinks seemed to be insect-like in their foraging, while others were more like insectivorous birds.

Now it is believed the imbalance of desert vertebrates has to do with the infertility of Australia's desert soils, and the kind of vegetation that infertility has produced; especially the characteristic spinifex. Spinifex is nutritionally very poor, but there is a lot of it — as much as 8000 kilograms per hectare. That makes spinifex an enormous food source for termites — which seem to prefer grasses that contain little nitrogen — but not for other herbivores. The abundance of termites (in some areas, such as the Tanami desert, there are 800 termite mounds per hectare) in turn means a great amount of food particularly suited to lizards and to the many invertebrate animals lizards eat.

As with marsupials — more so, in fact — there's a question mark over the origins and ancestry of Australia's reptiles. Some are thought to have been part of the original Gondwanan fauna that travelled with Australia on its journey into isolation. But others are closely related to families elsewhere in the world, and it is thought they entered from the north at various times over the past 15 million years — when Australia became close enough to Asia to permit colonisation across island chains and short sea crossings. It seems that at one stage at least — around two million years ago — land may have been continuous from Sulawesi (the Celebes) to Australia via Papua New Guinea; with Borneo connected to Asia, there would have been only one narrow sea gap to cross — what is now the Macassar Strait. Rafts of vegetation cast adrift by storms might have carried reptiles to new terrain. Whatever their true ancestry, reptile evolution and radiation have produced many specialisations, including some lizards unique to this continent.

Many have come to specialise in exploiting the few centimetres that make up the surface layer. That is where most termites are to be found, and moving just below the surface makes a good stalking technique for other prey, too. The first sign may be a tiny wave rolling along the sand, rather like the bow wave made by a mole's subterranean progress, but somewhat smaller: it belongs to a skink that 'swims' through the sand after prey.

But for every refinement of hunting technique there is a defensive strategy to counter it. The sand-swimming skink's favourite food, the sand grasshopper, is not only exactly the same colour as the sand, but buries itself until only its eyes are showing.

Legs are not much use to a sand swimmer, and as one line of skinks, the leristas, began to specialise in that mode of life, natural selection resulted in a gradual loss of limbs. The various stages still exist as living examples of evolution at work: from a species that still has all four legs of more or less normal length, but carries the

A uniquely Australian group of skinks (*Lerista* spp.) has adapted to a sand-swimming mode of life: their limbs have become modified in the process — in some species, to the point of virtual disappearance. *Lerista bipes* has no forelimbs, and only vestigial hindlimbs, all the easier to slip through the shifting sand.

The characteristic red sand of inland Australia has produced a matching colour in this grasshopper: camouflage is a good strategy for insects much sought-after as food.

Australia has given rise to a singular variety of lizards that have evolved snake-like forms. They are called flapfoot lizards for the vestigial limbs, but they move with a snake's sinuous motion, and their strike is as fast. This hooded scaly-foot (*Pygopus negriceps*) has just caught a spider.

hind pair folded on its back; to *Lerista xanthura*, which also still has four legs, but so reduced that they are no more than vestiges; to *Lerista bipes*, whose front legs have disappeared altogether (but which still has hindlegs), and *Lerista apoda*, which has no limbs at all.

Another lizard family unique to Australia, the Pygopodidae, or flap-footed lizards, has abandoned limbs in favour of a snake's sinuous motion. The family's name comes from the tiny flaps of skin that represent, in some species, all that remains of their former limbs. The physical resemblance to snakes is close: like the rest of its kind the hooded scaly-foot (*Pygopus lepidopodus*) moves its long, slender body through the sand in a very serpentine way. It reveals its true identity, however, by using its tongue to wipe its lidless eyes, and by the shape of the tongue itself: thick and fleshy, rather than the forked tongue of a snake. *Pygopus* can also lose its tail, then later regrow it.

The hooded scaly-foot's hunting technique is very snakelike. Having spotted its prey, a wolf spider that has just emerged from its sandy lair, *Pygopus* remains absolutely motionless — until it judges the moment right for a strike so swift it defies the eye. Unlike some other true snakes, the snakelike lizards are not venomous; instead of using poison to paralyse, *Pygopus* occasionally renders its victim immobile by biting off the legs before it consumes the body.

Lakes of Salt

The dunes of the sand ridge desert overlie and rechannel the ancient river courses, which drained into the huge inland lake that covered the interior until the onset of aridity and during wetter phases since. For many millions of years, Australia's rivers flowed to the sea until a slight tilt in the massive rock shield that makes up the continent's western half blocked their seaward passage.

It was the last major earth movement in the otherwise quiet continent, and it formed the vast inland drainage system which, through wet and dry spells, has determined the shape of life in the centre. For years on end, the rivers are sand and the lakes dry: all that shimmers on them is salt dissolved out of the rocks, carried into the lakes by the rivers and left there by millennia of evaporation. The largest of the clusters of salt lakes that remain to mark the bed of the great freshwater lake, hidden many metres below the present salt crust, is Lake Eyre.

Lake Eyre lies up to 15 metres below sea level — the lowest land in Australia. It is a sheet of salt 80 kilometres long, and almost as wide, with a total area of around 6000 square kilometres. It is difficult to imagine anything could survive on its surface, yet even amid the salt and the heat life signals its vigorous existence.

On a small rise of salt, two lizards are performing a series of almost balletic displays: leaping, bobbing their heads, performing sidesteps and push-ups with their forelimbs. The performers are male Lake Eyre dragons (*Amphibolurus maculosus*), jousting for dominance. They have just emerged from burrows beneath the salt crust, where they have spent the winter months in hibernation.

The dragons are a pale cream colour, beautifully patterned to match the shadowplay among the salt ripples and ridges. Now that spring has arrived, their pale cream is offset by bright breeding colours of orange-yellow markings on the sides and reddish-orange on the belly. In the first few weeks that follow the winter sleep, the dragons determine dominance with ritual jousts of feints and sidesteps. Sometimes the confrontations escalate into brief flurries of real fighting, when tails lash and jaws bite.

When the dragons have sorted out their hierarchy, female dragons emerge and the rituals move on to courtship. They also involve a series of stylised movements to signal desire on the part of the male and acceptance or rejection by the female. If she is not ready for mating, she waves one of her forelimbs to deter the

Lake Eyre dragons (*Amphibolurus maculosus*) thrive in Australia's most inhospitable region, the vast salt lake at the heart of the continent. They are highly specialised to cope with the heat, salt and extreme aridity: among other features, the eyelids are shaped as sunvisors to keep out the glare.

suitor: if that doesn't work, she rolls over on her back and lies still. Eventually, however, the dragon's courtly dance achieves its purpose: the female submits to his advances, and another generation of dragons is on the way.

The cones of salt that are the arena for dominance fights and the courtships that follow, are a central feature in the dragons' lives. They provide basking places and lookout points — and many of them provide food as well, for the mounds are often nest entrances for the ant colonies that are the main source of food (and water) for Lake Eyre dragons. The ants harvest microscopic algae that grow between the salt crystals: such a concentrated high-salt diet in turn makes the ants salty dragon fare indeed. Unlike some related lizards that void excess salt by 'sneezing' it out of a salt gland near the nose, Lake Eyre dragons simply store excess salt in their body fluids until the water from a chance rainfall enables them to flush it out of their systems. The dragons are also very efficient at preserving water: their rate of water loss through evaporation is less than half that of their nearest relative, which lives on Lake Eyre's sandy shores.

The dragons and the ants of the salt flats thrive in conditions that would defeat almost any other kind of life. Most of the time, their lives remain undisturbed — the salt beds on which they make their home remain dry. The runoff from the normal rains far to the north and east never makes it as far as the salt lakes of the centre:

Flash floods follow the rare, heavy rains, and sometimes catch animals unawares. This gecko finds temporary refuge on the limb of a tree.

Though inland Australia is an arid place, rain does fall — a
few times a century in such abundance that the deserts flood.
After the rain-clouds have passed, parts of the channel
country — the vast drainage basin in the east of the arid
zone — have turned into sheets of water.

the water soaks into the sands, or evaporates before it is halfway. But every now and then — perhaps only two or three times a century — a tropical cyclone veers far off course in the northeast, collides with a cold front moving up from the southwest and dumps huge rains across the channel country that drains half the interior into Lake Eyre. When the first waters sink into the salt bed and cover their domain, the dragons inflate their bodies and float on the surface. Many fall victim to the birds that come with the rains, but some make it to the sandy shores. Their colour changes to a deep grey, and their markings to match the pattern of pebbles on the lake beach. But even with the new camouflage, survival is much more difficult on the alien shores: the dragons have to compete with the resident lizards, and there are many more predators.

The Coming of the Rains

The rains bring hardship to the Lake Eyre dragons, but on the larger scale they bring a new lease of life to the arid regions. As the band of rain moves across the centre, every type of desert gets its share, and the first falls produce a montage of rare sights.

In a mulga tree, a gang of galahs turns the downpour into a shower: swinging by their beaks and hanging upside down, the characteristic cockatoos of the inland splash and play with the water — and wash their feathers in the process. The mulga tree itself is shaped like an inverted umbrella, so rainwater is funnelled down its branches, limbs and trunk and soaks into the ground where the roots are concentrated.

In a clump of spinifex, a gecko normally seen only at night drinks from raindrops rolling down the spears of grass. On the open sand between the spinifex, another lizard of a curious shape is also drinking, and in a most curious way. The lizard is the thorny devil — one of the dragon group, and its most fearsome-looking.

Moloch horridus takes its name from the Old Testament god to whom human sacrifices were made, but the only creatures to which the thorny devil presents a threat are the ants on which it feeds. The function of its armour of spines and sharp ridges is survival: partly to deter potential predators, partly — as now — to allow it to drink. For carved into the devil's skin is a network of tiny furrows that combine with the ridges and spines to channel moisture to the lizard's mouth. It is an ingenious system, designed to make the most of a heavy fall of dew or a passing shower.

But these are not passing showers. Soon great masses of water are moving across the arid heart of the continent. The channels flow, and the dry lakes fill. In some places the water trickles gently across the sands — in others, it swirls down creek beds in furious floods, carrying years of dry debris before it. It fills the cracked floors between the sand dunes and flushes a planigale from its day-time shelter. Half swimming, half running, the tiny refugee seeks sanctuary in a clump of spinifex.

It takes heavy rains to produce enough water to seep through to the reserves that run deep within the dunes, and that keep the desert's life ticking over during the long dry spell. Lighter rains only moisten the top layers, which soon dry out again.

As the water percolates through the sand, it wakes a burrowing frog (*Limnodynastes spenceri*) from a sleep that may have lasted years. Deserts would seem to be inhospitable places for frogs, yet 23 species live in Australia's arid regions. They are probably leftovers from lusher times, and have adapted to desert conditions by doing what most desert animals do: avoiding them. But frogs, with soft permeable skins, have special survival problems and take avoidance to the extreme, burying themselves deep beneath the parched surface for years at a time. To dig, burrowing frogs have a spadelike cutting edge on their fleshy hindfeet. Together, the feet work a little like a posthole digger, drilling a shaft beneath the frog's body and sinking it up to a metre below the surface. Some species take a water supply, stored in lymph sacs beneath the skin, with them. And to prevent water loss, some burrowing frogs slough off the outer layer of skin, which then encloses them like a cocoon. Two tiny pipes project from the nostrils through the cocoon to enable the frog to breathe during its long sleep.

Now the water soaking into its burrow signals the frog that it is time for a burst of activity. It struggles out of its protective casing, makes its first meal from the shreds, climbs to the surface and heads for the nearest flooded claypan, to breed with others of its kind that have gathered there for their brief taste of surface life. The water will not last long, and procreation must be swift: within 30 days, a new generation of frogs is ready to dig itself into posterity.

The claypan is stirring with other life, too. The touch of water has triggered the development of eggs that have lain long dormant in the clay. To prevent premature hatching in insufficient water, the eggs have been laid around the edges of the claypan, so the pool needs to be full before the water touches them. Within days, the claypan is aswarm with tiny shield shrimps.

On the surface the water has stimulated insects to hatch and breed — mosquitos, flies and beetles are on the wing, and within days pairs of dragonflies, joined in their mating flights, are skimming across the desert pools. Everywhere there is a frenzy to reproduce; to take advantage of the good times while they last. Within days of the waters' arrival, the wealth of insect food brings birds. Spearheading the invasion are the aerial foragers of the deserts, the kites, swooping low over the waters, hawking for insects.

The rivers run now, and swarm with fishes bred from the small

Frogs are surprising animals to find in deserts, yet many species thrive in inland Australia. Several have an extraordinary way of coping with droughts: like this waterholding frog (*Cyclorana* spp.), they lock themselves away in an underground cell for up to five years at a time, cocooned in a type of second skin. Rain soaking into their refuge wakens them from their torpor — they eat their way out of the cocoon and head for the surface to feed and breed.

reserve populations held captive in isolated pools until the rains came to wash them out. Some fish eggs — and even the adults of species such as the desert gobies — may have lain dormant deep within damp silt until the touch of water wakened them.

The floodwaters are highways for an invasion of bird life from other parts of the country — some from as far away as the wetlands of the coasts. Seagulls and cormorants, ibises and egrets come to feed in the waters, stalking the shallow edges, snapping, scooping up and spearing their way through feasts of fish. The abundance of food stimulates many of the birds to breed, and river red gums and coolabahs along the watercourses are crowded with nests.

The Deserts Bloom

The touch of water wakens new life everywhere. Soaking through the desert sands and stony plains, it transforms them with a myriad plants that appear as if from nowhere. Unlike animals, plants cannot avoid the desert's harsh conditions by hiding and have had to develop other strategies. When the central regions dried to desert, some groups were preadapted with features that enabled them to conserve water and to cope with heat. Among the plants preadapted for arid life were some of those that grew along the coasts where conditions were already desertlike. In parts of Western and South Australia, the arid regions extend to the coast and provided a path for coastal plants to colonise the interior.

Arid adaptations evolved independently in many Australian plant families. As dryness spread, some species could cope while others were forced to retreat: as a result, most of the arid plants have their closest relatives not in the desert, but in the neighbouring temperate and tropical regions.

Mulgas, desert oaks and spinifex are among the hardy descendants: they simply endure. When drought becomes severe some enter a kind of suspended animation. Sometimes trees and shrubs shed their leaves and almost shut down. Their cell sap has small cells with high salt concentrations, which enables them to retain water efficiently and to keep their metabolic processes at the minimum level for survival. In other plants, the leaves wither and turn brown, then revive after rain.

The tiny resurrection plants take the strategy to the extreme: to all appearances, they shrivel and die in a long drought. For years they lie dry and curled: yet when they feel the touch of water, they rise from an apparent death, fresh and green. Their extensive network of shallow roots takes up moisture quickly, and their leaves and stems can also absorb water directly. As the brown fronds unfold, they reveal traces of the vital green chlorophyll preserved through the long dry years, just enough to start the processes of

Plants have various ways of coping with the unpredictable rainfalls of the centre. This resurrection plant, a liverwort, lies shrivelled up and dead to all appearances, but within hours of rain, it swells with green again: the chlorophylls in its cells have resumed the work of photosynthesis.

photosynthesis again. Increasing amounts of chlorophyll are produced, and within 24 hours their resurrection is complete.

The other major plant strategy is that which paints the desert in instantaneous colours. Plants spring to life only when the deserts are, briefly, not deserts — when big rains bring back the lusher past for a short time. Great numbers of plants employ this strategy, locking themselves into time capsules: long-lived seeds. Protected by hard casings, they wait out the dry years — then, within hours of good rains, sprout forth.

Light showers are not enough; they do not produce enough moisture to leach out the built-in germination inhibitors that are part of the seed's chemistry. But with heavy falls, they bloom almost immediately to weave vast carpets of flowers: billy buttons, pink daisies, poached-egg daisies and peas of many hues. Among the most striking is Sturt's desert pea (*Clianthus formosus*), which sends its green tentacles reaching out many metres across the sand and embellishes them with tubular bells of vivid red, their tongues a shiny black.

When good rains fall in the arid regions, the dormant seeds of the ephemeral plants sprout, and within weeks the desert plains are carpeted with flowers such as these parakeelyas (*Calendria remota*). For the seeds of some species, a light shower is enough to trigger their growth; others need a good drenching. The result is an ever-changing pattern of successive blooms.

The desert plants that flower after rain produce vast quantities of seeds swiftly. Many will be eaten by birds and other animals, but enough will survive and lie dormant till the touch of the next rains.

Many of the arid regions'
permanent trees and shrubs
flower and set seed only when
there has been sufficient rain.

A veil of greens and pastels spreads over the desert. The tough, permanent shrubs have been waiting for the rains to flower; now they, too, put out their blooms. Species of *Swainsona* (a genus of the pea family that occurs only in Australia) become clothed in purple, pink and orange. Everlasting daisies paint the flat ground white and the higher, drier slopes yellow. A climbing daisy trails purple blooms with hearts of gold across low-growing shrubs. Poverty bushes offer the richest colour array of all — there are around 200 species in the *Eremophila* genus, and their tube-shaped, plain or patterned flowers cover every colour of the spectrum.

The rich colours also signal a wealth of food. The plants' entire strategy depends on producing huge volumes of seed as quickly as possible, so that by the time the desert dries out again there will be enough seed with a chance to survive till the next rains. In their urgent need to attract pollinators and to set seed swiftly, the plants provide copious amounts of pollen and nectar. Add to that succulent fresh green growth — and the flowers themselves — and insect populations burgeon . . . to become food for other animals.

Once the seed is set, it adds to a rich store of protein for small birds such as chats, zebra finches and budgerigars. The abundant food and water stimulate them to breed in enormous numbers. Even when the first rains were still falling, their breeding cycles were set in motion. It is usually seasonal changes in daily light cycles, operating on photosensitive cells in animals' brains, that tell the appropriate glands to begin releasing hormones; but in some of the nomadic desert birds the presence of plentiful rain can also act as a reproductive trigger, especially in spring and summer.

Like the other birds, the budgerigar (*Melopsittacus undulatus*) breeds rapidly and often while the good times last. The courtship of mutual preening is soon followed by a clutch of around six eggs; a month later the chicks are independent, and two months later *they* are ready to produce their own broods. In the meantime, their parents are already producing more chicks. Within a few months, a budgerigar population of a few thousand swells to millions, and clouds of brightly coloured birds are swirling over the deserts in flocks so dense they obscure the sun in their passing.

Budgerigars are well adapted to desert life: they are geared to survive the lean times with low metabolic rates (much lower than those of comparable birds in better endowed regions) and at the right times can breed quickly.

An Explosion of Life

While seasonal patterns always rule — albeit often faintly — desert life also promotes opportunistic breeding to cope with the arid cycles of long, lean years punctuated by brief bursts of plenty. Among many desert animals, populations contract to small numbers and retreat to refuges in the bad times; build up quickly and spread out in the good. A classic 'boom and bust' strategist is the long-haired rat (*Rattus villosissimus*) of the channel country. During the long drought, small populations survive in a few refuges along some of the watercourses. The burst of plant growth in the wake of the rains and floods stimulates the long-haired rats to breed. By eutherian standards gestation is a very short three weeks: litters number between five and ten, and the young are sexually mature at around 70 days. At these rates, numbers build up so rapidly that millions of long-haired rats are soon chewing their way through the channel country and the adjacent regions of the centre.

The long-haired rat is one of Australia's native rodents. It feeds on virtually anything edible, and as long as it can find food and water, it will multiply. Flesh in such volume means a feast for hunters — desert pythons and owls grow fat on the surfeit.

One predator, the letter-winged kite (*Elanus scriptus*), has tied its fortunes so closely to those of the long-haired rat that it breeds mainly when the rats swarm. A striking bird in shades of white marked with black, the letter-winged kite is unique among eagles and falcons in following its prey into the night. It has evolved special features to do so: larger eyes for night vision and wings that are more rounded than those of other kites, with broader tail feathers — both designed for silent flight and increased manoeuvrability at low speeds. The letter-winged kite scans for

Spinifex covers a third of inland Australia, and the spinifex hopping mouse (*Notomys alexis*) is often found in association with it. The mouse usually lives in social groups, sheltering from the daytime heat in communal burrows a metre or so deep. Like most desert creatures, it emerges only at night. It eats seeds and other plant matter, as well as insects. Again like many desert animals, it can survive without drinking.

prey low to the ground, circling and tilting on its long wings. Sighting quarry, it hovers with slow wingbeats, sometimes hanging motionless: then it stoops swiftly and silently, talons outstretched and wings thrown up so they almost meet.

The rats rule the kite's entire way of life: as the hordes follow the flush of new growth across the inland plains, the kites keep pace with them. Like all raptors they are normally solitary birds, but now they gather in flocks where the rats are at their densest. The coolabahs and bloodwoods along the watercourses become crowded with kites and their nests. Each tree has two or three nests, and when space is at a premium, several females have been known to use the same nest simultaneously.

The connection extends to the kite's nest, which is often lined with rat fur. Each nest will produce around four or five chicks: the male hunts, bringing food — rats — to the female and her brood every two hours or so throughout the night. He does not fly directly to the nest, but lands on a nearby branch and calls to his mate, who takes the food from him. The kites continue to breed as long as the rats remain abundant; but when their main food disappears, so do the kites, which live always on the brink of feast or famine.

For the moment, the good times continue everywhere in the desert. The abundance of plants and seeds not only enables the long-haired rats to move out of their drought refuges, but allows more specialised desert rodents to increase their numbers. The nine species of hopping mice (*Notomys* spp.) that inhabit the various types of desert belong to a rodent group that has been in Australia for much longer than the long-haired rats. The ancestors of the hopping mice probably arrived around fifteen million years ago, when Australia first began to dry out, and the group had time to become adapted for desert survival. Their distinctive hopping gait is fast and saves energy, and it is a trait hopping mice share with desert rodents elsewhere in the world. Another is their ability to survive without drinking, existing solely on dry seeds. Their digestive systems rearrange the seeds' constituent parts to produce water — in minute quantities, but enough to keep the mice alive.

Now, after the rains, there is not only an abundance of seeds but of water-rich green growth, too — more than enough to stimulate reproduction in the hopping mice.

Among the most widely distributed of their kind are the spinifex hopping mice (Notomys alexis), which live almost everywhere desert spinifex is found: the sandy plains and dune country of the inland. The mice live in communal burrows, which are dug out as a cooperative effort: each group regulates its numbers so there are never more than ten individuals in any one burrow complex. The burrows themselves are cunningly designed. When the females have young, the sloping access tunnels are plugged, and only vertical shafts remain open. Adult mice can enter or leave the nesting chambers, but the young cannot get out — and into trouble — until they are strong and agile enough for the climb. Few potential predators could fit down the narrow shafts.

With the plentiful food, there are hopping mice burrows every few metres in favoured areas. Though their gestation period of around four weeks is a little longer than that of long-haired rats, hopping mice can produce young as quickly: while females are suckling one litter, they can already be pregnant with another.

After sunset, the sands come alive as the mice emerge from their burrows to harvest seeds and feed on the fresh plant growth. Inevitably, their comings and goings attract the night hunters: snakes, marsupial carnivores and, sometimes, even a large spider that lies in ambush in a burrow.

One particular predator is the mulgara (Dasycercus cristicauda), a marsupial carnivore akin to the kowaris of the stony deserts. It is a thickset animal with red or sandy brown fur, a little smaller than the kowari but just as determined and fierce a hunter. Mice are the mulgara's particular prey, and it stalks them relentlessly. The trick is to catch hopping mice unawares, while they are feeding. Alarmed, their zigzag escape takes them out of danger at what for such a small animal is a remarkably fast four and a half metres a second. When the mulgara spots a mouse, it freezes for a moment, then makes a lightning pounce — one clean bite to the back of the neck, and the mouse becomes food.

The mulgaras, too, increase in numbers while the good times last: like most desert animals, their populations are partly governed by the amount of available food.

The explosion of life in the wake of the rains reaches its most dramatic form in Lake Eyre, the vast sheet of dry salt at the heart of the arid lands. It takes two consecutive wet years to fill the lake: the first year's rains saturate the subsoil of both the lake bed and the channels and rivers that drain into it, and follow-up floods are needed to fill it. The first waters dissolve the salt, and salinity levels reach many times those of the sea. Only specially adapted crus-taceans — the salt lake slaters and the brine shrimps — can sur-vive. Their eggs have lain in the salt beds since the previous floods decades earlier and hatch within 48 hours of being flooded. The slaters and shrimps feed on the tiny organisms that flourish in the salty, warm waters, and soon breed in dense swarms that in turn become food for the hardyheads and bony bream, salt-tolerant fishes that begin to arrive and breed in the lake.

The Desert Sea

As more water drains into the lake, the salt is diluted and layers of fresher water slide over the more saline layers. Both slaters and shrimps can tolerate a wide range of salinity — from very salty to almost fresh — and they continue to breed, providing food for the expanding companies of fishes flushed into the lake by floodwaters. Nutrient-rich silt is washed in to fuel the growth of algae and the range of animal life that feeds on them; as the lake fills, it is transformed from a desert of salt into a vast bowl of rich soup that attracts enormous numbers of birds.

It is a curious fact that despite their lack of permanent rivers and lakes, Australia's arid zones harbour a remarkable diversity of water and shore birds. Some are survivors from the original Gondwanan populations that remained after the inland lakes dried out: freckled ducks, banded stilts, red-kneed and inland dotterels, among others, have adapted to a nomadic existence, for even in dry times there is always some water somewhere. When one patch dries out, the birds simply move to another, migrating as far as the coast should the drought become particularly severe. Some have given up water life altogether: the Australian pratincole lives mainly in the stony deserts.

But now the birds' movement is to the centre, to Lake Eyre and its abundance of aquatic food. Freckled and pink-eared ducks and grey teal mass in thousands to breed and to feed on the crops of algae and microscopic animal life in the water.

In the shallows, red-necked avocets wade on long legs, swing-

A sixth of the continent's surface drains into Lake Eyre, but it may not see water for 30 years or more. It takes two consecutive years of high rainfall to fill the lake: the first to saturate the subsoils, and the second to top it up. Once full, the lake teems with fish and other aquatic life, and provides plentiful food to support huge populations of breeding waterbirds.

ing their heads from side to side, their bills slightly open to sift small animals from the mud. A close relative, the banded stilt, feeds almost exclusively on the brine shrimps that are now nearing the peak of their abundance.

A graceful white bird with almost-black wings and a chestnut band across the breast, the banded stilt (*Cladorhynchus leucocephalus*) is thought to be related to the long-extinct flamingos that once thronged the permanent and fresh inland lakes. The stilts survive as nomads in the arid regions, and gear their breeding to the sporadic blooms of brine shrimp: the filling of Lake Eyre brings the banded stilts from their entire range to establish breeding colonies that can number 20,000 nests. These nests are little more than shallow scrapes in the sand on isolated spits and islands.

The shining waters bring birds from halfway across the continent: sea birds — gulls, terns and cormorants — move in from the coasts, lake-hopping their way inland. When they reach Lake Eyre with its wealth of crustaceans and fish, they begin to breed. Silver gulls normally lay only two or three eggs, but the riches of Lake

Rednecked avocets (*Recurvirostra novaehollandiae*) are among the many species of waterbirds that converge on Lake Eyre to take advantage of its abundance. They stalk through the shallow inshore waters, sifting through the mud for brine shrimps.

Eyre boost many clutches to four or five, and the arrivals soon multiply into astronomical numbers.

The wave of life set in motion by the rains reaches its crest on an island where the most majestic of the birds that visit the desert sea make their abode — the pelicans (*Pelicanus conspicillatus*). A few weeks earlier, it was a slight rise in an expanse of salt and heat. Water now stands where the dragons performed their courtly dance, and reflects the circlings of the lake's new rulers. Nests — around 15,000 of them — cover the sandy rise.

Eggs have only just been laid in some: in others, the chicks are already well on the way to maturity. Their parents find limitless food nearby, and catch it in a feeding formation: circling to concentrate the fish, and dipping their bills in unison to harvest it.

The rains have long passed and the waters are evaporating in the dry desert heat, making the remainder saltier. The pelicans, like other sea birds, cope by means of special nasal glands that remove excess salt. Although the waters are diminishing, there will be food for many months yet; most of the chicks will grow and flourish, and the pelicans will more than double in number.

Eventually, however, the wave begins to break. The desert sun sucks the water from the lake, further concentrating the salt in what remains. The least salt-tolerant life dies off first, among it some of the algae and crustaceans that have been supporting the ducks and the avocets. They begin to depart, until long lines are streaming across the sky. Often half-grown chicks — those that have not yet learned to fly — are abandoned. The banded stilts will stay a while longer for their source of food, the brine shrimps, will continue to flourish even in water three times as saline as the oceans.

A shield shrimp (*Lepidurus* spp.):
a primitive crustacean tuned to
the interior's unpredictable
cycles of long droughts and
short times of plenty. Its eggs
may lie dormant for 25 years,
then hatch within days of being
immersed in water.

Right
The sandy spits and islands of
Lake Eyre become crowded
with breeding birds. There are
15,000 pairs of breeding
pelicans in this one colony.

For the black swans (*Cygnus atratus*), time is growing short. The water is rapidly becoming too salty to support even the relatively salt-tolerant water plants on which they have been feeding. Many of the cygnets have followed their parents into the water, and are learning to swim and to fend for themselves. But it is now a race against time, for the youngsters need to grow large enough and strong enough to fly before the food runs out.

As the waters retreat, they leave behind long lines of salt-killed fish to make a brief feast for scavenging gulls. But for the pelicans that can only fish in water, the diminishing supplies spell trouble. Their breeding instincts keep them trying to feed their chicks, but many of the baby pelicans have been too weakened by exposure to the relentless sun to take in the fish regurgitated by their parents.

Soon, the adult birds' urge for self-preservation takes over, and they join the exodus from the dying desert sea. It is a long flight back to the more permanent waters near the coast; the early departers may still find some pools along the drying rivers and chains of salt lakes to sustain them, but the birds that leave late find only salty mud or sand, and perish in their thousands.

The drying pools tell the burrowing frogs that their brief spell of freedom and reproduction is over and that it is time to prepare their solitary underground cells, away from the coming drought. Within a year or so, much of the desert sea is salt bed again, and the Lake Eyre dragons return to reclaim their dominion.

Much of the water evaporates, but some will sink into the sands to follow the ancient drainage network that lies just below the surface. The moisture moving through that buried system is the reservoir on which all life of the arid zone ultimately depends.

Spinifex Society

A good deal of the permanent life revolves around the spinifex, a group of uniquely Australian desert grasses. Spinifex evolved from the early sedges and grasses that themselves evolved in response to the onset of drier climates.

There are now around 50 species of spinifex, the dominant plant of much of the central and northern arid lands. In clumps bristling with yellowish green spear-like leaves, spinifex covers sand plains and rocky rises from horizon to horizon; sometimes in association with low shrubs and desert trees, but often on its own.

The spear shape of its leaves is an adaptation to scorching heat: they are rolled into tapering points to reduce evaporation. Spinifex roots drive deep into the sand to tap the moisture replenished by the rains, and through that hidden water, the spinifex makes possible a range of life remarkable for its variety and complexity.

Its presence might also explain why grasses are Australia's main arid plants rather than the cacti and other succulents typical of other deserts. In those deserts rainfall, though scarce, is more predictably seasonal and the plants store water in their tissues to last them between rains. That adaptation did not evolve to the same extent in Australia: the 'fossil' river systems buried beneath the sands distribute enough moisture to keep Australia's desert plants alive with the aid of deep roots and features such as the rolled leaves that keep water loss to a minimum.

As well as its deep tap roots, the spinifex sends out roots close to the surface to harvest what nutrients can be found in the meagre soil. In many types of spinifex, the clumps grow outward in ever-widening rings, with the older growth dying off in the middle. The rings provide spiky cover for many animals, offering protection from wind and sun as well as predators.

The spinifex pigeon (*Lophophaps plumifera*), also called the plumed pigeon, is one of the few birds whose life revolves around the spinifex. It lives mostly in stony, hilly country and its markings mimic the pattern of grass and stone. The flush of ephemeral plant growth that followed the rains has long gone, but it left a large stock of seeds in and around the spinifex tussock for the pigeons and other animals to feed on

Like other desert birds, spinifex pigeons do not need as much food as birds of comparable size elsewhere. The new crop of seeds will last them a long time: it will also help feed other spinifex dwellers. Seeds come in various sizes, and smaller seeds are harvested by the tiny grass wrens that forage in and around the spinifex, picking up insects as well. Insects are the main food for the spinifex bird (*Eremiornis carteri*), a warbler that hops along the grass stems to pick off small beetles and grasshoppers.

An aerial view of the centre's most characteristic plant growth: the ringed shapes of clumps of spinifex, a uniquely Australian group of desert grasses. Spinifex grows outwards, following the surface roots it sends out to seek nutrients in the sandy soil, and the older parts of the plant die off in the middle.

Arid Australia holds many surprises. One is the presence of a bowerbird, an animal normally associated with the lush and rich environment of a rainforest. But some areas of stony, hilly country carry enough vegetation to support the western bowerbird (*Chlamydera guttata*) in its labours of constructing an elegant, avenue-like bower, and decorating it with berries. This unusual desert inhabitant is often found in places where the fig *Ficus platypoda* grows.

As the insects of the tussocks are such sought-after food many are camouflaged, coloured and patterned to blend into the spinifex. A member of the silverfish family mimics form as well: its cerci are long and white, like the tufted seedhead of the spinifex. When the wind blows the seed away, the silverfish also lets go — its cerci flick about as the silverfish moves, to give the impression of a seedhead tumbling along the sand.

Insects are important members of the spinifex society. They feed on the plant material, and so become the next link in the food chain: the tough and resinous leaves are normally too unpalatable for larger animals. In one common type of spinifex community, tiny coccids suck the plant juices and in the process produce a sugary substance that attracts the spinifex ant. To protect the coccids and the food they produce, the ants build shelters out of the spinifex resins and the desert sand. The byres shield the sap suckers from the wind and sun — and from other food-seekers. The ants protect themselves, too, with covered runways that lead from the coccid farms on the leaves to their nests at the base of the tussocks.

Other harvesters are at work in the spinifex. It is too tough and resinous for larger herbivores, but for termites it makes good food.

The ceaseless cut and slice of termite jaws processes tonnes of spinifex into fuel and energy to sustain enormous populations; together with ants, termites are probably the most populous animals in the arid regions. In favoured areas, the ranks of their air-conditioned citadels rise metres high from the spinifex plains. Tunnels and the cover of night keep the termites out of sight most of the time, but there are skinks that know where to find them, where the tunnels break the surface.

Many of the ant species that live in and around the spiky hummocks are visible and active through the day, and their foraging lines also weave into the web that links the spinifex society. Many lizards eat ants: the thorny devil eats little else. With a curious rocking motion to confuse predators, it moves out from under the cover of the spinifex and takes up a station next to an ant trail. It can eat 5000 ants at a sitting, at a rate of around two a second.

Dragons, which blend so well with the patterns of sand and grass, use the spinifex as a base for swift sorties to snap up ants as well as any other small insects. Dragons and skinks are the daytime predators in the spinifex, but each species has its own niche in space, time or food source, and so keeps out of others' way.

Operating by day, however, means having to cope with heat. Reptiles have several means of regulating their body temperature. Not only are they far from the 'cold-blooded' creatures they were once thought, and surprisingly sophisticated in their thermoregulation, but their anatomy, coloration and behaviour are efficient heat shields or heat exchangers. Their undersides are light coloured to reflect heat from the sand. When they run, they do so swiftly and on the tips of their toes, bringing as little of the body in contact with the baking sand. Many change their skin colour from dark in the cool mornings and evenings (to absorb heat) to light in the heat of the day (to reflect heat). Several species of dragons gain extra warmth by 'bathing' with hot sand toward the end of the day, flicking it over their bodies with rapid scoops.

The pace of spinifex life quickens when the sun sets and the air cools. Animals that have spent the day shielded from the sun come out. Brilliantly coloured cockroaches feed on the dead spinifex litter and continue the process that keeps the nutrients moving through the system.

Trapdoor spiders join the cycle by ambushing the cockroaches, and they in turn become food for scorpions that search them out in their burrows. Some of the trapdoors are equipped with early warning systems — blades of spinifex laid on the ground and fanning out from the burrow, whose purpose is to signal food rather than danger. When an insect walks across the blades, their vibrations alert the spider and it makes a lightning grab. The heavier tread of the scorpion might also send a warning, but to no avail:

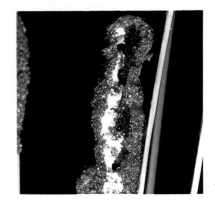

In some favoured places, spinifex supports one of the most fascinating animal relationships to be found in the interior. Spinifex ants (*Iridomyrmex flavipes*) build shelters from grains of sand stuck together with spinifex resin to protect the larvae of coccid insects, which suck the leaf sap. The ants feed on the larvae's waste — drops of sugary liquid.

scorpions have been found inside the trapdoor spiders' burrows, still eating the occupant.

When darkness is complete, the spinifex hummocks become busy with the comings and goings of geckos, which feed on insects. Their large lidless eyes, designed for efficient night vision, are kept moist and clean with regular wipes of the geckos' long, fleshy tongues. Geckos exemplify the lizards' successful exploitation of arid Australia: in one patch of spinifex desert there may be as many as 12 kinds of geckos. Three of them specialise in foraging for termites: three more range the bushes and low trees hunting the insects that live there. The third group, which forages around the spinifex litter and sand, ranges in size, and so avoids competition by hunting insects of different sizes.

Their soft, fleshy bodies make the geckos themselves attractive food for a range of predators; strikingly marked banded snakes and the desert death adder. Some of the snakelike legless lizards, themselves evolved from geckos, will also take geckos.

Predatory pressure has produced defences: the knobtailed gecko's head-shaped rear end deflects attention from the real thing, and several species autotomise, or drop, their tails if they are hard-pressed — a strategy common to some other types of lizards. Nervous reflex keeps the severed tail wriggling and distracts the predator long enough for its owner to escape, eventually to grow another tail.

The spiny-tailed gecko (*Diplodactylus ciliaris*) has developed a more aggressive alternative: the tail is armed with glands, and should a predator seize hold of it, the glands fire jets of a gluelike liquid to deter the attacker with a web of sticky threads.

Amid the Mulga

By sunrise, many of the spinifex dwellers have withdrawn to their nests and burrows, and there is only a network of tracks to point to the rich night life of the grass and sand. Where the sands overlie slightly richer subsoils, or give way to the vast stretches of red gravel soils that cover much of the interior, another characteristic arid plant dominates: the mulga. Depending on how meagre the soil is, it ranges in form from stunted shrubs to trees 10 metres high. Mulga belongs to the *Acacia* genus, the nine hundred or so wattles that form the largest group of trees and shrubs in Australia — a group larger even than the eucalypts.

Like the eucalypts, the acacias had their origins in the plant stock Australia carried away from Gondwana. Also like eucalypts, their ancestry remains obscure: they are not recognisable in the fossil record until around 25 million years ago. But whilst eucalypts arose only in Australia and are largely confined to the continent, acacias also occur in Africa, India and South America — all once part of Gondwana. They take rather different forms there; most of the non-Australian species have become armoured with woody thorns, presumably to protect them against the greater range of browsing animals in other lands.

Most of Australia's acacias belong to the group in which the leaves have become reduced to no more than vertically flattened stalks. The phyllodes, as they are called, have few pores compared with conventional leaves, to reduce water loss: a feature that enables acacias to survive in drier regions than eucalypts. The small group of acacias collectively called mulga became the dominant desert trees. Their phyllodes became further modified into pointed needles, often standing upright to present the smallest possible area to the sun. In severe droughts, the trees slow their physiological systems almost to a standstill, dropping leaves and sometimes even branches. After rains, their deep roots will tap the moisture trickling through the desert's buried drainage network to grow, to reproduce — and to support other life. Birds, lizards and small mammals live in and around the mulga communities, but as elsewhere, the most populous inhabitants are termites and ants.

In sheer numbers — both of species and individuals — ants and termites make up by far the bulk of Australia's animal population. There are at least 4000 species of ants alone, and there are more ant species in Australia's deserts than in any other arid region in the world. As well, many of the primitive ant groups that have died out elsewhere live on beside their modern descendants.

Ants play an immensely important part in shaping Australia's environment, especially its arid zones. Their tireless gathering of plant and animal matter keeps the desert's store of nutrients cycling through the system, and their nests and tunnels combine to form a vast cultivating machine that turns over and aerates the soils. Through their many and varied associations with plants, ants often determine which plants will grow where and how well — and so sculpt the landscape itself.

Mulga provides a backdrop for some of the most intriguing relationships between ants and plants. Many different species collect food from the trees in one form or another: one of the *Iridomyrmex* genus harvests the ruby-red lerps produced by sap-sucking coccids, and in so doing helps the tree by keeping away other, potentially more harmful bugs.

Other ants foraging on some species of mulga feed at tiny glands, near the base of the phyllodes, that secrete a kind of nectar at certain times. Why the mulga should supply so generously a food that costs so much energy to produce is not altogether clear. One theory is that these extrafloral nectaries serve to divert insect attention from the tree's small and delicate flowers and so prevent

Its belly hugely distended, this ant is a living honeypot — a storage system evolved by various *Campanotus* species to see the colony through the times when the nectar flow from mulga and other sources is reduced, or dries up altogether. The replete ant is being tended by a worker to release a drop of its sweet contents.

damage at seed-setting time. Whatever the reason, the effect is clear; the nectaries are a regular stop on the foraging patrols of many kinds of ants. Because the mulga's honey does not always flow, some have evolved an ingenious method of storing it.

Worker ants gather the nectar in their crops just behind their mouthparts and carry it to the nest, usually situated not far from the base of the tree. A narrow shaft leads to a complex of horizontal galleries deep below the sand. Hanging from their ceilings are what look like rows of translucent baubles. They are ants, their bellies hugely distended with nectar, turned into living honeypots for the good of the colony. The workers regurgitate their sweet cargo into the mouthparts of the storage ants: replete, the storage ants become virtually immobile, and thus use very little of the nectar for their own needs. When the mulga's nectar flow ceases, the colony turns to its living stores; ants in search of food visit the repletes and, stroking them with their antennae, stimulate them into releasing their nectar a tiny drop at a time.

The Hidden Rivers

The floods have long receded and the creeks and rivers have reverted to sand and stone, but water still flows underground. It supports stands of trees that flank the channel beds, sometimes in scattered pockets, often in almost unbroken double lines. Corridors of timber lead deep into the arid heart. The pale trunks of the eucalypts dominate the ribbons of woodland — coolabahs, ghost gums, and especially the majestic river red gums.

Red is the colour of their dense heartwood; it is covered by shiny white bark to reflect heat. Massive root systems tap the water deep below the sandy beds and draw in the nutrients, accumulated from the runoff of the surrounding plains, that also concentrate along the ancient drainage systems. The river reds drink prodigiously; their deep roots pump a tonne of water a day, and there is more plant tissue spread out below ground than above it.

A run of wetter-than-average years is needed for young trees to become established, and most of the growing effort in the first years goes into the development of root systems to reach the underground water to protect them from drought. Once established, the trees may live several hundred years.

Like other eucalypts, river red gums shed branches as they grow, creating opportunities for fungi and sometimes termites to invade the heartwood. As the trees sway in the wind, the pulp of broken-down tissue that is produced by fungi and termites is compressed, and cavities form. As time passes, more branches break off and open up the hollows.

River red gums (*Eucalyptus camaldulensis*) are among the most majestic of Australia's distinctive trees. Generous stands penetrate deep into the centre, lining the watercourses from which they draw the huge amounts of moisture they need — up to a tonne of water a day. The riverbeds are mostly dry sand, but the occasional floods recharge the moisture banks deep beneath the surface.

A galah chick waiting inside its tree-hollow nest for its parents to return with a cropful of food. It is about two weeks old, and it will be another six weeks or so before it is large and strong enough to climb to the nest entrance, a metre up, and fly. There will be no test flights — once it leaves the nest, it will not return.

The woodlands that line the desert rivers are the nurseries for many parrots. Most of their breeding is seasonal; the lengthening days prompt the release of hormones that stimulate their reproductive cycles and the trees come alive with parrots arriving to mate and rear young.

Most conspicuous are the cockatoos — galahs, pink cockatoos and white corellas. With loud cries breeding pairs squabble over nesting holes, then mutter softly as they perch together on a branch to preen each other. Partners greet with a bob of the head and a flash of their distinctive crests.

Preening strengthens the bond that will keep them together all their lives: long monogamous partnerships are a good tactic in a meagre environment, sharing the work of rearing young and eliminating the need for elaborate and energy expensive courtship rituals. Galah couples come back to the same nesting hole year after year. They rip away strips of bark from around the hole's entrance and polish the area with their beaks (not, as was once thought, to make the bark a slippery slide for predatory goannas, but to serve as a badge of occupancy). Other cockatoos find new nesting holes each season, and pairs spend much time prospecting for the right one: half a metre to a metre deep, and high enough to deter predators from reaching the eggs and chicks.

Although cockatoos breed seasonally, unpredictable cycles of drought punctuated by brief bursts of plenty also govern their reproduction. In drought years galahs reduce their clutches to one or

Galahs (*Cacatua roseicapilla*) pair for life, and male and female are rarely out of each other's sight. Perhaps the best-known of Australia's characteristic cockatoos, galahs range widely over the continent, following the crops of seeds as they ripen and fall.

two and, if bad times persist, may cease breeding altogether. In the seasons of plenty that follow good rains females lay four or five eggs, and may produce more than one brood.

When galah chicks fledge, their first flight takes them into a unique bird institution: one of the trees becomes a community crèche where all the young of the neighbourhood gather while their parents are away foraging. The fledglings while away the long hours learning to be galahs — grooming each other in a playful imitation of pair bonding; nipping off twigs and swinging by their beaks to strengthen the muscles that control that important feeding tool; and swooping through the trees in short practice flights.

When the adults return, their crops full of partly digested seeds, the crêche resounds with a cacophony of begging calls. Yet in all that confusion, each pair of parents unerringly recognises its own young. They lock beaks with their chicks before regurgitating food into their throats. After a few weeks, the young galahs begin to forage for themselves: close to the woodland nurseries at first, then further afield as their flying muscles and confidence grow.

By season's end, both adult and young cockatoos are moving across the arid plains. Their wanderings take them to all but the most desolate regions, feeding on seeds, bulbs, roots and fruits in season. Galahs are especially strong and fast fliers, and often travel 100 kilometres or more for a day's feeding, in crowds that can number two or three hundred. Pink cockatoos travel in smaller groups and stay close to cover, but they too wander over great distances.

Cockatoos prefer to feed in company, especially on the ground. There is safety in numbers, and at any one time at least one pair of eyes is scanning the surrounds for danger. Corellas form the most spectacular congregations: the sight of one group of birds feeding prompts others to join, which attract still more. The mobs grow until flocks of tens of thousands wheel across the plains. When they seek rest and shade in the heat of the day the sparse ranks of desert trees seem to blossom with birds, each branch dense with clusters of white.

A Pattern of Plains

The movements of the cockatoos and the other parrots of the interior are not random: they follow the patterns of vegetation concentrated along the dry rivers, creeks and flood-outs that still trace the ancient drainage system. Plant growth is most dense where there are even marginally more nutrients, and where moisture persists. The red gum-lined rivers of sand are the most dramatic illustration of this hidden resource, but fanning out from them are networks of creeks and channels that braid, sometimes almost imperceptibly, through the plains and scrublands. Over time, the movement of water has been an important agent in distributing the meagre soils of the interior, and has given rise to a mosaic of plant communities.

Sandier soils support stands of acacias such as prickly wattle and dead finish (so named because it was thought to outlast anything else). Scattered through the open spaces are eremophila bushes, whose berries are a favourite food of emus. Various hardy grasses grow in a range of conditions; among the most widespread are *Eragrostis*, 'neverfail', and Mitchell grass.

Saltbush and bluebush — plants marvellously adapted to cope with both salt and heat — flourish on saline soils. Their origins probably lie in coastal habitats, which are also saline and desert-like, and they may have spread inland from arid regions that border the sea. There are many saline plains in the interior: products of the 'great dry' that gradually sucked the water from the vast lakes and rivers and turned them into salt lakes and saltpans. Winds churned the salt, sand and clay of the dry beds into salt dust, and spread it across the plains.

To survive, saltbush and bluebush have silvery green leaves that reflect heat. They are also coated with wax and a thick covering of hair that maintains a stable layer of air, so reducing the drying effect of the wind. Finally, they also excrete the excess salt the plant draws from the ground with its water.

Saltbush uses salt to prevent its seeds germinating until there is enough rain to wash the salt away. Then the seeds sprout roots at the rate of 2 or 3 centimetres a day, enough to see the seedlings through a short dry spell. But the saltbush keeps other seeds in reserve: seeds that will only sprout after several good falls.

Birds of the Noonday Sun

On summer days, the stately sway of emus in full stride is often the only sign of life on the heat-baked plains. Other animals have retired to their burrows or to sparse shade, but the emus' double-layered coat of feathers makes them impervious to heat. They share a common ancestry with the other great flightless birds of Gondwanan origin — the rhea of South America, the ostrich of Southern Africa and the extinct moas of New Zealand. Their immediate ancestors are the cassowaries that still live in the rainforests of Queensland and Papua New Guinea.

On the way to adapting to life on the open plains, emus (*Dromaius novaehollandiae*) acquired longer legs and shorter toes for more economical long-distance walking, and a lighter body supported by a skeleton in which most bones are hollow.

Although the ancestral ratite birds lost the power of flight long before Australia became a separate continent, emus still have ves-

Unusually among birds, the male emu (*Dromaius novaehollandiae*) takes sole charge of incubating his mate's eggs, rarely leaving the nest and eating little during the eight weeks it takes for them to hatch. He will care for the chicks, shepherding them around, and brooding them under his feathers at night until — in about 18 months — they are large enough to fend for themselves.

tigial wings — short stubs about 20 centimetres long in a fully grown bird. There is a second indicator of their ancient lineage: in some parts of the arid regions emus feed on the fruits of the zamia 'palm', whose origins can also be traced to Gondwana. The zamia's fruits are so poisonous they would kill anything else, and the emus' immunity bespeaks a long period of coevolution.

Emus have also formed an intriguing association with a more recent plant. The seeds of nitre bushes are fitted with a salt-rich pericarp that prevents them germinating. Passing through the emu's gut removes the pericarp but leaves the seed otherwise intact, eventually to be voided with a ready supply of fertiliser. Emus eat large quantities of nitre fruit; and the more they eat, the more they help propagate one of their favourite foods.

The nitre bushes and the other plants on which the emus feed grow most readily and persist longest along the drainage lines, where the sand retains enough water below the surface to keep the plants growing and fruiting long after the adjoining areas are parched. Emus prefer high quality, nutritious foods such as fruits, seeds and fresh green growth, but even in favoured areas these tend to be sparsely distributed, so the birds spend most of the daylight hours searching through the better growth that marks the track of the subterranean waters.

They move slowly and their long legs use little energy, so some of the food they gather is stored in thick layers of subcutaneous fat: fat storages that are important not only to last the birds through lean times, but as fuel for breeding.

Unusual among birds, male emus perform the task of incubating the eggs, and they rarely leave the nest for eight weeks. The hen's part ends when she has laid her clutch — it is a considerable drain on her energies, for the eight or ten large green eggs she produces weigh around half a kilogram each. As soon as she has finished (sometimes even while she is laying the last of the clutch) the male squats over the eggs to begin his long vigil. Resting his long neck on the ground, he becomes torpid in the often cold arid winter. His body temperature drops about four degrees, and he hardly eats or drinks until his offspring have broken free from their shells.

When they hatch, the emu chicks' plumage is patterned with brown and yellow stripes to camouflage them in the grass and to conceal them from ravens and hawks. They stay with their father for around a year and a half, learning how the lie of the land points to areas of good food.

Kings of the Plains

The patterns of plant growth created and sustained by ancient drainage contours also shape the lives of the other great plains dwellers, the red kangaroos (*Macropus rufus*). They give the largest of the living macropods the two things it needs most: shade and green pasture. The trees and shrubs that line the channel banks give shelter from the sun; moisture left by the rare floods and sporadic rains concentrates in the flood-outs that fan out from the watercourses, and in the gilgais, the small depressions scattered across the plains. Grasses and herbs growing there stay green long into drought, and the kangaroos' cropping keeps them shooting new growth long after the surrounding areas have dried out.

Red kangaroos are majestic animals — when they rear up on their powerful hindlegs, chest thrown forward and balancing on their massive tail, males stand taller than a man. Usually only bucks are red — the smaller does are mainly blue grey in colour, and they are called blue fliers. Red kangaroos survive in large numbers in the inland by making the best of what is available, and by avoiding extremes. They move out into desert country only when there is plentiful food after big rains, and retreat to more favoured areas around the watercourses when conditions return to the normal pattern of long dry spells and sparse and patchy rainfalls.

Their daily routine conserves energy and avoids the stresses of what, even in the best of times, is a taxing environment. In the hot summer months, red kangaroos feed at night and ensure they are back in shade by sunrise. Because they are such large animals, shade is essential to prevent overheating: even the meagre shadows of trees and shrubs cut the sun's direct heat by up to 80 per cent, and dense shade is especially prized — larger animals often oust smaller ones from a favourite spot. Heat also radiates from the sand and to reduce their exposed body area, kangaroos dig themselves small depressions in which they lie.

With water so precious a commodity, the kangaroos cannot afford to sweat to any great extent — instead, they pant to get rid of excess body heat. In very high temperatures they lick their forearms, where there is little hair and a network of blood vessels close to the surface dissipates heat very efficiently.

Mobility is the key to survival on the plains, and red kangaroos need to be constantly on the move to find the young grasses and fresh euphorbias they prefer.

The variety of plant communities along the watercourses means the kangaroos confine their wanderings within well-defined home ranges of around 300 square kilometres or so. When there is enough rain to germinate seeds the kangaroos move to higher red sand areas where grasses and euphorbias are the first plants to shoot. They feed on the plants almost as soon as they break the soil surface, for they can bite very close to the ground. When the grasses on the sandy plains dry, the kangaroos move to the floodouts and gilgais where moisture and green growth persist longer. Even when the dry times return, the patterns of patchy rainfall mean there is a chance of a passing shower somewhere in the home range, enough to produce a flush of new growth where the drainage patterns concentrate the moisture.

Red kangaroos travel from crop to crop with the minimum expenditure of energy. When they feed, their gait is a cross between a crawl and a shuffle on all fours, but to travel long distances they adopt a fluid, elegant bound, with the long, heavy tail stretched out behind as a counterbalance. The tendons in their hindlegs work like springs, storing much of the energy of each bound to provide propulsive force for the next. Red kangaroos can reach speeds of 65 kilometres an hour, but cruise most comfortably and efficiently at around 20 km/h, using far less energy than a placental

Mature males competing for dominance usually come to blows only when they are of equal size and strength: normally, a strutting walk displaying sheer size is enough to deter a challenge. The shoulder and chest muscles are especially well developed for just this purpose. When males do fight, they grapple with the forearms, and lean back on their thick tail to thud the powerful hindlegs into their opponent's belly. To avoid disembowelment, the skin is especially tough in that region.

With eastern grey kangaroos, red kangaroos (*Macropus rufus*) are the largest living marsupials. Rearing up to their full height, males stand more than 2 metres tall. These two bucks are fighting for dominance: victory will secure sexual access to the females of the group.

mammal's four-legged gait at the same speed. Part of the saving comes from the way the bounding action helps breathing: instead of muscle effort, the up and down movement of the gut contracts and expands the chest cavity, sucking air in and pushing it out.

While the red kangaroo streamlined the basic mechanics of marsupial hopping into an efficient locomotion for its arid habitat, it also fine-tuned the marsupial mode of reproduction to match the unpredictability of its environment. Because marsupial young are born at such an early stage of development — in the case of red kangaroos, after a gestation of a month — they use little of their mother's energy; even in the pouch the developing embryos need very little milk for the first few weeks.

The red kangaroo's reproduction has evolved to take advantage of good food supplies while they last. Does are ready to mate two days after giving birth: the resulting fertilised egg develops quickly to a bundle of cells — a blastocyst — then lies dormant in the uterus while the young in the pouch is being suckled. When the joey begins to venture from the pouch (after around 190 days) and suckling tapers off, the hormonal changes that follow stimulate the blastocyst to resume its growth.

At any one time, blue fliers can have a joey at foot, another in the pouch and a dormant embryo in the uterus. Of the four teats, two are always in use; one for the joey developing inside the pouch, the other for the youngster finding its feet outside. And each teat provides different milk: the teat that feeds the pouch young is high on carbohydrates and low on fats, while the youngster at heel, which is burning up much more energy, receives milk that is very rich in fats.

The 'production line' system operates while there is good food. With does rearing three young every two years and females reaching sexual maturity as early as 18 months, red kangaroo populations increase rapidly. But when drought comes and food supplies diminish, the breeding cycle changes. Milk production drops, and the pouch young die when they are about two months old. This, however, still triggers the dormant blastocysts to develop, and there is a procession of embryos, all of which die until conditions improve and does can produce enough milk for their young to complete development.

Should drought persist, the reproductive machinery comes to a halt. The green herbage that is the red kangaroo's preferred food contains proteins and oestrogens that are vital ingredients in its reproductive process. When green food runs out, females cease coming into oestrus and males become sterile: a form of natural birth control that maintains a balance between the numbers of kangaroos and the country's ability to support them.

Millions of years of climatic change refined a range of checks and balances as plants and animals learned to survive in the drying continent. Fifty thousand — perhaps 120,000 — years ago, a new species arrived to become a major force in the making of the continent. The response of humans to the challenge of living here profoundly changed the nature of Australia.

CHAPTER FIVE

THE LAND OF FLOOD AND FIRE

The human use of fire as a tool to manage the landscape had a profound effect on the nature of Australia.

*I*n the pale hour before dawn, a song floats across the sea. Dark against the lightening sky, people sing a welcome to the day: they sing of what the day will bring, where they will go, the fish they will catch.

The song is as old as the sea by which its singers live. It has greeted many dawns on Australia's northern shores — human voices were first heard on the continent at least fifty thousand years ago, when the seas were low enough to be crossed from Asia. It may have been earlier still, but whenever it was, the sound of human voices signalled the arrival of a major force for change.

Humans were the latest in a series of immigrants. Once the raft that carried the continent ground into Asia, a way was opened for new forms of life: as soon as the gap closed to flying range, birds moved in, to join or compete with the original groups that had travelled from Gondwana. Bats also fluttered across — and found a vacant niche to exploit.

Winged insects were blown in (termite alates may have been among them), birds and bats carried seeds and a range of Asian plants, including figs, gained a roothold on the continent. For anything without wings the way was difficult, since formidable sea barriers remained. Rodents drifted on rafts of vegetation torn loose by flood and storm to found Australian branches of their families. Some reptiles — lizards, snakes and turtles — came too, possibly in the same way. In their various ways, the migrants and castaways played their part in

Speculation continues about when the first humans set foot in Australia. Most informed opinion still favours an arrival time of about 50,000 years ago, when sea levels were low enough to permit relatively short seacrossings from the southeast Asian islands, where the first Australians were thought to have originated. But there is also evidence that it may have been a good deal earlier, perhaps as long ago as 120,000 years. Whenever it was, the places where the ancestral Aboriginals first landed have long been reclaimed by the sea.

shaping the nature of the continent. Then, a whim of wind and tide swept a simple craft — possibly no more than some bamboo poles lashed together — beyond the hope of return to its island home, and launched its occupants on a voyage beyond the horizon.

The arrival of human immigrants injected for the first time an element other than chance into the play of the forces that shaped the nature of Australia. The uniquely human ability to control the environment, to some degree at least, would bring profound changes to a continent where chance had been the sole ruler.

The origins of the first Australians lie in Southeast Asia, part of the Old World within which humans evolved. At times of low sealevels the region from Vietnam and Malaya to the islands of Bali and Borneo, became a single continent known as Sundaland. And as the human species evolved, it spread through the tropics and subtropics of the Old World, including all of Sundaland.

Much of the land was covered in dense forest, and clearer open woodlands and seashores, with their wealth of food, became avenues of exploration and expansion. Simple rafts evolved into more complex craft made of bamboo poles tied together. The maritime skills acquired, together with accumulating knowledge of winds, tides and currents, allowed sea-crossings and enabled humans to colonise the chains of islands that spread out east of Sundaland across Wallacea — the archipelagos strung out between modern Indonesia and Australia-Papua New Guinea.

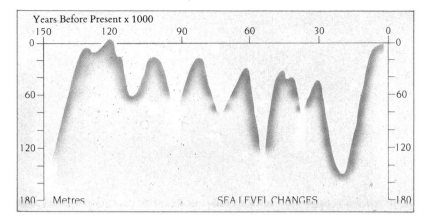

Changes in sea level during the last 150,000 years.

Even when the seas were at their lowest, as much as 250 metres below present levels, immensely deep channels still separated the islands of Sundaland. But the channels were narrow; even today, many of the islands are only a few kilometres apart and, because they are high volcanic lands, one is clearly visible from another. Over thousands of generations, the search for new territory led the early humans ever eastwards. Some colonisation would have been accidental: wind shifts must have turned many inshore fishing trips into unplanned migrations.

By 60,000 years ago, the world was moving into another ice age. Vast volumes of water were locked into the great ice sheets that extended north and south from the polar regions, the withdrawal of the seas exposed even greater landmasses and the world's climate grew cooler and drier.

Australia, Papua New Guinea and Tasmania were joined in the vast continent of Greater Australia (sometimes called Sahul). The northwestern shores extended up to 500 kilometres further than today, and the nearest island — present-day Timor — was only 90 kilometres away. Further north, the distances between New Guinea and the islands westward toward Sulawesi and Borneo were similarly shortened. The first humans to arrive in Australia might have come either way, and separate groups might have used both. Whichever point on Australia's jagged northern coast saw the first human landfall has long been reclaimed by the sea, and imagination must build on the circumstantial evidence supplied by science to form a picture of the landscape encountered by the first arrivals. In the relatively cooler and drier climate of the time, the wide plains of Greater Australia were probably covered in savannah woodland, dissected by broad rivers flowing down from the New Guinea highlands.

Although it was a new land, many of its features would have seemed familiar. Australia's north lies on the southern edge of the monsoonal tropics and its climate forms a continuum with that of the Sundaland and Wallacean regions through which the settlers had edged their way. The coastlines were fringed with mangroves and other shore communities rich in familiar fish and shell foods. They would have recognised many birds — especially fishing raptors such as the sea eagle, which ranges widely through Southeast Asia, and whose flight was a reliable guide to fish-rich waters.

Many plants were reassuringly familiar: there were patches of rainforest quite like the forests their ancestors had skirted in the Old World, but because it was the height of the global ice age the climate had moved to the dry end of the spectrum, and in northern Australia (where the dry seasons were probably drier and lasted longer than they do today), much of the vegetation consisted of drought-adapted plants, dominated not by the eucalypts now so characteristic but by stands of more ancient *Callitris* and *Casuarina*.

Among the new animals the first Australians encountered on their arrival in the continent was the largest marsupial that ever lived: *Diprotodon optatum*. It was nearly 3 metres long, and 2 metres high at the shoulder. It was one of the last members of its family of giant browsers and became extinct between 15,000 and 25,000 years ago.

The first people found many familiar vegetables — of the plants used for food by modern Aboriginals, at least twenty-nine also grow in the ancestral Sundaland. Some preparation techniques are still used: methods of leaching poisons from yams, palm nuts and mangrove seeds are similar to those employed by Indonesian islanders. Tradition dies hard, and a preference for the island foods of the forebears of northern Australia's Aboriginal people lasted through a thousand generations. But if many plants were familiar to the first arrivals, some animal life was not. When their ancestors first crossed the deep sea channels that separated Sunda from the island clusters of Wallacea, they left behind the animals typical of the Old World: deer, elephants, tigers and monkeys.

When they arrived in Sahul, they found animals with deerlike faces, which hopped on their hindlegs and whose does carried their young in pouches. The people spreading south from what is now Papua New Guinea saw even odder variations: deerlike hoppers that climbed trees. Instead of monkeys, possums and cuscuses climbed and lived in the forest canopy. Instead of tigers, there were wolflike hunters; instead of elephants, diprotodonts roamed the savannah woodlands. What all had in common was the pouch. It did not take the first Aboriginal people very long to experiment with marsupial meals, once they had become familiar with the behaviour of these new animals and had adjusted their hunting techniques to suit.

Learning the Country

The first generations retained some of the ways of their ancestors, and adapted to the demands and opportunities of an environment that mixed the familiar with the new. Life depended on knowing the country: what it had to offer, and when. The appearance of a certain star, a bird, flower or insect came to mean that rain was coming, that fish were running, that certain animals would soon be plentiful, that yams or ground nuts were ready for digging, or that wild fruits were ripe.

Watching the behaviour of animals taught much about seasonal rhythms. The large saltwater crocodiles northern Australia shares with the monsoonal regions of Sunda were familiar and feared, but their eggs made good food in the wet season for anyone who could slip past the female guarding her nest. In the upper reaches of the rivers and in the billabongs of the north, the first people found another type of crocodile, much smaller than the saltwater giant.

Its breeding cycle was also keyed into the rhythm of the wet and dry seasons, but while the estuarine or saltwater crocodiles nest during the wet, Australia's second species of crocodile nests during the dry season. The small freshwater crocodiles (*Crocodylus*

The saltwater, or estuarine, crocodile (*Crocodylus porosus*) is one of the animals that far north and northeast Australia shares with the monsoonal regions of southeast Asia. 'Salties' possibly colonised the continent when its long voyage from Gondwana took it into tropical latitudes about 15 million years ago. Crocodiles are an immensely ancient group, and have survived virtually unchanged for 200 million years — they are the largest survivors from the age of dinosaurs, with whom they shared a common ancestry.

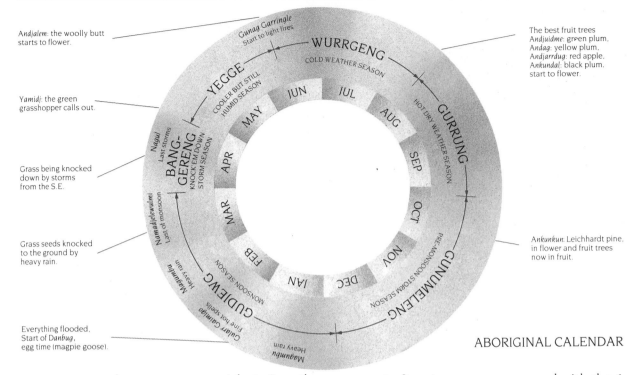

Andjalem: the woolly butt starts to flower.

Yamidj: the green grasshopper calls out.

Grass being knocked down by storms from the S.E.

Grass seeds knocked to the ground by heavy rain.

Everything flooded, Start of Danbug, egg time (magpie goose).

The best fruit trees
Andjuidme: green plum,
Andag: yellow plum,
Andjarrdug: red apple,
Ankundal: black plum.
start to flower.

Ankunkun: Leichhardt pine. in flower and fruit trees now in fruit.

(calendar wheel labels)
Gunag Garringle Start to light fires
WURRGENG COLD WEATHER SEASON
YEGGE COOLER BUT STILL HUMID SEASON
GURRUNG HOT DRY WEATHER SEASON
Nagul Last storms
BANG-GERENG KNOCK 'EM DOWN STORM SEASON
Namadjelewulmi Last of monsoon
GUUMELENG PRE-MONSOON STORM SEASON
Magumbu Heavy rain
GUDJEWG MONSOON SEASON
Gulurr Garringu Fine hot spells
Magumbu Heavy rain
JUN JUL AUG SEP OCT NOV DEC JAN FEB MAR APR MAY

ABORIGINAL CALENDAR

An Aboriginal calendar, showing the seasons recognised by the people of the Kakadu region of Arnhemland in the Northern Territory.

johnstoni) — they grow up to 2 metres or so, compared with the 6 metres of their saltwater relatives — time their reproduction so that their offspring have a good chance of hatching during the abundance of food that comes with the floods.

When the dry season is at its most intense, the females leave the water to search for nesting sites in the sandy river banks. They dig many trial holes before finding one that has the right soil consistency and dampness (which will influence incubation temperatures), and one that is safely above likely flood levels. Unlike the saltwater crocodiles, which guard their nests, freshwater crocodiles abandon theirs until they are due to hatch.

Over hundreds of generations, as the first Australians spread along the shore and followed the rivers, they learned the nuances of northern Australia's landscape. It is a landscape that has changed many times since humans first moved through it. Rising and falling sea levels and accompanying swings from drier to wetter climates and back again have seen the plains expand and contract, turn into saline mudflats, give rise to saltwater lagoons and become laced with lakes and swamps. The freshwater floodplains of today, with their intricate lattices of rivers, creeks and billabongs, are only a few thousand years old, but similar environments have existed in the past — governed as they still are, by the annual cycle of wet and dry seasons.

The floodplain of the East Alligator River in far north Australia: rich soils and annual inundations produce an abundance of plant and animal life.

The jabiru (*Ephippiorhynchus asiaticus*), or black-necked stork, is the only Australian member of the family. It strides through the shallow water of billabongs and freshwater lagoons, probing with its long, sharp bill for fish. This is a young bird — it still has some of its juvenile plumage, which eventually will become a bold combination of white and glossy green-black,

The dry is at its driest just before it ends, and the little water that remains on the plains becomes the focus for masses of waterbirds. Jabiru, herons and egrets stalk the shallows, spearing fish crowded in the diminishing waters. On one of the remaining lagoons, a flock of tens of thousands of water whistling ducks seems to roll across the surface as birds at the rear fly to the vanguard of the flock, and the air is filled with the whistling of wings and voices.

For the human hunter-gatherers, lagoons in the dry were a rich store of bird and fish food and became important links in patterns of seasonal movements. Magpie geese became a favourite quarry, and the centre of elaborate annual hunting rituals. Toward the end of the dry, the evening skies fill with endless streams of magpie geese coming together to camp on the lagoons and drying swamps. The hunters would take up station in trees across the birds' flight path and knock the birds out of the air with throwing sticks. The trees fringing the swamps and lagoons make daytime camps for colonies of flying foxes or fruit bats, which served as food — and the phases of their lives served as seasonal signs. When the black flying fox (*Pteropus alecto*) begins to give birth, the onset of the monsoon is not far away.

The birth itself is a remarkable event that seems to defy gravity. In the usual resting mode for flying foxes, the pregnant vixen hangs by her clawlike hindfeet. Arching her head and neck upwards, she

A large flock of water whistle ducks (*Dendrocygna arcuata*) rests by a billabong in the heat of the tropical day. In the dry season, they concentrate on permanent waters, and disperse in the wet when the swamps fill and the plains flood. They feed on aquatic grasses, waterlilies and other aquatic plants.

prepares for the birth by licking her vagina; after perhaps an hour, the baby makes its appearance head first. Once its head is clear, the young rests for several minutes twitching its ears and moving its head. Then the rest of its body emerges; the mother cradles the newborn in her wing and guides it to her nipple. Then she chews through the umbilical cord and eats the placenta.

For the first three weeks mother and young are inseparable, and baby accompanies her everywhere — flying, feeding and resting. It is soon too large and too heavy to be carried about, and is left in the daytime camps with groups of other young while the parents forage. The bond between mother and young remains close: when she returns from feeding, she suckles and grooms her offspring, and will continue to do so until it is about four months old and can fly.

In both behaviour and appearance, the fruit- and blossom-eating flying foxes are quite unlike the much smaller insectivorous bats. Both flying foxes and 'true' bats are classed as members of the same order (the Chiroptera, or 'wing-handed ones'), largely for convenience. Recent evidence has, however, highlighted the obvious and long-recognised differences between them and it appears each group evolved independently; that flying foxes may have evolved from primitive primate groups and that they are, in fact, flying monkeys.

As the wet season approaches, other new life stirs in the night. Calls from within eggs buried in a sandy river bank signal that a new generation of freshwater crocodiles is about to emerge. The female has been patrolling the river close to the nest as hatching time draws near, and now the calls bring her ashore. In what for reptiles is a remarkable display of parental care, she helps the young make their way into the world; scraping with her front claws, she digs out the eggs and helps them hatch by rolling them gently between her jaws. When the dozen or so hatchlings have emerged, she takes them in her mouth one or two at a time and carries them to the water. Then she joins her brood in the river — and mounts a protective patrol, for crocodile hatchlings make attractive food for a range of predators, from barramundi to other crocodiles.

The female has timed her egg-laying well: her brood has hatched late enough for the young to take advantage of the abundance of insect food that comes with the wet season, but not so late that the nest is at risk of being flooded by the rising waters.

To the Escarpment

The timing and duration of the wet season are unpredictable: there is often a series of false starts. Clouds form, storms roll in with violent rain squalls, then dry but still humid weather returns for a spell. Experience taught the early hunter-gatherers that the first storms meant it was time to move to higher ground: as the seas rose again and reclaimed the plains, later generations found higher ground further inland, until eventually they arrived at the great escarpment beckoning on the horizon. Once hundreds of kilometres of plains separated the walls of rock from the coasts; now, with the rising sea levels, only a relatively narrow band of plain remained for their dry season wanderings.

In the wet, when much of the country was flooded, they sought refuge in the rock shelters and overhangs of the escarpment. On the long, rainy days, they turned the rock walls into galleries for their art — the earliest rock paintings in the world — recordings of important features and events. The oldest of the works, which date from perhaps thirty-five thousand years ago, were made by coating hands and grass with wet pigment and pressing them against the rock. As with all art, fashions and styles changed: techniques improved, were lost and sometimes returned.

Around twenty thousand years ago, during the most recent ice age, the people who occupied the rock shelters in the wet seasons

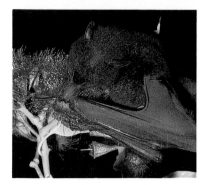

A black flying fox (*Pteropus alecto*) feeding on the blossom of a swamp bloodwood — eucalypt and paperbark flowers are the preferred food of these animals. They spend the days in mangrove or paperbark swamps, in camps that may number hundreds of thousands of individuals, and fly to their feeding grounds only after sunset.

A black flying fox gives birth: the baby's head has just emerged. It will remain in this position for 10 minutes to an hour or more taking stock of the surroundings before finally completing its emergence into the world. Although well developed, it cannot fly as yet and for the first month of its life, the young bat clings to its mother, gripping her fur with its claws, and her nipples with recurved milk teeth.

Atop the pitted and eroded Arnhem Land plateau, an ancient sandstone massif, formed from sediments laid down as marine deposits 1800 to 1400 million years ago. It is about 230 kilometres long, and 180 kilometres across at its widest point. The eastern face forms a continuous rock wall, an escarpment that rises out of the plains to heights ranging from 90 to 240 metres.

painted large, naturalistic images of themselves and of the animals they hunted. The pictures were drawn in outline, then filled with an ochre wash. Many of the animals can still be recognised: wallabies and possums, echidnas and bandicoots, pythons and freshwater crocodiles. There were also animals that have long since disappeared: thylacines, which vanished from the mainland four or five thousand years ago, and which survived in the isolation of Tasmania until recently; and long-beaked echidnas, which now occur only in Papua New Guinea.

The diverse company of giant mammals — all but the two monotremes are marsupials — that flourished in Australia in the Pleistocene epoch which ended 10,000 years ago. The animals are shown with an Aboriginal hunter — with whom many may have coexisted — to show comparative size.

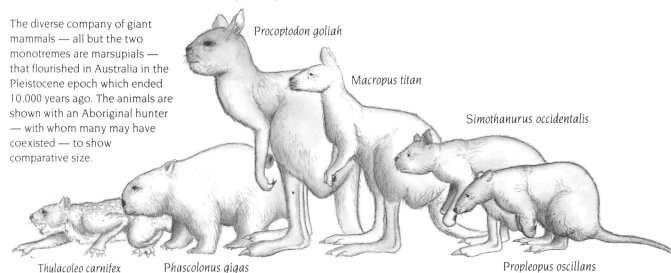

Procoptodon goliah

Macropus titan

Simothanurus occidentalis

Thylacoleo carnifex

Phascolonus gigas

Propleopus oscillans

Most intriguing are portraits of animals that have no modern equivalents, and that are thought to be representations of some of the last survivors of the age of giants — the megafauna that are otherwise known only from fossils. One picture possibly represents the extinct *Sthenurus*, a massive, blunt-faced kangaroo that may have been as much as 3 metres in height. Another suggests *Palorchestes*, a large browsing marsupial (about the size of a cow) with a tapirlike snout. And there is even a likeness of *Thylacoleo*, the marsupial lion — one of these animals' main predators.

Thousands of paintings cover the cave walls, overhangs and fissures in the escarpment. Many are overlain by layers of later works; others have faded to the faintest of outlines. But together they build into a remarkably complete record of a people and their world, and chart clearly the changes that overtook that world.

The megafauna occupy but a small part of the record, which suggests they vanished quickly once humans entered the picture. The companies of animals changed to correspond with periods of high and low sea levels: land and freshwater animals in pre-estuarine times, with a change of emphasis to different mammals, birds and fish when the coastlines and estuaries advanced and brought those animals within range of the people of the escarpment. The populations using the caves also ebbed and flowed, keeping pace with the relative abundances of food supplies that came with climatic changes.

The escarpment itself forms the massive front wall of an immense sandstone massif, first laid down as lime sediments in a shallow sea almost two thousand million years ago. Time, wind and water have carved the escarpment into huge pillars and stacks, sheer cliffs and stairways of giant sandstone steps. Rivers have carved their way through the plateau to form narrow, winding

The rock walls of many caves and overhangs of the Arnhem Land escarpment bear a record of a people and their environment that goes back more than 25,000 years. There are paintings of various recognisable species of fish, and portraits of animals now or once common in the region: echidnas and quolls.
The paintings were made during the wet seasons, when the Aboriginal people withdrew from the flooded plains, and sought shelter in the escarpment.

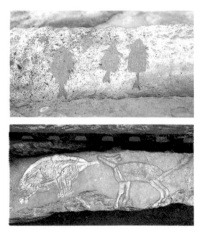

Aboriginal man

Zygomaturus trilobus

Diprotodon optatum

Sarcophilus laniarius   Zaglossus hacketti   Zaglossus ramsayi

Palorchestes azael

Hand stencils — made by pressing the hands against the rock, and blowing pigment from the mouth — are one of the earliest and most common forms of Aboriginal rock art.

In the thousands of years of the history of Aboriginal rock art, styles, subjects and fashions changed. In the earlier period, simple, dynamic lines depicted the people and the animals they hunted.

A later style of Aboriginal rock art: paintings such as this one, probably of a long-necked turtle, are more intricate and reveal something of the internal structure, as in an X-ray picture.

gorges. The roof of the plateau is a barren place, scoured by millennia of monsoonal rains. Most of the vegetation is in the valleys and gorges where soil has accumulated and where there is shelter from the wind and sun of the dry season.

Water, soil, rock and shade combine in different ways to create distinct habitats, each with its own plants and the animals that come to feed on them. Fig trees have established themselves here and there on the sheer rock. Their roots spread, searching out minute cracks and fissures where moisture collects and runs.

Coming of the Monsoon

The season of storms gathers in intensity: the winds change to the northwest and are warm and heavy with moisture. Black clouds tower above the escarpment, rimmed and shot through with the gold of the dying sun. The clouds burst, and the escarpment and plateau become a vast catchment. The fissures and crevices in the sandstone channel the waters into the gorges, sending them flying over precipices in waterfalls 200 metres deep.

Sometimes so much rain falls in such a short time that the flash floods rushing across the plains take animals by surprise. Entire populations of dusky rats drown; in places, the floods are aswirl with carcasses. But some animals manage to find refuge in scattered trees: a large goanna clings to a dead treelimb, just out of the water's reach; pythons coil in a paperback fork, within a tongue's flicker of a wet and shivering marsupial mouse . . . but normal predatory instincts are suspended in this common crisis. Once the initial buildup of water subsides — in a few hours, or a few days — some of the refugees will be able to make their way back to more or less dry ground. Others will tire, and perish.

The larger, more mobile animals move to high ground earlier, when the plains' grasses dry. Rock outcrops, outliers of the escarpment cut off by erosion, become islands in the flooded plains; wet season refuges for a range of animals. Agile wallabies (*Macropus agilis*) and the more solitary, elusive black wallaroos (*Macropus bernardus*) find grasses and herbs growing within the shelter of the rocky crevices.

Waterlife is prolific during the wet: aquatic plants grow and flower, the water surface is busy with insects, and with the birds and fishes that hunt them. Archer fishes (*Toxotes* spp.) shoot down insects from overhanging vegetation with jets of water — their accuracy all the more remarkable for the fact that they must allow for light refraction between air and water. If they miss, they sometimes jump out of the water to reach their prey. Jacanas, crested with bright red combs, seem to walk on the water: their extraordinarily long toes spread their weight so that even the flimsiest water weeds can support them.

The Arnhem Land plateau is a vast water catchment,
recharged by the heavy rains of the wet season. Rivers
come flying over the edge of the escarpment, making
spectacular falls 200 metres deep.

The pig-nose turtle (*Carettochelys insculpta*) lives in the freshwater lagoons and rivers of Australia's top end. Its reproduction is tuned to the unpredictable arrival of the annual monsoonal rains. The eggs are buried on the sandy banks and shores, and hatch only when floodlevels rise sufficiently to completely immerse them in water.

One of the larger honeyeaters, the blue-faced honeyeater (*Entomyzon cyanotis*) ranges widely, from the southeast to the tropical north. Though it does take nectar, it feeds mostly on insects which it finds an abundance in the monsoonal top end.

The slightly higher plains fringing the flooded paperbark forests turn into swamps in the wet season, and grow dense crops of wild rice, spike-rush and other sedges: food and nesting material for the magpie geese. The vast flocks that had gathered toward the end of the dry began to break up into breeding groups with the arrival of the first storms. Now the wet season is well advanced, and the sedges have grown tall enough to hide the birds and their nests. 'Building' is perhaps too complimentary a description: the birds simply pull down clumps of rushes into a rough platform on which they lay their eggs.

Magpie geese (*Anseranas semipalmata*) are neither magpies nor geese, but uniquely Australian birds — possibly, as their generic name suggests, an ancestral form of both geese and ducks. They are well adapted to both the wet and dry season: their feet are partially webbed, to cope with water, yet clawed to enable them to roost in trees. They also have strongly hooked, powerful bills that can dig through soil and mud for bulbs and tubers.

Breeding is organised in a way that may be a response to the stresses of a monsoonal existence: instead of pairs, magpie geese often form triangular relationships. Each male has two mates (usually one female is older), both of which lay their eggs in the same nest. One advantage of such a *ménage à trois* may be that the younger female learns the skills of brooding and chick care from her senior: another is that with incubation chores shared, each bird has shorter spells on the nest and more time for feeding.

A Time of Plenty

The breeding swamps, with their thousands of egg-filled nests, are a rich source of food for both animal and human predators. Goannas and water pythons move purposefully through the swamps, their progress marked by the alarmed honking of nesting birds: up to 70 per cent of the eggs may be lost by the end of the season. The eggs made good food for the Aboriginal hunter-gatherers, too, and gathering them became an important event on their seasonal calendar.

In parts of the north, Aboriginals cut strips of bark from euca-lypts on the margins of the swamps and fashioned them into canoes with broad, upward-sloping bows to slide over the swamp grasses. Ten or so canoes would fan out across the swamp, each poled by one hunter standing in the stern. With a goose nest every few metres, the canoes were low in the water by the end of the day. Egg hunts could last many days; the gatherers spent the nights cooking geese, huddled over small, smoky fires on platforms built in trees above the swamps.

Deep within the escarpment looming over the swamps and flooded plains other, less conspicuous, animals breed in their teeming thousands, providing bounty for other kinds of hunters. Soon after the wet began, hordes of bentwing bats (Miniopterus spp.) began gathering in an escarpment cavern. All are females, and they come together to give birth to young in concert with the abundance of insect food that comes with the wet. One cave may hold a hundred thousand or more bats: its rock floor lies buried under metres of bat dung. Bats first blew into Australia about 25 million years ago; there are now around 60 species, which makes them the most successful of the placental mammals to colonise the continent. Bats are abundant in tropical Australia (where they first arrived), and the clefts, crevices and gorges of the escarpment make ideal roosts. Some become the stage for a singularly dramatic display of animal behaviour.

Soon after sunset, the bentwings begin to stream out of their caves in dense black swarms. On a rock ledge close to where the cave openings are narrowest — and where the bat streams are thus at their most dense — pythons have come to feast. They weave their bodies into the stream like supple fishing rods: with such a multitude, the snakes take their time — but when they strike, they are fast and accurate. Sometimes the pythons tuck one bat into a coil, to eat later, while they catch more.

On rock ledges deeper inside the cave, large green tree frogs crouch in ambush. They are watching for young bats flying for the first time, which come to grief trying to navigate their way out of the narrow tunnel. After 20 minutes or so the last bat squadrons have

A Children's python (*Liasis childreni*) devouring a bentwing bat it has just snatched from mid-air. The pythons take up station near the narrow cleft where the bats come streaming out for the night's foraging, extend their bodies into the stream like supple fishing rods, and take their pick.

A moving wall of bat flesh:
some caves in Australia's
tropical north become home to
colonies of 100,000 bats at
breeding time. All these are
female bentwing bats
(*Miniopterus* spp.) and their
young. Breeding females
gathered in such vast numbers
generate great body heat to
produce the high temperatures
needed to rear their young.

made their way into the night, and the casualties are being digested by the snakes and frogs. Even after they have run that
gauntlet, the bentwings may not be safe: as they scatter through
the woodlands and paperbark forests of the flooded plains to hunt
insects, some may fall prey to large, carnivorous ghost bats.

By the time the young bentwing bats are flying, down in the
swamps the first of the new generations of magpie geese are hatching. The goslings hatch when the water levels in the swamps begin
to fall: they spend only a day or so on the nest, then all three
parents lead the twelve or so chicks through the tangled spike
rushes and wild rice in search of seeds and bulbs. The goose camps
are bordered by areas where couch, millet and paspalum grasses
grow. They produce seed at about the time the young magpie
geese hatch, and the adult geese bend the stalks down with their
clawed feet to bring the seedheads within reach of young beaks.

This is also the time when in the deeper lagoons the young of
the jacanas take their first tentative steps. Managing their long,

awkward feet on the tilting and sliding waterlily leaves takes some learning, and makes the baby jacanas especially vulnerable. While the mother patrols the family's territory and drives off intruders, the father guards the young. At the slightest sign of disturbance, he scoops the chicks up beneath his wings and carries them swiftly away from danger.

The sight of magpie goslings and jacana chicks, accompanied by winds shifting to the slightly cooler southeasterlies, were signs that told the bands of hunter-gatherers that the vegetable crops of the lagoons and flooded forests were ready for harvesting. Lines of women and children moved through the water, bending down or diving beneath the water to gather the roots and tubers of the water plants. Particularly favoured were the sweet-tasting tubers of the waterlilies: the tubers are the plants' food reserves, built up during the wet to last them through the dry, and they make reliable and nutritious fare.

On drier ground, various yams provide rich stores of carbohydrates and many fruits are ripe on the trees and bushes. Most of the plant foods were common to other monsoonal regions, but a little experimentation added a number of new, distinctively local items to the menu.

At least 35 different fruits and 34 vegetables became part of the Aboriginal diet at one time or another around the seasonal calendar. Their food preferences were to have a subtle effect on the landscape: as the bands moved around their territories, their faeces spread seeds of fruit trees and other food plants into new areas.

A series of what the Aboriginal people came to call the 'knock 'em down' storms heralds the end of the rainy season. The squalls

A storm looms over the floodplains of Kakadu, heralding the end of the rainy season. The local Aboriginals call them 'knock 'em down' storms — the wind and rain flatten the grasses and other plants that grow tall during the wet.

of wind and rain flatten the tall speargrass into sodden mats. After the last of the heavy rains, the waters subside and small green grasshoppers call to signal the season of plenty. Many of the smaller, more delicate plants choose this time — when the risk from destruction by heavy rain has passed — to set their flowers. And this is the time when many reptiles and mammals breed.

There is a second flush of insect life, and bees are busy collecting nectar from the prolific blooms. The honey becomes a prized food for the human foragers; to find it, a small, bright feather is tied to a bee, which then shows the location of its hive — usually in a tree hollow. Such a concentrated energy food made a welcome supplement to the daily diet, and was relatively easy to gather. Collecting protein in the form of animal flesh required more effort. One reliable source was the daytime camps of the black flying foxes, and the huntsmen made regular raids.

At this time of the year, the flying foxes themselves are preoccupied with procreation. The young born at the beginning of the wet season are becoming independent, and their mothers are ready to conceive again. The segregation of the birth time has ended, and males and females are back together. There is constant squabbling over mating rights: older, more powerful males establish territories (perhaps only a metre or so in diameter, but large enough to court and mount females) and keep away other males. Courtship is often a protracted affair, and involves much mutual grooming and licking before the pair copulates.

The imprint of the people on the landscape was but slight during the wet seasons. They joined the crocodiles, eagles and the larger marsupial carnivores as major predators, and their impact was probably no greater. In their wanderings, they changed the distribution of some plants and rearranged plant communities in minor ways. On the whole, however, humans and their activities merged with the natural patterns of the wet seasons. But when the rains ended, when the waters began to recede from the floodplains and the tall grasses began to turn yellow in the woodlands, the human presence became a visible, powerful force in the landscape.

Firesticks as Tools

For mobile hunter-gatherers, living off the land necessarily means moving through it. The long, dense plant growth that shoots up in the wet and that is knocked down by the storms that end the season, makes much of the land difficult to traverse. At the same time, the upsurge of life produces an abundance of animals — among them many venomous snakes, including king browns and death adders — which made travel and camping hazardous.

As soon as the weather becomes drier, the Aboriginal people begin their annual burning regime, to clean up the country' and promote fresh new growth and mosaics of vegetation that favour animals sought after as food. Their method of managing and controlling their environment through the use of fire has come to be called 'firestick farming'. Over their 40,000 plus years of occupation, the Aboriginal firing regimes changed the face of the continent.

The Aboriginal fire regime promoted regrowth in various stages that made mosaics of vegetation — patchworks of open areas scattered with denser thickets. Such a blend is ideal for prized prey like these northern brown bandicoots (*Isoodon macrourus*), which shelter in dense growth by day and feed in the open at night on insects, berries and seeds. With a gestation period of only 12½ days (the shortest known for any mammal) bandicoots are fast breeders and become plentiful in the good conditions created and maintained by fire.

Snakes were among the people's greatest fears, for they had no cure for a venomous bite. What they did have was prevention . . . in the form of fire.

The people began burning the swamps as soon as they began to dry out, to get rid of old plant growth: matted and tangled layers of grass would make it harder for magpie geese to nest and find food in the next nesting season, and magpie geese were important for meat and eggs. They knew, too, that the first flush of fresh green growth would attract agile wallabies, and make them easier targets for their spears.

When burning through the woodlands and open forests early in the dry season, they lit fires during the windiest time of the day so the winds would bend the flames forward, and keep them from scorching the valuable fruit trees. Care was taken to burn only certain areas at a time; the effect was to create a patchwork of fire breaks to keep wild fires in check.

In some places — the food-rich but vulnerable patches of rainforest and vine thickets — fire was banned altogether. Smoke from fires lit there would blind the people, according to one tribal proscription. The effect was to keep a valuable food source intact.

As the cooler months gave way to intense heat later in the dry season, burning eased off. The only fires still lit in the woodlands and open forests were for the hunt, since with plant food running low there was a greater need for meat. Hunting fires were often set in a horseshoe shape, with a narrow gap at one end. As fleeing

A northern woodland, regenerating after fire. Frequent burning tended to favour fire-tolerant vegetation such as eucalypts.

Inside a nest of termites (*Mastotermes darwiniensis*) — workers, nurses and soldiers, each caste with its appointed task. Only the workers can process the cellulose, the chief ingredient of the wood and grass that are the termites' food. They digest it, and feed it by mouth or in faecal pellets to the colony's other inhabitants.

kangaroos and wallabies came rushing through the only opening in a wall of flames, spears and clubs awaited them. Birds of prey came hunting along the fire front: the first signs of smoke brought great numbers of black kites and brown falcons to wheel and swoop through the columns of smoke, hooking up insects, lizards and other small creatures trying to escape the fire.

Over time, Aboriginal burning shifted the mix of plants in the landscape. Initial firings denuded the soils of fire-sensitive vegetation, and left them vulnerable to erosion — especially on hill slopes, where the monsoonal downpours might wash away the entire top layer of soil in a few seasons. But eventually fire-tolerant trees and shrubs, plants that could come back from frequent burnings, extended their hold and anchored what was left of the soils. The character of the woodlands changed: they became more open, and grasses spread.

With the grasses came the animals that fed on them. In the tropical north, that in the main meant not the herds of large mammals that roam the grasslands of other continents, but one particular group of much smaller grass-eaters, the termites. Tropical grasses carry relatively few marsupial grazers; there are kangaroos and wallabies, but not nearly as many as might be expected and not nearly as many as are found further south. One reason may be the generally poor quality of the soils, which means the grasses are not particularly nutritious. But they make rich fare for termites, which cope with the torrid climate by insulating themselves in an environment of their own making.

The plains of northern Australia are dominated by
innumerable termite mounds, castles of clay that house
the Australian equivalent of the grazing herds of
mammals found on the grassplains of other continents.

This strategy makes termites one of the most powerful forces at work in the tropical landscape: individually tiny and helpless, together they determine the very shape of life. Through harvest and storage, they lock up vast amounts of organic material; by tunnelling and nest building, they turn over the soil.

Usually hidden from sight in tunnels and galleries, the termites' dominating presence becomes visible through their 'cities' rising above the savannahs and the grasses covering the woodland floors. The city walls are a rock-hard mixture of clay, termite saliva and faeces, built up millimetre by millimetre by hundreds of thousands of termites: some of the clay castles rise 6 metres. The walls make such good insulation that, whatever the conditions outside, the inside temperatures remain at a constant 30 degrees, with close to 100 per cent humidity. One species of termite has developed architectural and air-conditioning skills to an even greater degree. Because the monsoons leave low-lying areas waterlogged much of the time, termites cannot retreat underground to escape the heat as those in other areas do. So they build their mounds to expose the largest surfaces to the sun for the shortest possible time — by making the mounds long and narrow and by aligning them north to south, they keep one side cool at any one time.

Favoured by the Flames

The termite food of cellulose is the main ingredient in wood as well as in grass, and many termite species harvest their cellulose from timber. Not all are mound builders — some have nests underground and inside trees — but all send intricate networks of tunnels and galleries radiating throughout the grass and woodlands, from one clump of grass to another, from tree to tree, into the dead and fallen wood. Covered runways climb rock faces to reach the grasses and trees clinging there, and run up the sides of trees to get at the dead wood in the crown.

Wood-eating termites prefer eucalypts, but what began as a simple attack by parasites has evolved into a curious two-way deal that works to the advantage of both. It is a partnership in which fire is an indispensable ingredient, and one that affects the lives of many other animals. Eucalypts as well as grasses were favoured by the more frequent fire that came with humans. They had features that enabled them to cope with regular searings better than trees such as the native pines and oaks. Eucalypts had thick bark to shield their heartwood, and the ability to sprout again from trunk and roots. Gusts of hot air carried seeds to colonise new areas.

As eucalypts extended their dominion, so too did the termites that depend on them. Their partnership consolidated the advantage conferred by the flames. The guiding principle was simple: the eucalypts provided the termites with food and, as a result, gained extra food themselves: an important benefit in Australia's impoverished soils.

As well as favouring eucalypts in a general sense, fire also played a direct role: the scars left at the base of the trees by the passing flames weaken what is otherwise an almost impenetrable defence, and allow the termites entry. Once inside, they rapidly hollow out the central part of the trunk and the main branches. The heartwood is soon turned into a pulp that the termites mould into nursery chambers. Every branch of the host tree is mined for wood, and foraging parties are sent into neighbouring trees: one colony may come to harvest as many as twelve eucalypts over an area of half a hectare. More than 80 per cent of northern Australia's eucalypts are being hollowed out in this way at any one time.

The eucalypts' habit (helped by wind and fire) of shedding branches leaves openings that are valuable to many animals.

A fifth of northern Australia's birds, a quarter of its reptiles and half its mammals use tree hollows for nests and shelters. And in return for their lodging, the animal tenants supply their hosts with nutrients in the form of droppings, leftovers and nest litter.

Hollow-users give the north's eucalypt communities their distinctive character. Typically, woodland and forest spread from the floodplains to the base of the escarpment — scattered groups and

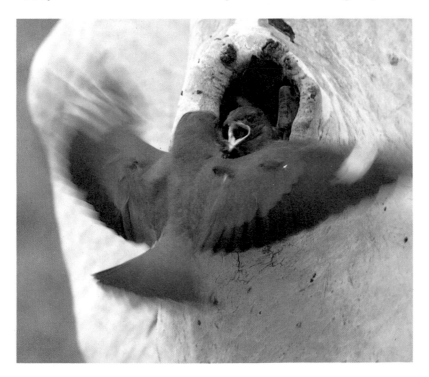

Termites hollow out eucalypts and create nesting space for many animals. A dollar bird (*Eurystomus orientalis*) brings a meal of mashed insects to its young. The birds migrate from Papua New Guinea to breed in these woodlands.

open woodland on the poorer, stonier soils, denser forest on richer ground. The ground is carpeted with grasses, and in more fertile areas there are understoreys of shrubs. Stringybarks and woollybutts are dominant, and provide hollows in generous measure.

The hollows come in different shapes and sizes, and at various levels to suit different animals. The tree-dwellers make up a varied company through the seasons. Among the many birds that nest in the hollows are red-tailed black cockatoos and northern rosellas, which move in flocks through the canopies to crack gum nuts, harvest their seeds and bring cropsful back to their chicks inside the trees. Kingfishers dive for insects and small reptiles on the woodland floor. Dollarbirds, which migrate from New Guinea to breed, take their insects on the wing. Much of that prey also finishes up inside the trees as food.

At night, other tree dwellers become busy. Sugar gliders emerge from their hollows and sail to a woollybutt still in flower to feed on nectar. A northern brushtail possum (*Trichosurus arnhemensis*) feeds on the leaves of a stringybark, and snatches moths and other insects when it gets the chance. A northern quoll (*Dasyurus hallucatus*) slips out of its capacious nest near the top of the tree and runs head first down the trunk to hunt the woodland floor for anything that stirs, from large insects to small marsupials and rodents.

Perhaps Australia's best-known reptile, the spectacular frilled lizard (*Chlamydosaurus kingii*). It is mostly arboreal, though it also forages on the ground for insects and small vertebrates. It measures about 220 mm from snout to vent, with the tail twice as long again. The frill normally lies in folds around the neck and is erected by opening the mouth when the lizard is alarmed. Its other characteristic feature is to use only the hindlegs when running.

Red-tailed black cockatoos (*Calyptorhynchus banksii*) were the first Australian parrots to be illustrated — by Sydney Parkinson, Joseph Banks' draughtsman on the *Endeavour* in 1770. These magnificent birds are especially abundant in northern Australia where flocks of up to 200 may gather to roost and feed, eating a wide variety of seeds of trees, shrubs and grasses.

Before daybreak all have returned to their hollows, bringing back the nutrients they have gathered and processed: honey, leaves, insects and animal flesh. Some will be passed on, directly or as milk, to their young. Some will be spilt, some wasted, some recycled and excreted. Individually, it may not amount to much; but in the aggregate it is a feast in an impoverished environment, and gives eucalypts an advantage over trees that do not have a hollow-forming relationship with termites.

Eventually, of course, the termites may kill their host: the hollowing weakens the tree so much that wind or fire will topple it. And that may be the end of the termite colony itself: the falling tree smashes the mound, leaving it open to invasion, and a range of animals — lizards, spiders and ants — comes to gorge. More usually, the termite nest has grown so large and solid that it outlasts the tree in which it began perhaps 50 or 60 years earlier.

Trails of Fire

What prompted the people's first movements out of the areas of the early landfalls can only be guessed at: natural human curiosity — a desire to see what lies beyond the horizon — was probably part of it. One reason might have been an increasing population outstripping the local food supplies, or food dwindled through drought, which would have had the same effect. A band of hunter-gatherers needs a large tract of country to support it, especially while it is still getting to know the terrain.

There is no accurate way of reckoning the numbers of the first arrivals: perhaps several small groups came in within a few years of each other and combined; perhaps the entire Aboriginal population arose from one small band of immigrants. In theory, it is possible for a single craft to have carried a founder population: a man and two women would be enough to produce up to around two thousand descendants in a thousand years.

Differences in the size and form of the skeletons of some of the early people have given rise to theories that two, perhaps even three, distinct human races arrived at various times in prehistory, and that modern Aboriginal people descended from a mixing of those early waves of immigrants.

The more temperate, better watered regions were settled first. Only when population increased further, and with it knowledge and experience of making harsher land yield life, did humans venture to the continent's arid core. Whatever the routes of colonisation, most of Australia was occupied by 30,000 years ago, and probably all of it by 20,000 years ago.

None of these dates can be accurate, of course: new archaeological evidence keeps turning up, and timescales are revised constantly. One recent find dates a human settlement near Sydney at possibly 46,000 years ago — which means the southeast was occupied a good deal earlier than previously thought. A similarly tantalising lack of conclusiveness attends the question of how many humans lived in Australia before Europeans arrived. After the initial explorations and occupations the population probably increased rapidly, then settled at a more or less constant level, with some fluctuations between harsh and good times.

Estimates of that level have ranged from as low as a hundred thousand people to more than a million, with most informed opinion clustering around 300,000. Population densities varied from several people per square kilometre in food-rich areas such as the Murray-Darling basin, to perhaps one person per 100 square kilometres in the desert regions, while seasonal movements were a common feature among the hunter-gatherers. Likewise, their journeys would have varied according to the environment — from perhaps only a few hundred metres at a time along lake shores and rivers to many hundreds of kilometres in arid land.

There was variation, too, in the size of groups. The base unit was usually an extended family of one or two men — commonly brothers — and their wives and children. Four or five of these groups formed a band that came together more or less regularly.

An Aboriginal 'mortar and pestle', a stone mill to grind the seeds that became a more common part of the hunter-gatherers' diet over the past five thousand years. Though not as popular as berries and other fruits, seeds — especially of grasses — became a more reliable and abundant source of food in the changing Australian environment.

Full-scale tribal gatherings were held only on special occasions, when there was enough food to sustain large numbers of people in one area. There were at least three hundred separate tribal groupings, each with its own distinct language.

Fire continued to be the focus of all life: domestic, material and spiritual. It was the family hearth and the tribal temple, the source of warmth, protection and spiritual strength. Its heat reduced pain and stemmed the flow of blood from wounds. Fire was central to many rites of life and death. Before giving birth, a woman made fire to produce ash with which to clean and dry her child. In initiation ceremonies, fire marked the passage to manhood. Fire rituals were to evolve into spectacular forms: conflicts within some tribes were resolved in ceremonial fight-dancing where participants brandished torches 5 metres long. In death, fire kept away evil spirits, consumed the possessions of the dead . . . and in some tribes, the dead themselves. Cremation was practised on the shores of Lake Mungo 30,000 years ago.

In daily life, fire was a practical and flexible tool, wielded with casual expertise by both sexes. Women were adept at using fire to fell dead trees for firewood, to flush small animals from burrows and hollow logs, and to clear small areas of litter to dig for yams and insect larvae. Men used fire to harden spearpoints, to clear paths in regions of dense plant growth, to signal to other groups and of course, to hunt.

Shifting Mosaics

In the monsoonal north, the annual cycle of wet and dry was fairly predictable and in combination with both natural and controlled fire, produced regular annual patterns of growth and decline. In the drier inland, rain was both scarcer and less predictable. Life was tuned to years of drought broken by short seasons of plenty. Before the human advent, fire was probably a random and scarce occurrence — but should lightning start a burn, especially during the long dry times, the plains turned into seas of flame. The fires might not stop until they reached natural breaks such as deserts of sand and stone. Such huge fires, although rare, seem to have favoured large and very small animals over medium-sized varieties. Large, mobile animals such as kangaroos and the bigger wallabies could escape and return for the new growth. Very small animals could find refuge beneath rocks or underground, and enough food in the post-fire debris to survive. Medium-sized animals, in contrast, would have both their food and their shelter burned away.

Once humans moved into the central regions (probably during more favourable times, their descendants gradually adapting to harsher conditions), there was a change. Fire was kept to a smaller scale, a patchwork of burns. The burnt ground kept natural wildfires in check and, over time, produced a mosaic of vegetation in varying stages of growth and composition. The time span was both greater and less predictable than it had been in the north: there new growth might spring up in days or weeks, but in drier regions the ground might lie fallow for months or years before a chance rainfall wakened the dormant seeds.

When rain does come, there is a rush of growth. First short-lived ephemeral plants put forth their flowers and seeds, then wither and die as the longer lived grasses sprout; grevilleas and hakeas shoot from burned stems and buried tubers, or rise from the seeds released by the fire. Each stage brings its own mix of animals. The flowers attract the nomadic birds of the inland. White-plumed honeyeaters and crimson chats come to feed on the nectar and the insects propelled into life by the plants' brief bloom. Later, the new crop of seeds feeds wrens, pigeons and nocturnal foragers such as hopping mice.

Aboriginal fire, rain and time blended with variations of soil and terrain to produce plant communities that suited a variety of animals. Especially favoured were medium-sized marsupials — bettongs, bandicoots and hare-wallabies.

Aboriginal fire created a mix of old and new vegetation, and therefore of shelter and food. Some of those patterns persist in areas of the inland: in the Tanami region of the centre lives the tiny rufous hare-wallaby (*Lagorchestes hirsutus*), called *mala* by the Aboriginals. The mala's wellbeing is very much governed by the right

A mala, or rufous hare-wallaby (*Lagorchestes hirsutus*), feeding in spinifex country that is regenerating after fire. It is one of the small to medium-sized marsupials that benefit from the mosaics of vegetation promoted by the Aboriginal regime of patchy, small-scale and regular burning.

Bilbies, or rabbit-eared bandicoots (*Macrotis lagotis*), are among the animals that thrive on the smorgasbord of plant food produced by patchwork burning. They emerge from their desert burrows at night to forage. This one is digging out a cache of seeds gathered and stored by harvester ants in their nest.

kind of fire. The patchiness of Aboriginal burning leaves part of the vegetation untouched: clumps of old spinifex provide the mala with its shelter, from which it moves to new growth to feed on the seedheads and young leaves of the euphorbias and grasses.

Fire is also important to the bilby (*Macrotis lagotis*), a member of the bandicoot family. It is among the loveliest of marsupials, with soft blue-grey fur, a slender white-tipped tail and long, delicate rabbitlike ears. Unlike the mala, bilbies do not need the plant growth for shelter (they excavate a deep burrow in the sand) but rely on the variety of foods created by the Aboriginal fire regime: seeds, bulbs, fruit and fungi, and insects and their larvae.

Like many arid-zone animals, bilbies can survive without free water as long as there is the right mix of foods to provide moisture. Their reproduction is also governed by the availability of food: while there is enough of the right kind, they breed.

With fire such a potent force, it reached into every plant and animal community. Like the malas and bilbies of the Tanami, the woylies and tammar wallabies of the jarrah forests of southwestern Australia depend on fire, and it has shaped their behaviour in curious ways. The right kind of fire — hot, but not too hot, at the right time — once every seven years or so, maintains the forest understorey thickets of heartleaf. The heat of the fire cracks the heartleaf seed cases and allows them to germinate. It keeps the thickets dense enough to provide cover, but not so dense that they are difficult to move through.

The thickets are central to the lives of both animals: the tammars for shelter, the woylies — the local name for the brush-tailed bettong (*Bettongia penicillata*) — for food. The woylies feed on underground fungi that they dig from the soil around the bushes. And more frequent fire maintains open patches of varied kinds of grasses for the tammars (*Macropus eugenii*) to graze. The different food sources mean different social lives. Tammars are more social: concentrated grazing brings them together. The woylies' main food of fungi is more patchily distributed, so it pays them to establish individual territories. So strong is their attachment to home that it takes more than fire to make them leave. When fire visits the forest — what for other animals would be a real crisis — they do not panic. They move calmly ahead of the flames until they reach the limits of their territory: then, if they have not been able to find refuge, they simply double back through the smoke and flames.

The fire triggers a burst of growth, not only among the seeds of the heartleaf and other plants that have lain dormant, but also of the fungi that are the woylies' main food. They eat the fleshy core but the spores, the fungal equivalent of seeds, pass through their digestive system intact. A fourth ingredient now enters the mix: after fire, fungi and woylies come the scarab beetles. The beetles feed on the droppings and bury them, so replanting the fungal spores to ensure another generation of growth.

The sequence is a cycle: many of the fungi the woylies feed on grow with the roots of heartleaf, and help them extract nutrients from the soil more efficiently. Fungi whose spores have passed through the woylie's gut enhance the growth of heartleaf more than those whose spores have not. So in eating the fungi the woylies help to maintain their habitat — and their survival.

Patterns of Change

Precisely where Aboriginal burning began and natural fires left off in this complex cycle is now impossible to tell. On the larger scale, too, it is often difficult to measure the precise extent of Aboriginal influence. Their advance across the continent coincided with some dramatic fluctuations in the climate, climaxing in a particularly sev-

Procoptodons were giant, short-faced kangaroos that flourished with the spread of open woodland and grassland as Australia became drier over the past two million years.

ere period of intense droughts, cold hard winds and permanent snow on the southern ranges that reached its nadir around eighteen thousand years ago.

The forests retreated even further, woodlands became more open, grass plains extended and many animals were swept into extinction — including the last of the giant kangaroos, diprotodonts and flightless birds twice the size of emus. The shift to aridity probably began their decline; extremely large size makes it more difficult for animals to cope with sudden climatic swings. The decline may have been hastened by the Aboriginal firestick: and for some species the death blow may have been dealt by the direct use of fire to trap animals that otherwise might have proved difficult prey.

In parts of Australia, people and megafauna coexisted for many thousands of years. Most of the extinctions occurred in the arid and semi-arid areas around ten thousand years before they did in

There was a great diversity of browsing and grazing kangaroos and wallabies — which provided prey for marsupial carnivores. The largest and fiercest was *Thylacoleo carnifex*, the size of a leopard. Aboriginal burning and hunting may have contributed to the extinction of both the megafauna and its predators: the last of the giants vanished about 10,000 years ago.

the more favoured regions of the southeast, which would tend to suggest climatic change as the more important cause. Yet when the southeastern extinctions did occur, they did so during a relatively wetter and more benign climatic phase — which in this case suggests human hunting was the decisive factor.

Not all the megafauna became extinct: some survive in 'dwarfed' form. There is good evidence that the eastern grey kangaroo (*Macropus giganteus*) is a direct descendant of the Pleistocene giant *Macropus titan* which, at more than 2 metres in height, was half a metre taller and weighed half as much again. The Tasmanian devil's direct ancestors, common on the mainland, were also much larger — as were those of the wombat. The same processes that led to the extinctions of the megafauna in all likelihood also caused the 'dwarfing' of some forms. The effect was probably not a reduction in size within a population of a species, but rather a geographic shift in populations of different sizes: as the larger animals died out, smaller forms of the same species may have moved into vacant niches.

Human changes to the landscape probably played a part in the process as well. Climatic change influenced the patterns of human movement across the continent, and therefore the effects of their fires on the landscape. In the depth of the most recent ice age, the most severely drought-stricken regions may have been abandoned altogether. The loss of those lands was balanced by the vast areas on the continent's margins from which the sea had withdrawn (though even in those more favoured coastal regions life must have been hard). Around sixteen thousand years ago, the climatic pendulum began to swing back again and the seas began their final and most dramatic rise. In 10,000 years they climbed 150 metres. By 12,000 years ago Tasmania had been cut off from the mainland; by 8000 years ago the last connections with Papua New Guinea were broken. Levels stabilised at around their present mark about six thousand years ago.

To the tribes of the coastal plains, the invasion of the seas must have seemed terrifyingly swift. Some might have seen their entire hunting grounds disappear within a generation: on the flatter coasts, land was lost to the sea at a metre a day. The advance of the seas sent its effects rippling far inland: rainfall increased again, and people moved back into the interior.

In the north, the coastal people were pushed back to the escarpment as the plains narrowed. The rock paintings in the escarpment galleries began to reflect the advancing sea with images of marine and estuarine animals: barramundi and saltwater crocodiles. With the climatic changes came increasingly fierce electrical storms, recorded in many paintings of Namarrgon, the mythical lightning man.

Namarrgon, the mythical lightning man. His picture appeared more frequently with the fierce storms that accompanied climatic change. The stone axes protruding from his head, and attached to his knees and elbows, struck the clouds and released the lightning, represented by the band encircling his body.

A New Invader

Around this time, another new image begins to appear in the record. It looks somewhat like a thylacine, but it is in fact a new predator that arrived on the northern shores about five thousand years ago. The latest invader was the dingo, a very early form of dog. How it arrived in Australia is still the subject of argument: with a late arrival of Aboriginal immigrants is one thought; with early Asian seafarers, as living food supplies that escaped, is another. Either way, dingoes spread quickly to every part of the continent.

Their radiation may have been helped by humans. Dingoes probably insinuated themselves into Aboriginal life, scavenging around the camps for food, and graduated to sleeping companions: frosty nights in the centre are still called 'three-dog nights'.

Dingoes are very adaptable animals, feeding on carrion as well as a large range of live prey, from insects and lizards to wallabies and kangaroos. With large prey, the strategy is pursuit — keeping up a sustained pace over long distances to wear the quarry down. They form packs, rather loose arrangements that break up and reform to suit changing circumstances. Only the pack leader has the right to mate when a bitch comes on heat: a system that helps keep dingo numbers within the limits of the country's ability to support them.

Their flexible life style soon made dingoes masters of the bush, and in their conquest of the continent they displaced and outcompeted their marsupial counterparts, the thylacines. In a sense, dingoes were harbingers of later invasions: they showed how swiftly the natural equilibrium could be disturbed by the introduction of a new element.

After perhaps fifty or more millennia of occupation, the Aboriginal people had achieved their own equilibrium with the continent. Far from being the timeless and changeless land of popular perception, Australia has been swept by dramatic change many times, change in which the Aboriginals often played a major part.

There is a tendency to overestimate the Aboriginal people as the original conservationists — environmental managers carefully wielding their firestick with an eye to the long-term future — perhaps in a reaction against the original underestimation of them as 'the miserablest people on earth'. But, like all humans, their concern was with survival. And, like all hunter-gatherers, survival meant leaving something for tomorrow. They had a complex system of proscriptions, the effect of which was usually to maintain animal and plant reserves. Some of the inland tribes had taboos on hunting kangaroos in certain areas: areas that corresponded to the animals' last refuges in drought. Similarly, some water sources

The dingo (*Canis familiaris dingo*) is a comparatively recent arrival in Australia — though just when or how remains a matter of vigorous scientific debate. The oldest reliable fossil has been dated at about 3000 years. It is generally agreed that it has not been here for much more than 5000 years. Since then, it has become a major predator on the mainland, displacing the marsupial thylacine. Dingoes have a flexible social system — they are solitary hunters of small game but form packs to bring down larger prey such as wallabies.

were out of bounds until all other sources had been exhausted.

The Aboriginals were well aware of the immediate and short-term effects of their burning practices, and became highly skilled at turning these changes to their greatest advantage. But they had no way of knowing the longer term impact on the landscape and its plant and animal communities. How were the natural balances altered? How many species were lost? There is still no precise way of knowing; too many climatic and environmental variables are interwoven with the human factor.

Nevertheless, the changes they brought — mainly through fire — had been slow enough to allow plant and animal communities to adjust. The effects of some of those changes flowed back into their own lives. The shift to grasslands (if not initiated, then maintained and extended by the firestick) saw seeds become an important part of the Aboriginal diet from around five thousand years ago. Grindstones appeared, and harvesting techniques — again, often using fire — were only a step away from farming.

Seeds were especially important in the arid regions: though neither sweet nor particularly flavoursome, they were more dependable and predictable than popular foods such as berries and other fruits. If a plant produced enough seed to be worth the effort of collecting it, it was added to the menu. In central Australia, 75 different plants were harvested for seed, ranging from ground-hugging plants such as pigface to grasses such as woollybutt and native millet to trees and shrubs, including mulga and prickly wattle. One common way of harvesting seeds was to break seed-laden branches from the trees and to stock them in stook-like piles at the base of the trunks. After a few days' drying, the seeds would be easy to collect.

In the fertile river valleys of the coastal regions of the southeast and southwest, Aboriginal life came to have many elements of what in other parts of the world would evolve into the first farming communities: semi-permanent villages, sometimes of stone huts, grew up in areas rich in food. Stone traps used the rivers' ebb and flow to harvest fish. In one area of Victoria's western districts, a complex network of canals was dug to channel and farm eels.

In the coastal plains of Western Australia, rich yam grounds supported villages of perhaps 150 people for a season every year. They lived in clusters of solid huts, clay-plastered and turf-roofed. A network of well-defined paths connected the villages and their 'gardens'. In what came close to cultivation, some of each clump of yams would be left in the ground. But as well as the digging stick, fire was used as an agricultural tool. Bulrushes were cultivated by fire: burning the leaves caused the edible roots to become even more nutritious. Pastures were managed: river plains and woodlands were fired in a regular annual pattern to produce crops

An Aboriginal fish trap on Hinchinbrook Island, off the northeast Queensland coast. Such traps were built by many coastal and river tribes, with the walls shaped so that fish flushed in at high water would be left stranded on the ebb, to make an easy catch.

of green grass for kangaroos. Complex rules governed firing —
each family had its own range, and only it had the right to burn
there: its intimate knowledge of the terrain directed the flames to
their best effect. Knowledge meant control, and Aboriginals had
many words for fire; a separate word for each of its many forms,
uses and effects, and for each stage of the burning cycle.

What had begun on the northern shores a thousand generations earlier as a pattern of random burnings had evolved into a
sophisticated system of land management by fire. Especially in the
southeast and southwest of the continent, the result was a distinctive landscape of rolling, grassy downs with widely spaced trees.

In one of history's ironies, the Aboriginal people had prepared
the ground for the invasion that would end their way of life. For to
European eyes, their land seemed like the parklands of home, with
pastures just waiting for cattle and sheep. The view of the time was
nicely reflected by one of the early arrivals:

> . . . as they have been passing from creation, they have per-
> formed their allotted task; and the fires of the dark child of the
> forest have cleared the soil, the hills and the valleys of the
> superabundant scrub and timber that covered the country and
> presented a bar to its occupation. Now, prepared by the hands
> of the lowest race in the scale of humanity . . . the soil of these
> extensive regions is ready to receive the virgin impressions of
> civilised man . . .

(J.C. Byrne, 1848).

Sails of doom. Paintings of fully-rigged sailing ships appear at the end of the Aboriginal pictorial record, heralding a new invasion. The tradition of making rock art all but ceased.

CHAPTER SIX

THE END OF ISOLATION

A stark illustration of the impact of European settlement:
Mt Lyell mine, Queenstown, Tasmania. Much of the hill
country was cleared to supply the mine, and the
sulphurous fumes from its workings killed what remained.

*T*here is a piece of blighted land in western Tasmania where nothing lives. The earth is as dead as the moon, killed by a mine that took the trees and spewed them back as sulphurous fumes. The scoured hills stand bare and pale as bone. Their eerie pallor brings tourists, and keeps the town alive — because now the mine is dying, too.

Not far away, loggers are bulldozing a road into one of the island's last remnants of rainforest. Wielding fists and boots, they wade into the human barricade of protesters trying to stop them. Later, shots are fired at the protest leader. It is a new twist to that laconic description of the way European Australians were seen to treat their bush: shoot anything that moves, chop down anything that doesn't. But the shots, the boots and fists signal an important change: a century ago, no-one thought to protect the hills against progress.

Yet for every battle won, more are lost. Across the mountains, one of the last wild rivers on earth continues to run free, saved from damming by a massive surge of public outrage. In the same region, a lake of rare and precious quality lies drowned — protest could not save it. In this region of rainforests, mountain rivers and lakes, one of the last wilderness regions on earth, the dilemma that has faced European Australians ever since they arrived continues: how to survive in this deceptive land without turning it into a wasteland.

It took decades for some plantlife to return to the scoured landscape: it is not altogether welcomed by local people for the denuded slopes have become a tourist attraction.

It took a long time for the dilemma to be recognised, and it is still a long way from being resolved. But at least there is a growing realisation among Australians that their environment is not a limitless resource, to be plundered without price. That realisation finds its clearest expression in places such as the wilderness areas of southwestern Tasmania, where the lines of battle seem straightforward: the forces of exploitation seeking to protect jobs and livelihoods ranged against the forces of conservation, seeking to protect the last remnants of natural grandeur. In fact, the dilemma is more easily resolved there than in many other parts of Australia, where it is less obviously dramatic but far more pervasive.

It is difficult to come to terms with an environment whose true nature remained elusive for so long. Now that it *is* being revealed, recounting the part played by European Australians in the making of Australia often becomes a litany of gloom, doom and destruction. In terms of how the continent was and how it is now, it is by and large a depressing story . . . and who wants to be told a depressing story?

In terms of human survival, however — of one species' successful colonisation of a new habitat — the story of European settlement seems a more encouraging tale: sixteen million individuals

Lake Pedder in southwest Tasmania — as it was. Its unique quality now lies drowned under metres of dammed-up water: a long and bitter campaign could not save it from the island state's hunger for hydroelectric power.

living more or less comfortably, more or less protected against predators and the extremes of climate, more or less buffered against the booms and busts of resources, feeding and supporting themselves with enough left over to feed individuals of the species elsewhere.

A success story, surely? After all, agricultural Australia is only about the size of France, and the land is much less fertile.

Well, yes and no. There have been successes, but evaluated even within the narrow context of the human species, they have been at a cost in environmental degradation that poses a real threat to our long-term wellbeing. Resources are our capital, and we have been living on that capital . . . and depleting it, for despite our fond imaginings, our capital is by no means inexhaustible. In

European settlement has disadvantaged many native animals, but some have benefited, at least in the short term. The Tasmanian devil (*Sarcophilus harrisii*) is mainly a carrion feeder and appears to have become more abundant since the introduction of grazing stock increased its food supply. Young devils quit the pouch at about 15 weeks of age, and stay in the nest for another 15 weeks before venturing out to accompany mother on her foraging trips.

Opposite

Australia harbours some of the world's last areas of virgin wilderness: this view was taken above the Franklin River in southwest Tasmania, still running free in a victory for the forces of conservation.

the two-thirds of the continent that is arid or semi-arid, the processes of degradation triggered by factors such as overgrazing and the introduction of exotic plants and animals have, in some areas, passed the point where they can be economically reversed: they are beyond repair, and will continue to decline steadily.

In higher rainfall areas, the picture seems to be brighter: agricultural productivity has shown steady, sometimes even spectacular increases. Through the inventive use of new agricultural techniques such as minimum cultivation, spray seeding and selective herbicides, yields will continue to increase. But there, too, the cost is mounting: with more intensive exploitation, the land will not be able to rest and remain resilient. More (and more expensive) fertilisers, herbicides and pesticides will have to be added to keep the system functioning as its vulnerability to pests and weeds grows.

In Australia's agriculturally most productive region, the Murray Basin, salinity has become a major problem through the combined effects of clearing, which, through the removal of the natural pumps of the native vegetation, causes ground water levels to rise, flushing salts to the surface and destroying the irrigation schemes that distribute and concentrate salt levels.

We are still looking only at the prospects for our own species; and then only at where the next generation's food and water is going to come from. Begin to consider other less tangible factors, such as emotional wellbeing — who wants to live in a land of dust and goats, to queue for permits to climb a mountain or visit a beach? — and beyond ourselves to our fellow creatures. Contemplate the staggering losses of animal and plant communities, and the threatened loss of more, and we are back to a depressing story indeed. So where did we go wrong — and, more importantly, what do we do now?

Some might say the answer to the first is in coming here in the first place, which is not immensely helpful (besides ignoring the fact that most of the early arrivals had no say in it). It is more constructive to address that question by examining how the European invasion and settlement of this continent can be seen as a natural force, the latest of a number of forces that have shaped the nature of Australia. And when we allow for the fact that alone of all those forces, we have the ability to recognise what we are doing and, through that to direct and modify our activities and their results, we may be well on the way to answering the second question.

Origins and Beginnings

European settlement of Australia began with the arrival of Arthur Phillip's First Fleet in 1788. The soldiers and convicts who were the founding fathers and mothers of the penal colony carried with them not only material provisions — livestock and plantstock,

much of which would prove singularly inappropriate for Australian conditions — but a stock of knowledge, ideas and preconceptions that were the product of a culture fashioned in an altogether different world. Not least important among the ideas was the one Christians had formulated from their Bible: that man was separate from and superior to the rest of creation, and therefore had a God-given right to exploit nature for his own benefit.

That older world had been cleared, cultivated and farmed for centuries: a world of robust soils, worked and reworked; of strongly defined seasons, of evenly spread and predictable rainfall and temperate climate, a world also in which human society had evolved into a complexity of haves, of have-littles and of have-nots; where property, especially land, was the index of social worth.

It was the need to find a new place to dump the unwanted criminal and political products of that society that provided the impetus for the first settlement of Australia; with the added consideration that even if the place wasn't worth much, there was still some strategic advantage in grabbing it before someone else did.

So there they were in 1788, on the shores of Botany Bay; the unwilling led by the ill-equipped. The first penal colony had little impact beyond the narrow strip it occupied on the coast. It had enough problems keeping itself alive. Soldiers and convicts made reluctant farmers, and with unsuitable tools and techniques trying to till land where nothing was as it seemed, the colony came terrifyingly close to starvation.

The original human inhabitants might have offered advice on how to live very well on what the land offered, but such an idea could not occur to those who looked on the Aboriginal people as little more than savages to be pitied and who (like people everywhere) carried with them concepts impossible to abandon. Nowhere else in the world, or in history, have immigrants been able to cast aside their heritage — however inappropriate. In any case, many of the natives were soon killed off by the diseases carried by the new arrivals: a smallpox outbreak killed half the local Aboriginals of the Sydney area in 1789.

Even if the new Australians had had a better grasp of agricultural skills, practices that had evolved in the old world of rich soils and strong seasons would have been of limited use in the new one, where seasons were a vague and movable feast and where much of the soil was either marshy or sandy. But *Homo sapiens* is supremely adaptable, and it did not take the first settlers long to see the possibilities as well as the problems of this new land.

If nothing else, Australia seemed to offer limitless stretches of land, a passport to social worth and wealth. It was the first free men — emancipated convicts, retired officers, some immigrants — all hungry for land and impatient for wealth, who began the push into the interior. The final catalyst for that push was another lesson in the realities of this deceptive land: a severe drought from 1813 to 1815 caused a massive shortage of food in the narrow coastal strip of the first settlement and led to a desperate search for a way over the Blue Mountains that hemmed it in like prison walls.

Once over the wall, there seemed to be no end to the grazing country. An early settler was to recollect '. . . plains and "open forest", untrodden by the foot of the white man, and, as far as the eye can reach, covered with grass so luxuriant that it brushes the horseman in his saddle; flocks of kangaroos quietly grazing, as yet untaught to fear the enemy that is invading their territory; the emu, playfully crossing and recrossing his route; the quail rising at every step; lagoons literally swarming with wild-fowl . . .' (W.H. Haygarth. *Recollections of Bush Life in Australia*, 1848). The pioneers found pastures that seemed cultivated and almost European: like farmlands that had been planted with trees and grass, and then abandoned. And indeed, they were farmlands of a kind: the product of 50,000 years of Aboriginal burning. They had created this landscape with their firesticks.

Those original Australians looked upon the advancing Europeans with their flocks of sheep and herds of cattle as the spirits of the dead — slain warriors returning with gifts of abundant meat. Sometimes they thought they were the spirits of rival tribes, and attacked them.

When the Aboriginal people realised that what they were facing was an invasion of their land, the fighting intensified. In places the line of the pastoral advance became a warfront. Shepherds' huts and homesteads were attacked, their occupants killed, the stock maimed or driven off. The settlers retaliated with vengeance. Shooting parties hunted down the guilty and innocent alike. 'No wild beast of the forest was ever hunted down with such unsparing perseverence as they are. Men, women, and children are shot whenever they can be . . . these things are kept very secret . . . some things I have seen that would form as dark a page as ever you read in the book of history . . .' (F.J. Meyrick, *Life in the Bush*, 1840—1847. A *Memoir of Henry Howard Meyrick*, 1939).

High as the deathtoll from the direct conflicts was, it accounted for only a fraction of the eventual decimation of the Aboriginal people. In some districts, people deprived of their traditional food sources were given poisoned flour. Disease, especially smallpox, carried off whole tribes. Venereal infection took its toll in both deaths and a reduced birthrate. Within 60 years, the estimated 250,000 Aboriginals of southeastern Australia had been reduced to perhaps a tenth of that number.

Between the bullets and the viruses, Aboriginal resistance collapsed, and the scattered survivors were driven to the fringes of the new order, to cling to life as best they might. Not the least part of the tragedy was the loss of a rich store of knowledge about the land, its plants and animals, built up over 50,000 years of human occupation. The extinction of the Aboriginal way of life, especially their way with fire, would have an important effect on the land-scape.

Hard Hooves and Soft Feet

Within 50 years, all the viable grazing land in southeastern Australia had been occupied: sometimes legally, often not, for the colonial government found it difficult to keep up with the pace of expansion, let alone to control or regulate it.

By 1860, the southeastern quarter of the continent carried 20 million sheep and four million cattle; 30 years later, cattle numbers had doubled, the sheep had increased fivefold and had spread to every part of the country except the desert interior. In the process, vast tracts of the original Australian bush had been made over into a landscape to suit the alien animals and the people who depended on them for their livelihood.

As part of the same process, the cattle and sheep themselves underwent a transformation. Early trial and error (and later increasingly sophisticated breeding techniques) mixed and matched sheep breeds from such disparate sources as Africa, Germany and Spain to turn the early flocks of disease-ridden, hairy and rather stunted creatures into hardy animals, well attuned to the rigours of the climate and with fine fleeces much valued on world markets. Selective breeding also tuned the cattle to the demands of the environment.

Through human intervention, the exotic animals had an advantage where natural selection might have worked against them. But while they soon were ready to cope with the demands of the new environment, the environment was totally unprepared for them.

Sheep, unlike wallabies and kangaroos, are very sociable animals. Their instinct is to herd together, forming a protective ring against the wolves of their ancestral home. They stay close to each other while they feed, multiplying the impact of their most destructive feature on Australia's fragile soils: their hard hooves.

Up to 1788, no hoof had ever been imprinted on Australian soil: a mere century later, 432 million hooves were trampling it to dust, tamping it down so hard that fragile roots could not penetrate it or water sink in to it.

The effects did not take 100 years to make themselves visible. Early sheep runs were centred on river frontages and natural watercourses: sheep prefer not to graze more than around 5 kilometres from water, and as flock numbers increased, overcrowding quickly led to overgrazing and erosion. The river valleys that beckoned so lushly only a few years earlier turned into dustbowls.

The more sensitive native grasses disappeared and the hardier, tougher species took advantage of the disturbed ground. One valley in North Queensland had to be abandoned within ten years: the succulent grasses had been eaten out, replaced by spear grasses so sharp they punctured the sheep's skins.

In the Riverina district of New South Wales, the shifting balance of vegetation produced another hazard. There, the palatable grasses were supplanted by patches of native bush called Darling pea. It is both poisonous and addictive, and 'pea-struck' animals will eat nothing else. Their gait changes to a high-stepping stagger, and the poison compels them to walk in a straight line — not swerving even for a tree.

For native animals, changing vegetation patterns had far-reaching effects. Animal communities that, on an evolutionary timescale, had only just begun to adjust to the subtle changes that came in the wake of Aboriginal occupation, would be completely disrupted by the upheavals accompanying this new invasion. Smaller animals — bettongs, potoroos, bandicoots — had both their cover and their food supplies eaten away from them. Larger animals, such as wallabies and kangaroos, gained temporary advantage from the changing pastures.

How complex the impact of European settlement could be was measured in the New England region. When it was settled in 1850, kangaroos and wallabies were not numerous. Twenty years later they had increased so much that the pastoralists were petitioning the government for help. Bounties were offered, and eastern grey kangaroos were killed in tens of thousands. As their numbers fell,

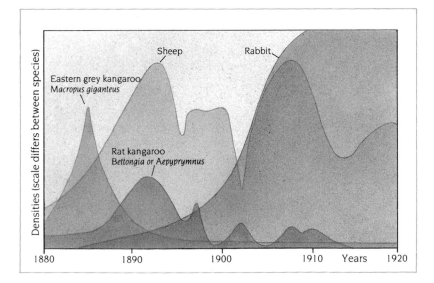

Patterns of extinction: changes in the relative abundance of native and introduced herbivorous mammals on the New England tablelands between 1880 and 1920. The diverse community of native animals was all but replaced by rabbits and sheep.

red-necked and swamp wallabies flourished for about two decades, then declined in their turn. Denser plant growth for a time favoured two kinds of rat kangaroos — then they disappeared as conditions changed again. Finally, bridled nail-tail wallabies, rare until then, had a brief period of abundance . . . then became extinct.

Of the varied company of native herbivores, each species was favoured in turn by changes set in train by European settlement. By 1920 the company had all but vanished, and only sheep and rabbits were left.

With variations, the pattern was repeated wherever European stock opened up the country. Interwoven with those effects was the disruption of the traditional Aboriginal way of managing the land — chiefly Aboriginal use of fire in regular seasonal patterns. Many animals had come to depend on the variety of vegetation created by Aboriginal burning mosaics. In effect, the Aboriginal people were farming the continent: altering the environment so useful plants and animals were encouraged. When the Aboriginals vanished or abandoned their traditional ways, the mosaics disintegrated and the animals that depended on them disappeared. In Western Australia, the brush-tailed bettong (the woylie); in the central regions, the western hare-wallaby (the mala); in the southern half of the continent, the rabbit-eared bandicoot (the bilby): all were at least partly dependent on the plants fostered by burning. They might have coped with that disruption alone, but added to the competition from European stock and other introduced animals, the challenge proved too great.

All are now rare, found in only a few small refuges. Of the eastern barred bandicoot, once abundant in the eastern quarter of the continent, all that survives on the mainland is a single tiny population, clinging to existence in a car dump on the outskirts of a Victorian country town. Many similar animals have become extinct.

Alien Invaders

The same processes that saw the smaller native animals vanish helped the advance of their alien competitors and predators. Chief among the former was the rabbit; among the latter, the fox. Both had been introduced (rabbits with the First Fleet, foxes in the 1840s or 1850s) as part of a continuing drive by the Europeans to improve what they saw as an inferior environment: Australia did not have much in the way of suitable animals to chase and kill, so more familiar creatures were imported from home.

A squatter named Thomas Austin had 24 rabbits sent out in 1859 — he turned out 13 to breed up for sport. Later, more escaped from his property at Barwon Park in Victoria's Western District. Ironically, several earlier attempts to breed rabbits for food for the young colonies had failed. But these were a hardier breed, and they made the beginnings of a ruinous plague.

The country might have been made for rabbits. The climate of much of southern Australia is like that of the Mediterranean, where rabbits originated. The rabbit likes short grass — and the European advance had ensured there was plenty of that. Even in times when there wasn't, the rabbit's tastes are broad enough to enable it to survive on almost anything . . . and the sandy soils of much of Australia make burrowing easy.

Given all those advantages, it was hardly surprising that rabbits bred like rabbits. The figures go like this: a rabbit doe can breed every month for five months, producing an average of four kittens per litter. At any one time, she may have four kittens playing outside the burrow, four just about to open their eyes in the nest, and another four growing in her womb. By the end of the season, females from the first and second litters will themselves be producing. In theory, it is possible for a single pair of rabbits to have produced 62,064 descendants by the end of their third season.

With everything favouring the young's survival individual rabbit colonies grew rapidly, to the point where overcrowding triggered dominant rabbits to expel the immature young and subordinate does. The exiles move only as far as they have to: usually just outside the territorial limits of their colony. Eventually they establish their own colony, which in time will produce its own outward movement: so rapidly did the rabbit population grow that this normally slow process accelerated into an ever faster conquest. The banks of rivers became the main routes for the invasion; by 1875 rabbits had penetrated far inland, confounding those who claimed the semi-arid country would stop the plague.

Along the way, the rabbits helped dispossess the bilbies, the rabbit-eared bandicoots once common across the southern half of the continent. The invaders took over the bilbies' burrows and extended them for their own use: vast stretches of country were pitted and delved with warrens.

Entire sheep runs were abandoned. By 1880, leases to two million acres (810,000 hectares) of mallee country had been forfeited — the sheep sold, the owners gone to Queensland. The rabbits would soon follow them. Seven years later, the valuable saltbush and bluebush country of northeastern South Australia had been turned into a desert. Every plant had been killed over hundreds of square kilometres: in their desperate hunger, rabbits ringbarked the trees and shrubs as high as they could reach, and ate every seedling.

Higher rainfall country could recover from rabbits, but the vulnerable semi-arid regions could not. It had already been pushed to its limits by sheep grazing, and when the rabbits came it had no resistance left. As well as killing every plant, the rabbits' burrows made the soil even more vulnerable to erosion, and the land was left in ecological tatters.

Ever more desperate measures were tried to stop the rabbit, and failed: costly fences did not halt their advance; trapping, shooting and poisoning had little effect on the population growth. The animals that might have been the rabbit's natural predators, and that might have been at least of some help in stopping them — the wedgetailed eagle and the dingo — had themselves been poisoned and shot in huge numbers for their supposed predation on sheep and lambs. And human predators, men paid to trap and exterminate rabbits, had a vested interest in not altogether exterminating the source of their income.

As the rabbits extended their dominion, they aided the advance of another, more secretive invader: the fox. It had been imported to provide sport, but the importers hadn't foreseen that, freed of the natural constraints that held rabbits and foxes in check in their own environment, both would run wild in this new one.

The rabbits provided food for the foxes; where rabbits went, so did the foxes. But foxes eat many other things, too, and in their own way would have as great an effect on the native fauna as the rabbit would have on the flora: following a poison campaign against rabbits in one area of Western Australia, the numbers of native mammals crashed suddenly.

Victims of a misunderstanding: a row of wedge-tailed eagles (*Aquila audax*), Australia's mightiest bird, falsely accused of killing sheep and lambs, and executed. The misunderstanding arose from seeing them feed on animals which had in fact died from other causes. For many years, bounties were paid for the eagles' destruction, a practice that has ceased since the realisation that their main prey is rabbits.

Ringtail possums, bandicoots and woylies vanished almost overnight. The cause was not the poison laid for the rabbits, but foxes deprived of their standard fare. But there was a sting in the tale for the foxes: many West Australian plants of the genus *Gastrolobium* are loaded with highly toxic sodium fluoroacetate (incidentally, the main ingredient in the 1080 poison used against rabbits). Native mammals that feed on the plants are immune but themselves become poisonous to exotic predators, and some of the foxes that made meals of possums perished.

Ground-nesting birds and their eggs are especially at risk: mallee fowl, for example, lose a third of the 25 or so eggs buried in their mounds to foxes. Male brush turkeys engaged in mound maintenance also present foxes with an easily stalked target. Even when rabbits remain the major part of the fox's diet, its less intensive predation on the native birds and mammals can still be devastating, for many of the smaller native animals have low population densities and even small losses can mean extinction in an area.

A study in South Australia found that Murray River tortoises are losing 93 per cent of their eggs to foxes, and the population is dwindling. Foxes are a problem for native carnivores too, for they compete for food as well as for living and breeding space.

Like rabbits, foxes have become part of the Australian ecology — and economy: how big a part is illustrated by the fact that Australia is the world's largest exporter of fox furs. In 1980/82, for example, 531,607 furs worth $15 million were exported.

Domestic cats have also become successful Australians. Many were released in New South Wales to help control rabbits, and soon spread to every part of the continent. In one Victorian district, there are four feral cats per square kilometre: a high density indeed, and one that means intense pressure on wildlife. Like foxes, cats prefer rabbits and rabbit-kittens and help keep their numbers down, but they also take native animals. There have been suggestions that cats may be forming subspecies to tackle different-sized prey — as well as familiar 'cat-sized' cats, some specimens have been trapped that weigh 10 kilograms.

After the Goldrush

The forces of change accelerated and intensified when the discovery of gold triggered a rush of people into the country in the 1850s. Australia's population doubled, then doubled again. Because Australia is a dry and flat continent, its relatively few rivers and even fewer harbours and estuaries became natural focal points for settlement. The goldrushes, with their influxes of people and spin-offs of wealth, generated rapid growth that saw the coastal settlements swallow up the natural wetlands and harbours.

A sugar glider in its nest in a tree hollow. Many species of Australia's mammals, birds and reptiles rely on tree hollows for nests and shelter — clearing the woodlands reduced populations and saw some species vanish altogether.

Much of the native life was pushed out: the great concentrations of magpie geese that camped in the wetlands around infant Melbourne disappeared as the city grew. Eventually the city's effluent created new, artificial wetlands in the form of sewage farms — rich feeding and breeding grounds for a wide range of waterfowl, from black swans and pelicans to ibis and various species of ducks — but for the magpie geese the substitute came too late, for they had suffered the additional pressure of being hunted for their succulent flesh to feed growing numbers of people, and are now found only in far northern Australia.

There were pressures in other directions, too. As the gold petered out, tens of thousands of diggers looked for an alternative livelihood. Many drifted to the towns and cities. Many others turned to farming. The insatiable hunger of the goldmines for timber — for struts and supports, and as fuel for the steam engines that powered the workings — had already swallowed up vast tracts of woodland and forest in and around the goldmining areas. Now there was demand for more land for farming and grazing, putting greater pressure on woodlands and forests.

The effect on the native animals, especially those dependent on tree hollows for shelter and breeding space, was predictable: great numbers were lost, and several species became extinct. Australia-wide, at least 15 of the continent's 245 native terrestrial mammals have become extinct since 1788. With as many as half of the continent's woodland mammals, as well as many birds and perhaps a quarter of reptiles dependent on tree hollows in one way or another, the impact of the loss of such vast areas of habitat is obvious enough.

A male and female broadfaced potoroo (*Potorous platyops*), as depicted by John Gould. It is all we will ever see of them — like 14 other species of native animals, they are extinct (22 more are endangered), casualties of the ecological disturbance caused by European settlement.

Gippsland — an oil painting by Isaac Whitehead (1819—
1881). The very scale of the bullock team and its driver
suggests the early settlers' view of these mighty forests as
an inexhaustible source of rich timber.

Timber harvesting and export was a major industry in early Australia. Of the most valuable timber, cedar, barely a tree was left standing 50 years after the first axeblow fell. Of the great belt of forest and woodland that all but encircled the continent on the eve of European settlement, there is only a third left and inroads into the remainder continue apace.

Neither did it take long for some of the other effects to become obvious. Robbed of its anchors, much of the soil washed away. Clearing the forests increased rain runoff and worsened the floods that had always been part of the system. With no plants and roots to break their force and with diminishing layers of soil to soak them up, the waters cut deep, jagged gullies down and across the slopes of the denuded hills and valleys.

Clearing so much of the forests put pressure on what remained. On the tablelands of New England, the grasslands that replaced the woodlands made ideal breeding places for a multitude of insects which, at certain stages of their lives, moved into the remnants of woodland to feed. The birds, traditional defenders of the trees, had lost many of their breeding places, and their depleted ranks were no match for the hordes of insect attackers.

That, plus the interplay of factors such as drought and fungal infections of root systems, reduced the trees' resilience to a point where no recovery was possible. The inevitable result was dieback on a massive scale: bleached skeletons of trees standing in silent ranks that stretch from horizon to horizon.

To serve the need for timber depleted native forests could no longer meet, vast tracts have been replanted with the softwood *Pinus radiata*. It grows faster than native trees, is more manageable, and makes more useful timber than the native softwoods.

Pine plantations also create a biological desert. Little grows in them, and most native animals that grew up with eucalypts cannot live in the immigrant forests. There are some exceptions — some cockatoos have developed a liking for their seeds. But pine trees do not offer the hollows they need for breeding. Many native mammals feed on eucalypt leaves, or on the insects that feed on the leaves. Resinous pine needles are no substitute.

There are signs, however, that at least one native mammal may be adapting to another part of pine trees — their tender, green young shoots. Surprisingly, that mammal is the koala, which was always thought to rely exclusively on eucalypt leaves and then only those of a select few species. It is the young males among the koala populations, driven out to establish their own territories, that have been found to have an exploratory nibble at the pines. But even if it does turn out that koalas can survive on pine, their preference for the growing parts of the trees will not make them welcome visitors, let alone residents in the new forests.

Koalas, now promoted as the characteristic animals of Australia, have also long characterised the confusion and ambivalence of European Australians' attitudes to their environment. When Europeans arrived, koalas were not particularly abundant: predation by the Aboriginal people and dingoes kept their numbers down. With both Aboriginals and dingoes driven off, however, koala populations surged to such an extent that they came to be a valuable resource for pelts. In Queensland, times were hard in the 1920s: the government of the day needed some cheap votes, and an open season was declared so rural workers could earn extra money with koala pelts. In three months, 600,000 pelts were taken to market. The government fell at the next election. The koala numbers never recovered. But the slaughter caused a nationwide outcry, rallied the fledgling conservation movement, and so served to help create a counterbalance to the prevailing forces of shortsighted economic exploitation.

The invasion of foreign plants proved a boon for some native birds: the gang gang cockatoo (*Callocephalon fimbriatum*) relishes the berries of the introduced hawthorn bush such as *Crataegus*. Only the adult male has the red crest and head.

Koalas are protected today, but uncertainty surrounds their future. Reproductive disease is affecting some populations, possibly exacerbated by changes in their habitats. The disease renders a percentage of female koalas infertile, leading some researchers to predict eventual extinction. Others say the koala/bacteria relationship is the normal host/parasite one, but the balance could be tipped against koalas if other factors — road-deaths and a shortage of suitable food trees, for example — begin to produce abnormal levels of mortality.

Probably the greatest risk for the koalas, as for the other native animals, continues to be the loss of their natural habitats. Partly in recognition of this danger, and partly to foster native timbers, commercial plantations of eucalypts are being established on an increasing scale. They provide more niches for native animals than the introduced pine, but because they tend to be uniform stands

— all the same kinds of trees, all the same age — and because they lack a rich understorey, they do not have the diversity and complexity of the original forests.

In the meantime, natural woodlands continue to die. In Victoria, the loss has averaged 1 per cent per year over the past 25 years: in one area, river red gums die at the rate of 3320 trees each year. In Tasmania, 55 per cent of trees on private rural land were lost over 32 years. Halting the decline needs the support of rural landowners, who control almost two-thirds of Australia: 500 million hectares of agricultural land, compared with only 27 million acres (almost 11 million hectares) protected in national parks and reserves. Farmers, embattled by declining prices and rising interest rates, are nevertheless beginning to see the value of preserving trees — and of planting more. Native trees, they know, repair some of the problems clearing has brought in its wake. Strips and patches of woodland help control erosion, provide valuable shelter for stock and crops, and a home for birds and other native wildlife that help keep insect pests under control. But tradition — even one as young as Australia's — cannot be changed overnight: while tree clearing may be allowed as a tax deduction in some states, tree planting may not.

Remaking the Land

For the early Europeans, clearing the land was the first stage in remaking an alien landscape. There were fixed concepts, born of eighteenth century notions, concerning the nature of beauty, what the landscape should look like, and what was beautiful. Australia failed the test, and was looked upon as a second-class environment at whose demolition the world would shed no tears. John White, a surgeon with the First Fleet, called it 'a place so forbidding and hateful as only to merit execration and curses'. Wrote Anthony Trollope, 'It is taken for granted that Australia is ugly'.

Acclimatisation societies were formed to import familiar plants and animals. Of the long list of imports, some failed, but many succeeded beyond dreams and became nightmares, like the rabbits. It was not only animals; the list of plants introduced — mostly deliberately, sometimes accidentally — grew year by year: forget-me-nots for the homesick. Like the animals, the native plants were the products of an isolated evolution; in their natural state, they could resist invaders, but even a slight disturbance created a breach in their defences that quickly saw them overwhelmed.

One of the most dramatic cases was that of the prickly pear. Originally imported as hedge plants and as food for a beetle used in the process of making dye for soldiers' uniforms, it eventually came to infest 120,000 square miles (over 31 million hectares) of brigalow and belah country in southern Queensland and northern

One of the more unlovely of the wave of animal immigrants that followed the end of Australia's isolation: the cane toad (*Bufo marinus*). They were imported from Hawaii to eat the native beetles that were attacking the crops of sugar cane in Queensland. The toads made no difference to the beetles, but themselves became a major pest and threat to wildlife. At last report, they had penetrated as far north as the Northern Territory. But back where *Bufo* was first released, large numbers are being wiped out by a bacterial disease.

New South Wales. So bad was the infestation that some home-steads were walled in by impenetrable barriers of prickly pear 6 feet (almost 2 metres) high. Eventually, the barriers were brought down by a moth from Argentina — *Cactoblastis cactorum* — whose larvae bore through the middle of the plant, and kill it.

The disturbances that came in the wake of European settlement had other dramatic consequences. For more than 40,000 years — possibly as many as 120,000 years — the Aboriginal people, with their patterns of regular burning, kept the woodland and forest floors free of scrub and dry litter. Once they were driven out, the patterns changed. Dense scrub grew where the ground had been clear, and the falling bark and leaf litter built up into thick layers of fuel. The European strategy in the southeast was to prevent fire, but inevitably lightning, accident or criminal design would spark off the first flames somewhere. On a bad day, fuel buildup rendered tinder dry by a long hot summer would combine with hot north winds to set the country ablaze. Days that would burn themselves into the annals of national disaster were Black Thursday in 1851, Black Friday in 1939, and Ash Wednesday in 1983.

Golden Harvests

Successive waves of immigration, prompted first by the discovery of gold and later by the demands of the 'populate or perish' theories, meant ever-closer settlement and ever-greater pressure on the land. Farmers followed the pioneering sheepmen further inland: many of the grazing lands of the early decades were turned over to the clearing axes and fires, and the ploughs.

Wheat sought to rival wool as a source of wealth: the pursuit of that end produced some remarkable innovations . . . but also some tragic mistakes. In tracts of semi-arid mallee woodland, the arrival of the stump-jump plough solved the problem of tilling soils that thinly covered the subterranean thickets of stubborn mallee roots — the lignotubers that serve these eucalypts as food stores. Later, the world's first combine harvesters rolled through Australian wheatfields. They gathered grain cultivated from new strains bred to flourish in the dry warm climate.

South Australia set its sights on becoming the granary of the southern hemisphere. It was not as rich in wool as other states, and had no gold, but its sandy plains were reckoned ideal for growing cereals. As well, the long fingers of the Spencer and St Vincent's Gulfs pointing up from the Australian Bight put seaports within easy reach of farming country. But if wheat doesn't need much rain, it does need some, and at more or less predictable times. The reality of the unpredictable climate still had to be learned.

After a drought in the mid-1860s, the Surveyor-General, G.W. Goyder was commissioned to find the climatic limits to

Prickly pear — a plant introduced to make ornamental hedges, and as food for beetles used in a dye-making process — ran wild across vast tracts of outback Queensland and New South Wales, a nightmare plague rivalled only by the rabbits. In some places it grew 2 metres tall, in dense 'crops' of 500 tonnes to the acre.

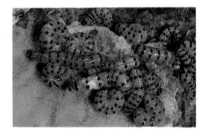

One of the first instances of successful biological control: larvae of the moth *Cactoblastis cactorum*, introduced from Argentina in 1925. About 3000 million eggs were distributed to landholders. The hatched larvae bore through the plant tissue, and kill it. Within a few years, the prickly pear was beaten.

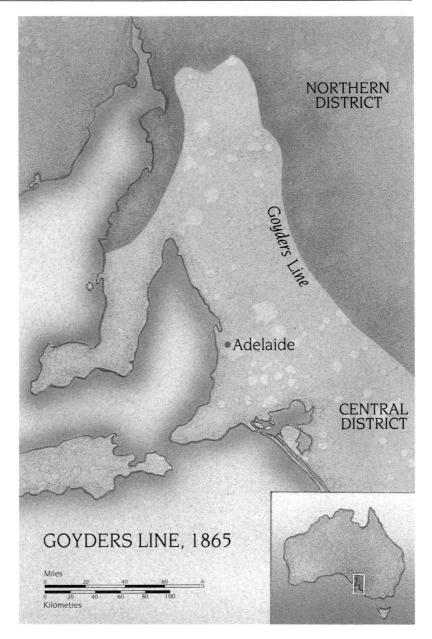

NORTHERN
DISTRICT

Goyders Line

•Adelaide

CENTRAL
DISTRICT

GOYDERS LINE, 1865

Miles
0   20   40   60   8(
0   20   40   60   80   100
Kilometres

Goyder's Line — famous more for its breaching than its observance. G. W. Goyder, a South Australian Surveyor-General drew his line of reliable rainfall after a great drought in the 1860s. It was promptly ignored by the land-hungry with disastrous results.

wheatland expansion. He drew a line based on a careful study of rainfall and vegetation, and stressed that even within the line crops might sometimes be at risk. But a run of good seasons persuaded the land hungry that Goyder was wrong, and they poured north across his line. Railways were pushed into the interior, towns were planned and built to serve what were confidently expected to be flourishing wheat-growing communities. The optimism was boundless: no matter that there was no water on many of the farms into which the semi-desert had been carved: water was fetched in bullock carts from springs in the hills many kilometres away.

The belief of the time was that rain would 'follow the plough': breaking up the soil would improve the absorption and evaporation of water, increase the moisture in the atmosphere, and so bring more rain. The early years seemed to vindicate the theory: there were good rains and bumper crops. But then the inevitable happened. The rains failed one season, then the next, and the next. The ploughed soil turned to dust and blew away, the farms were abandoned. All that remained of the hopes and dreams were the ruins of the stone houses, and the ruins of the land.

But whether wheat fails or thrives, there is a toll on the land. It is evident in Victoria's mallee country, where clearing for wheat produced massive erosion and sand drift: hot northerly winds carried dust storms as far as the coast and 'browned out' Melbourne. It is evident, too, in the wheatbelt of Western Australia, where clearing programmes often left not a tree standing. The removal of these natural pumps allowed the subterranean water level to rise and to flush salts to the surface. The creeping blight of salinisation turned large areas into wasteland — good for neither wheat nor bush.

For the native animals the arrival of wheat cultivation meant drastic changes . . . but not always predictable changes. Cockatoos, characteristically Australian and largest of the continent's parrots, found the coming of wheat a mixed blessing. It is a measure of the complexity of ecological interactions that such closely related birds should yet react so differently: some species thrived, some held their own, and some went into a sharp decline.

Corellas and galahs, birds of the semi-arid grass plains, extended their ranges into the new wheat areas. For them, wheat was just a better class of grass, and they multiplied rapidly — in some farmers' eyes, to pest proportions. But seeing is not always believing. Flocks of red-tailed black cockatoos (*Calyptorhynchus banksii*) also descended on the wheatfields: it turned out that they were not after the grain, but the seeds of a pernicious weed, called Double G, that had been introduced with it. The red-tails' normal food is the hard-cased seeds of native trees and shrubs, and their sharp, powerful bills proved a precise match for the Double G. A flock of red-tails can clean up many thousands of seeds at a picking, helping the wheat farmers combat a weed while maintaining a hold on life themselves.

Yet for the red-tails' closest relative, the white-tailed black cockatoos (*C. baudinii*), the coming of wheat spelt doom. They depend much more on woodland than the other cockatoos, because a large part of their diet is the larvae of wood-boring insects. Using

The changes wrought in the Australian environment by European settlement could affect even closely related species of native animals in dramatically different ways: some cockatoos flourished, others went into decline. Sulphur-crested cockatoos (*Cacatua galerita*) continue to fare well, taking advantage of introduced crops such as oats and maize. But on the debit side, the continued clearing of woodland is reducing the number of nesting hollows.

For many thousands, possibly millions, of years, locusts have been swarming in a belt sweeping down inland eastern Australia. Planting wheat and other grain crops in that belt turned the swarms into plagues. One swarm of *Chortoicetes terminifera* can chomp its way through a hundred tonnes of cereal in a day. Plagues break out every 15 to 20 years, but aerial spraying with insecticide has become so efficient that in the last major outbreak in 1984, 87 per cent of the locusts were destroyed and most of the crops saved.

their sharp bills they slice into the bark to extract the grubs. No woodland — no grubs — no white-tails.

For a very different reason, the diminishing woodland is also forcing into retreat what is perhaps the loveliest cockatoo of all, the rose-tinged pink cockatoo, *Cacatua leadbeateri* (universally known as the Major Mitchell). It is not the introduced crops and weeds that are the problem; unlike the white-tail, its rose-tinged relative has adapted well to those. What they do need is a lot of breeding space. In the original woodland, pink cockatoos established large territories around their nesting hollows to ensure they had enough food for their growing chicks. The wheat crops and weeds brought abundant food, but the Major Mitchells still would not nest closer than 2 kilometres to each other, and there simply isn't enough woodland to go around. Like the white-tails, their lives are governed by tradition, and they cannot change their ways.

In the long run, the vanishing woodland of the wheat country threatens the survival of all cockatoos in these regions (including the species currently thriving on the introduced food), for cockatoos need tree hollows in which to nest. As the tattered remnants of woodland age, die and collapse, the supply of nesting hollows will diminish — and the cockatoos with them.

The expansion of the wheatlands in southwestern Western Australia also meant upheaval for another bird. Emus in that region move between the arid lands, where cyclonic rainstorms produce seeds and fruits in late summer, and areas nearer the coast, where winter rainfall brings green feed. The wheatlands lay across the emus' seasonal paths, and the birds arrived for their winter food just when the crops were ripening. In some years, unstoppable armies of emus marched through the fields. The problem might have been solved by leaving corridors of natural vegetation, but such ecological understanding was still some decades off. Instead, the farmers of one district called in their own army: a machine-gun detachment was dispatched to the emu front in 1932, but withdrew without inflicting many casualties.

Learning the Reality

The early settlers could not foresee the effects of the changes they set in train. Even had they been able to, the dictates of economic survival left little alternative. In any event, the land was there to be conquered, made to serve human needs.

It served them well. In the four decades after gold was discovered, progress was swift and produced a prosperity that put Australia among the richest nations in the world. The population rose sevenfold to three million, the vast majority still concentrated in the coastal cities and towns. There, they enjoyed a standard of living a great deal better than that offered by the Old World at the time, and a far cry from the privations of the first generations.

The wealth was built on an abundance of resources, drawn from the new land with energy and ingenuity. Although there were failures and setbacks along the way — sometimes on a tragic scale, as with the South Australian wheat crash — it was overall a swift and successful expansion. If the physical conquest was soon accomplished, the emotional conquest would be a long time coming. The reality of the land had to be learned. Fire and drought were still seen as calamities, freaks, instead of as integral to the nature of the continent. There had been several droughts since European settlement, but they had been confined to individual regions and had not usually lasted longer than two or three years.

The drought that began in 1895 came to grip almost all the settled continent, and was to last eight years. There have been many droughts since, but the one that spanned the centuries is still remembered as the 'king drought'. It marked a turning point in Australians' emotional discovery of their land.

Drought comes stealthily. One dry year does not make a drought; only hindsight can mark its beginning and end. The pastoral country had been overstocked in the good years, which the optimism of the time had determined were the norm. Pastoral expansion had been aided by the discovery of artesian water, the sinking of wells and bores and the building of dams. As the drought tightened its grip, there was still water. But the overstocked pastures were soon eaten down to the bare dust and the sheep and cattle, generators of much of the country's wealth, began to die in their millions — not of thirst, many of them, but of starvation. The number of sheep fell by almost half, from an estimated 106 million in 1891 to 54 million in 1902. The number of cattle dropped from 12 million to 7 million.

The croplands dried to dust. The Victorian wheatbelt, new claimant to the status of the southern hemisphere's granary, produced virtually no wheat for export for three years in a row. What it did produce was millions of cubic tonnes of ploughed soil, which blew away in huge, swirlng dust storms. Tens of thousands of farmers were ruined. As they slid into debt and bankruptcy, so did the small towns dependent on them.

The Great Drought began a lean time from which rural Australia would not fully recover for another half-century. It proved a sobering lesson in the real nature of the continent, and it taught again the inappropriateness of the European experience.

When land was divided for farming, the traditional size was a square mile (259 hectares) — generous by European standards and perhaps adequate in good years, but in the long run far too small to be economically viable. In the desperate struggle to remain sol-

Drought is part of the nature of Australia, not the freak calamity that the early settlers thought it to be. Animal numbers are geared to the unpredictable cycles of feast and famine. Kangaroos breed and flourish while they find sufficient nourishment — when food and water become scarce, hormonal changes render the males sterile and the females infertile. If conditions remain severe, many perish, but some always survive somewhere to form the nucleus of the next population growth.

vent, the farmers were forced to work and overwork every corner of their land. 'Conservation' meant no more than trying to stop soil blowing away.

An old enemy reappeared in rural Australia's battle for survival. The long drought temporarily halted the march of the rabbits, but with its end they were soon on the move again. In a desperate effort to stop them invading the west, a fence was built that stretched 1832 kilometres from the port of Esperance to the tropical coast beyond Port Hedland. While the fencers were still wiring the netting to the posts, the rabbits had already reached the coast.

The campaign against the rabbit was not a singleminded one, for the animal had become an important part of the economy for some sections of the population. It was the poor people's food, and king rabbiters could earn more than gun shearers. In 1906, 22 million frozen rabbits were exported, earning Australia more than the frozen beef shipped out that year.

Even among those who realised that unless the rabbit was destroyed the country faced ruin, conflicts of opinion often led to inaction and missed opportunities. As early as 1887, the New South Wales government offered science a £25,000 prize for a sure way of beating rabbits. Louis Pasteur, working in France, found that the chicken cholera virus wiped out rabbit colonies, but the authorities would not allow the virus to be released in Australia for fear of infecting other fauna. About a later virus idea, the *Melbourne Age* was to write, 'It had to be admitted that there was something frightfully repulsive about a wholesale propagation of disease even though it were only a rabbit plague. To cover the sweet earth with a filthy virus which living animals are to communicate to one another is a horrible idea'.

It would not be till 1950 that the revulsion was finally overcome: the myxomatosis virus was released, and within three years most of Australia was free of rabbits — perhaps 90 per cent of the population had been wiped out. The war had been virtually won.

After the initial wholesale massacres of the 1950s, rabbits might have been exterminated altogether if there had been a swift and coordinated mopping-up campaign. But the opportunity was lost: there was no framework for such a programme, no authority that could direct it. By 1955, rabbits were beginning to breed back . . . and some were resistant to myxomatosis. Viruses have a vested interest in maintaining a host population; natural selection favours weaker strains that allow hosts to live. New, more virulent strains are now being thrown into the fray, and the challenge for science is to produce more effective strains faster than rabbits can acquire resistance.

The long and bitter struggle against the rabbits marked another stage in the discovery by Australians of the true nature of their continent, which had begun so traumatically with the great drought.

Taming a River

The drought slowed the pace of progress — but did not halt it altogether. In fact, it stimulated the development of grand schemes to harness Australia's largest river.

The Murray-Darling river system drains a seventh of Australia's land surface. It has its origins in the Great Dividing Range, the barrier that traps most of the rain before it can cross to the vast hinterland, and returns it in a multitude of short, fast-flowing rivers that water the fertile eastern strip. A few of the streams drain to the west, and eventually combine to form the Murray-Darling, the fourth longest river system in the world. But length does not necessarily mean volume; the amount of water it carries is relatively small on the world scale, and enormously variable. The total runoff of all the rivers and streams in Australia is less than that of the Amazon, or the Nile. Because the continent is so flat, most rivers roll slowly and their courses meander so much that any given river distance is three times the direct distance. Even in moderate floods rivers burst their banks, and the water flows out into a myriad billabongs and back reaches.

Life along the Murray-Darling has adapted to survive droughts, and when floods come, to take quick advantage of the conditions that favour new life. That adaptability finds its most dramatic expression in the majestic forests of river red gums (*Eucalyptus camaldulensis*) that grow in the Murray's back reaches along the Victorian border. For much of the time they stand in dry ground, but they rely on the river to supply them with more or less regular inundations to replenish nutrient and moisture levels. Equally importantly, the gums need floods to germinate and transport their seeds. But they also need floods to drain away again eventually, or else they drown. In the natural cycle, the river's overflow lakes fill during floods and drain again in the dry.

Since European settlement, however, the Murray-Darling system has become the major source of water for the populations of rain-starved areas through which it makes its slow, meandering way. The Murray in particular has been dammed, locked, weired and reservoired to provide water for settlements along its banks and to serve a chain of irrigation schemes that now help to produce half the country's food and fibre.

Disrupting the rivers' natural flow has had a series of interlocking effects, both on the river itself and on the country on each side. In places natural overflow lakes have been dammed and regulated to make permanent reservoirs, and the red gum forests have drowned, their skeletons mirrored in the still water.

Reducing the river to what is in effect a series of static pools has made it increasingly difficult for aquatic life to survive. Native fishes — golden perch, silver perch, Murray cod — have had migratory

The 'king' drought of the turn of the century stimulated schemes to harness Australia's largest river system, the Murray-Darling. Natural overflow lakes were dammed permanently, and great forests of river red gum drowned. Lake Menindee, near Broken Hill, New South Wales.

routes to traditional breeding waters barred by locks and dam walls. Many breeding places had already vanished in earlier operations that cleared the river of snags for paddle steamers, snags that had served the fishes and other water life as nesting sites.

The once-abundant freshwater crayfish, the Murray lobster, has disappeared from all but a few stretches of the river, as has the mighty Murray cod. One reason for the diminishing river life has to do with the cooling effect of storing the river's water. Water drawn off from storage is taken from lower levels, which tend to be cooler than surface water and to contain less oxygen. Water discharged from the gigantic Hume Reservoir lowers water temperatures downstream by as much as 6 degrees in summer: far too cold for native fish to spawn.

Adding to the pressure is competition from introduced fishes, notably the European carp, which has become the aquatic equivalent of the rabbit in many of Australia's inland waters.

Originally from Asia, the carp was taken in the Middle Ages to Europe, where it was cultivated widely for food. There are records of it being introduced into Australia as early as 1872, but it has reached plague numbers only in the past few decades. It is a hardy fish, thriving in tough conditions and breeding prolifically: mature females about 65 centimetres long lay an average of half a million eggs at a time, and can spawn several times a year. What makes the carp a particular pest is its method of feeding: it stirs up mud from the bottom, sucks in the debris, consumes what is edible and expels the rest. The clouds of sediment prevent sunlight reaching the bottom, stunting the growth of aquatic plants and ruining the river for native fishes that require clear water. As with rabbits, a viral weapon offers the only hope of ending the carp menace, and researchers are experimenting with a prototype.

The harnessing of the great river has brought harmful changes, whose effects extend far beyond the system itself. The water drawn from its storages to irrigate the river plains produces not only food, but a creeping blight that is increasingly destroying the land's productivity: salinisation. The blight is the same as that laying waste to many dry land farming areas, but its mechanism is different. The tonnes of water pumped on to the land raise the level of the underground watertable and flush the natural salts nearer the surface, there to accumulate as the water evaporates. So far, 120,000 hectares of irrigated land have simply been salted away.

And the problem flows back into the river itself; as the surplus water drains back, it carries salt with it. It has been estimated that one and a quarter million tonnes of salt flow down the river each year — double the natural amount.

The Drive Inland

The increased population and closer settlement that followed the goldrushes, and which prompted the harnessing of the Murray-Darling and the development of irrigation schemes, also had the effect of pushing pastoralists further inland to open up the dry interior for their flocks and herds. The discovery of the Great Artesian Basin and the development of mechanical means to tap these subterranean waters with bores and wells allowed stock numbers to rise swiftly. As had happened in the more temperate regions, the smaller macropods such as bettongs and medium-sized marsupials such as bandicoots saw their habitats reduced or vanished altogether with the advance of the European grazers.

But that same advance brought benefits for the large kangaroos — the eastern and western greys, the red kangaroos further out into the drier country, and the euros in the semi-arid hill country

The large number of artificial watering points enabled kangaroos to move out from the watercourses that had been their tra-

A dramatic contrast: the paddock on the right, near Wentworth in southwest New South Wales, has been grazed only lightly. The country is resilient if it is given a fair chance.

ditional centres, and the grazing patterns of sheep and cattle also changed the pastures to the advantage of kangaroos. When the European stock first moved into the interior, the vast plains were covered in long, dry grass and, in some regions, with saltbush. The dry grass sheltered small marsupials but did not suit the large kangaroos, which prefer short, green pick. The sheep and cattle grazed the tall grasses down, robbing small animals of their shelter but causing fresh, perennial grasses, so attractive to kangaroos that they have been called marsupial lawns, to sprout.

Similarly, the saltbush — which kangaroos avoid, but which European stock like — was eaten out, and replaced by grasses that suited the kangaroos. More water, more food: for red kangaroos, whose reproductive system is geared to the prevailing conditions, they added up to a continuing stimulus to breed.

With artificially induced good seasons generated by the advent of pastoralism, many of the inland's sheep stations ended up carrying more kangaroos than sheep. Their combined grazing puts enormous pressure on the land, especially when the climatic cycle turns inevitably to drought.

Many of the rangelands of the interior have been degraded beyond repair. Erosion has silted up natural waterholes, and overgrazing in the mulga woodlands has created open ground where grass-eating termites thrive for a time, extending their colonies enormously. Eventually they die out, probably for want of food, and leave huge areas of hard, impermeable termite-bed on which grass will not grow for many decades.

Overgrazing quickly reduces the land's carrying capacity, both of native animals and of introduced stock. After the first rapid in-

The effects of overgrazing: devastated land in the Flinders Ranges, South Australia. Stripping away the fragile groundcover left the thin layer of more fertile topsoil vulnerable to erosion, and reduced the country's ability to absorb the infrequent rains, leaving the trees to die.

crease, stock numbers fluctuated wildly — crashing in bad seasons, rising again in good, but never regaining the levels produced by the initial, soon exhausted, wealth of the virgin plains.

Especially in lean times, kangaroos came to be seen as competitors for food with sheep and cattle. The impression was heightened by the sight of large mobs of red kangaroos clustered on the few remaining patches of green feed: the same feed on which introduced stock depends. In fact, competition may not be as severe as at first thought. The kangaroos' diet has been found to have a higher percentage of grasses than that of sheep and cattle, and a lower proportion of browse plants. Neither do they eat as wide a range of plants as introduced stock.

Nevertheless, there is enough overlap for kangaroos — both the western and eastern greys, as well as the red kangaroos and euros — to be seen as pests and to permit as many as three million a year to be shot with official sanction, and perhaps as many again illegally. The official culling policy underpins a commercial industry that exports kangaroo products worth around $13 million a year. Though the bulk of the trade is made up of the three large kangaroos, there are also kill quotas for rufous wallabies, Bennett's wallabies and whiptail wallabies in various regions.

The official line is that culling is necessary to keep kangaroo populations from reaching pest proportions, and to safeguard their long-term welfare by not allowing numbers to outrun food supplies. Opponents of kangaroo killing argue that the official quotas are based on inaccurate and incomplete population counts, and that in any case it is far from proven that kangaroos are the pests graziers say they are. They point to the problems of adequately policing a killing zone that covers a third of Australia, and the dangers posed to even seemingly abundant species by illegal killing that may outnumber the official quotas (which themselves are based on questionable data).

The kangaroo-kill controversy highlights some elements of the dilemma in which Australians find themselves in trying to come to terms with an environment their actions have helped create. That there are so many kangaroos is, in all probability, due to the way the pastoral advance rearranged the ecology of the rangelands. That dealing with them has become more than simply an economic question, and now includes aesthetic and ethical considerations, is some measure of the way Australians' relationship with their land has matured.

For the pioneering pastoralists, any problems posed by (or, at least, perceived to be posed by) increased numbers of kangaroos were compounded by those caused by introduced animals that had run wild in the wake of European settlement. Of these, rabbits were by far the most destructive. Even when myxomatosis arrived,

Donkeys (*Equus asinus*) were imported from Europe in 1866 as pack animals and transport teams. Turned loose after motor transport ended their usefulness, they thrived in the arid regions of Western Australia and South Australia, where conditions are very similar to those of their ancestry in the semi-deserts of the Middle East. Donkeys can survive on much coarser vegetation than horses, and compete with cattle and sheep for food and water.

it was not as effective in the drier inland because it is best spread by mosquitoes in moister country. The rangelands continue to be plagued by uncountable hordes of rabbits, especially when there is a run of good seasons. They graze the country bare, ringbark and kill trees, dump subsoil from their warrens on the surface and accelerate erosion.

Other animals are contributing their share to the damage. In some areas, goats rival rabbits as a destructive force. Goats eat any kind of plant matter, and strip the country bare: current estimates of numbers range as high as two million.

Donkeys, turned loose when motor transport ended their usefulness, bred up into enormous herds that often outnumbered cattle: some stations in the Kimberley region of Western Australia carried 5000 cattle — and 10,000 donkeys. Over the past decade 164,000 donkeys have been shot in the area and shooting campaigns are managing to keep numbers down elsewhere. The latest estimates put the number of feral donkeys in Australia at around ninety-five thousand.

Wild horses — brumbies — also compete with stock for food and water. As settlers and stock moved away from the coastal areas, a continuous trickle of horses was set free or escaped into the bush. They bred into pest numbers, and some of the methods to get rid of them were hideous, even by the tough standards of the times. Thousands of brumbies were rounded up and run into yards. To avoid a great pile of dead horseflesh, several dispersal techniques were refined. One was for the horses to be forced through a crush, one at a time, and their throats slashed. The dying horse would gallop almost a kilometre before it fell. Another was to fix a rusty blade to a pole and then to jab each horse in the belly. Death by tetanus took a week — and a considerable distance. Another method was a shot behind the left shoulder into the heart: this was called the three-mile range, since a dying horse would usually manage that distance.

In dry times, waterholes and dams were fenced off and wild horses left to die of thirst. A refinement was to put out poisoned water — more painful, perhaps, but at least it worked more quickly. Such methods are no longer used; shooting now gets rid of unwanted horses. As with all animals, numbers fluctuate with the cycles of drought and short times of plenty — there are currently reckoned to be around 175,000 brumbies, with possibly as many as 80,000 in the Northern Territory south of Tennant Creek.

Of all the animals running wild in the interior, the camel has made itself most at home in the driest parts. Camels can travel much further from water than horses: indeed, they were initially imported because of their ability to survive in the desert. Among the first were 33 from India, for the Burke and Wills expedition of

1860. Later, camels were used to haul freight in the inland and for construction work on the transcontinental railway in 1914. As with donkeys and horses, mechanised transport also made camels obsolete and they were allowed to run free and multiply. There are now thought to be around 30,000, most of them in the sand ridge dunes of central and central-western Australia.

The great weight of new animals brought into the inland by the European expansion — both by accident and by design — meant a feast of both carrion and live prey for the resident carnivore, Australia's native dog, the dingo. It had been all but exterminated in the more closely settled areas, but as flocks and herds moved inland, dingo numbers there probably increased in response to this sudden plenitude of easy meat. Sheep farmers in particular came to regard dingoes as major pests. Losses at lambing time could be heavy, and grown sheep also made easy prey with their habit of bunching together in the face of danger.

In fact, the dingoes' predations probably had far less impact on the outback stations' productivity than the more insidious effects of overgrazing and rabbits, especially when exacerbated by the vagaries of the climate. But dingoes were a tangible enemy against which a blow could be struck. Even so, they proved an elusive target: not poison, bullets or the trapping skills of cunning doggers could keep their numbers down. Eventually, a fence was built to keep the dingoes out of the sheeplands: at 9660 kilometres, the longest fence in the world. With regular patrols and repairs, it has proved a reasonably effective barrier. Dogs still get through, but in low enough numbers to be controllable. With the reduced threat, sheep are safer — but so are the kangaroos that sometimes compete with them for food. Emus, too, are more plentiful inside the fence than outside it.

Feral horses (*Equus caballus*) digging for water in a dry creek bed in the MacDonnell Ranges west of Alice Springs. They are called brumbies, after a Private James Brumby, who is said to have turned the first of them loose in the 1800s. Many herds still run wild in outback Australia — like the native animals, their numbers fluctuate with the cycles of drought and seasons of plenty.

Australians have a fascination with fences: if a problem can not be fenced in, it can be fenced out. Some work, many do not: rows of fences did not stop the rabbits spreading their destruction across the continent. This is the famous dog fence, at just short of 10,000 kilometres, the longest in the world. Built to keep dingoes out of sheep country, it is patrolled and repaired regularly, and does its job reasonably well.

The Rangelands Dilemma

Beyond the fence, further inland, is cattle country. Dingoes are less of a threat to cattle than sheep, though they will attack calves if they have a chance. Most of the time, however, a dingo will hunt smaller prey — whatever is most abundant at any one time. (And that usually means rabbits, which might make dingoes more a help than a hindrance to the pastoralists of the central rangelands.) But dingoes are peripheral to the central issue of whether the arid and semi-arid lands are capable of sustaining an economically sound and ecologically responsible grazing industry at all. They carry only about 20 per cent of Australia's total livestock, on an area many times greater than that carrying the rest — much of it fragile semi-desert especially vulnerable to disturbance.

Part of the problem is that while there is a clear relationship between overstocking and land degradation, it is often a case of one guess being as good an another as to exactly how much stock is too much. Only South Australia has set maximum stocking rates in its arid regions: understanding of the land's reality there has come a long way since early government policy, which required pastoralists to stock their properties with up to a hundred sheep per square mile (259 hectares) or lose their lease.

Even if precise figures are difficult to establish in such an unpredictable environment, it would seem sensible to leave a wide margin for error. Long before the obvious indicators of degradation — trampled soils, erosion, loss of plants — there are biological warnings. The decline of smaller native animals is one; another is big mobs of large kangaroos, numbers far greater than the land used to sustain. The shift in balance warns that the land is changing in ways that will lead to its ultimate destruction, both for introduced stock and, ultimately, the kangaroos themselves.

How the warning system operates was revealed by a study in the Pilbara region of Western Australia. When sheep were first moved there in the 1890s, red kangaroos and euros were the dominant herbivores, but in modest numbers. The kangaroos lived on the river and creek floodplains, where they fed on a mixture of nutritious grasses; the euros were largely confined to the hills and ranges where there were caves for shelter, some water, and where they fed on the seedheads of spinifex.

Once sheep arrived, and with them the provision of artificial watering points and the introduction of exotic grasses, the balance began to shift. Euros were able to come down from the hills and compete with the sheep and kangaroos for the more nutritious grasses. Initially there was plenty of food for all three. Sheep numbers increased enormously; so did the euro populations, and to a lesser extent the kangaroos. By the 1930s, sheep numbers peaked

Australia grew prosperous on the sheep's back, but in many places the ecological price was inordinately high. There is a better understanding now of the nature of the continent, to underwrite more appropriate management for the long-term wellbeing of the land and its inhabitants.

at around three-quarters of a million. There were double that number of euros, and red kangaroos were being shot as pests in their thousands. Then the changes that had been working their way through the system began taking their toll. Graziers had been burning their pastures in winter to promote fresh green growth. What it also promoted in the longer term was spinifex, which gradually began to move out of the hills to the adjoining plains, and to replace more nutritious grasses.

When severe drought came in the 1940s and finally killed the better grasses, only euros could survive and breed on spinifex. The first to disappear were the red kangaroos: almost the entire population died. Sheep numbers also collapsed; though individuals could just survive on spinifex, it was not nutritious enough to keep them breeding. Only the euros flourished. Though like the others, they preferred more nutritious grasses if they had the choice, they were well adapted to a diet of spinifex. In less than half a century, the rich pastures that initially produced such a wealth of wool had been transformed into semi-deserts of spinifex, good only for euros. Once-thriving sheep stations were abandoned.

And as the artificial watering points, the bores and dams, fell into disrepair and collapsed, the euros also came under pressure and their numbers began to dwindle. The end of the story may well be their disappearance too, leaving only the spinifex.

In hindsight, the rise in the euro numbers can be seen as the first omen of the ultimate collapse. In the same way, the large mobs of red and eastern and western grey kangaroos that gather on some of the semi-arid and arid rangelands elsewhere in Australia may be seen as heralds of ultimate ruin for the grazing industry in those regions.

Already soil erosion, degraded pastures and even dead woodlands are widespread. Soils stripped of their groundcover become much hotter, and the roots running in them may perish. That is what may have contributed to the death of vast stretches of the characteristic mulga woodlands — swathes 160 kilometres long — in southern parts of the Northern Territory.

If kangaroos in large numbers are a danger signal pointing to degradation, kangaroos themselves can also point to a way for the land to survive. After all, they have been surviving successfully in the inland since before it became arid.

Red kangaroos especially can serve as a model: they are the most widely distributed species in the inland, and their fodder is the green herbage that is also important to stock. The essential pointers lie in the way they cope with drought, for drought is the norm in the inland. Within their large home ranges, the reds are nomadic: they move to where green feed persists, or where rain has fallen locally. They breed in good times, and stop in bad; and in

A euro, or common wallaroo (*Macropus robustus*), one of the three largest kangaroos. It inhabits rocky hills and stony rises. In Western Australia's Pilbarra region, a sudden rise in its numbers, accompanying a movement on to the plains, proved to be a warning sign that European grazing practices were changing and harming the country. Studying the population dynamics of native animals may prove a useful guide to better land management.

drought it is the young that die, not the breeders.

Of course, biologically and ecologically, the introduced European stock could not hope to emulate the success of the native herbivores . . . but European technology can bridge the gap.

Nomadism can be achieved through the use of transport; road and rail can carry stock swiftly away from imminent drought to more favourable areas. It means holdings need to be extremely large to cover a range of conditions: smaller stations would not have the necessary flexibility. To simulate the kangaroos' restricted breeding is simply a matter of herd control, as is infant mortality: in lean times, young could be transported away, or killed off.

Kangaroos are acutely sensitive to changing conditions. A distant line of clouds may signal a chance rainfall, and the mobs set off for the green pick that follows.

Introduced animals — or, at least, their human managers — also have a system that tells of changing conditions. The infant science of remote sensing offers a valuable tool in the management of the continent's resources, including its pastures. Instruments aboard satellites scan the spectrum of radiation reflected from the earth's surface, from the long wavelengths of radio to microwaves and infrared, through visible light to the extremely short wavelengths of ultraviolet, X-rays and gamma radiation. Australian scientists have developed comprehensive techniques to translate the information supplied by the satellite sensors into an immediate overview of any particular part of the country, down to areas as small as 30 square metres.

Among other things, patterns of drought, overgrazing and erosion become instantly recognisable. The use of remote sensing techniques in the management of rangelands is already being demonstrated in two states. Western Australia has reclaimed eight badly degraded pastoral stations in the West Kimberley region, and is using Landsat information about patterns of erosion and vegetation to restructure them into new and ecologically more viable holdings. South Australia has developed a rangeland package of information for the pastoralists of its arid hinterlands about grazing patterns and the distribution of feed.

Providing the information is one thing — ensuring it is used to the best effect is another. Two centuries of over-exploitation have built into an economic, social, political and cultural juggernaut whose impetus will be difficult to arrest, much less reverse. Even if the latest technology and knowledge is put to the best use, improved management techniques may only be a short-term palliative. It may already be too late: there may no longer be a safe way to graze many of the arid and semi-arid rangelands, a way that does not turn them into manmade deserts.

One thing the satellites show is that the deserts are expanding. A third of the interior has already been degraded to the point where desert is the only apt description, and another third is at risk. And of Australia's pastoral and agricultural area, 51 per cent needs repair, at a cost that in 1975 was already estimated at $675 million.

If grazing livestock in the interior (or at least large areas of it) indeed has no long-term economic or ecological future, as various indicators seem to say, then a carefully managed tourist industry may well offer the best economic and ecological alternative.

Australia's arid heart and its spectacular landforms offer much scenic wealth. But careful management is the key: uncontrolled hordes of tourists charging about the landscape can be almost as destructive as grazing livestock. Tourism has grown so swiftly in the more scenic areas — the number of visitors to Uluru (Ayers Rock), for example, rose from 42,000 in 1971 to a projected 220,000 in 1987 — that adequate strategies to deal with them had difficulty catching up. As early as the 1960s, it became clear that the hotchpotch of accommodation that had grown up around the base of Uluru was totally inadequate to deal with the tourist influx, and that it created damaging pressure on the rock and its surrounds. It took another 25 years for a new tourist complex to be built, 14 kilometres out of harm's way.

Though tourism will inevitably produce its crop of problems, they are likely to prove more tractable than the subtle complexities of the pastoral impact on the arid regions. Economic and political realities, however, indicate that phasing out the grazing industry (even in the more sensitive areas) doesn't seem a likely option.

Top End: the Last Frontier

The dilemmas of European settlement; of balancing economic wellbeing with the welfare of the land, find some of their most vivid expressions in the wet-dry tropics of the Top End. It is a torrid land, hot all year round, with dramatic swings between a wet season of monsoonal rains and a dry that turns the region into semi-desert. Neither is it an entirely predictable cycle: there are years when winter rains interrupt the dry, and dry spells punctuate the summer monsoon. The somewhat fickle starts and ends of the wet and dry, and their violent contrasts — between flooded billabongs, swollen rivers and plains flushed with life in the steamy warmth, and those same plains cracking in the heat of the dry with the rivers reduced to chains of muddy pools — produce special challenges of survival.

The amount of moisture in the soils alternates from that found in a hot, humid rainforest to that in a hot, dry desert. Animals and plants have adapted to these extremes with various strategies: many species of birds, mammals, fishes and some reptiles escape the stresses of the dry by moving to refuges. Plants, which cannot move, stop growing and some rely on food stores in their root systems to tide them over — food that sustains some of the animals. Many trees shut down their systems and drop their leaves.

Most annual vegetation dies at the end of the wet, and dries out to become fuel on which fire feeds. Although less intense, fires are more frequent in the grass-floored forests and woodlands of the wet-dry tropics than they are in any other part of Australia. Before the arrival of the Aboriginal people, the frequency of fires depended indirectly on temperature and annual rainfall — which in turn were determined by the prevailing climates of the time — and directly on the frequency of lightning.

For at least the past 40,000 years, the major cause of fire has been Aboriginals, who changed both the patterns and frequencies of fire, with consequent changes for the plants and animals.

The Top End was where the Aboriginals' ancestors first established themselves on the continent. With its wealth and diversity of food sources, it remained among the most densely populated regions of Aboriginal Australia and, as elsewhere on the continent, the European advent disrupted traditional Aboriginal ways of living with the land. The original people disappeared from large areas of the Top End, and their way of life changed greatly in the remainder. Among the more immediate changes were an end to traditional Aboriginal fire regimes in many areas. As a result fires burned more erratically later in the dry season and more destructively. The effects of the changes are still working through the system, and it will be some time before their impact on plant and animal communities (and the landscape) is revealed in full.

There are other changes initiated by European settlement whose impact already is all too clear. Ironically, those changes were generated by the first attempts to establish a presence — attempts that failed. Small military garrisons were established in the first half of last century in a few places on the far north coast, including Port Essington on the Cobourg Peninsula, and Melville Island. They were set up to be self-sufficient, and supplied with small herds of cattle, pigs and domestic water buffalo imported from Indonesia.

Each of the settlements lasted only a few years: heat, disease and crop failures took their toll, and the tiny colonies were abandoned. The surviving animals were turned loose. Not surprisingly, those imported from other tropical areas — particularly the buffaloes and the pigs — went on to thrive in an environment that seemed to offer them a ready-made niche, unoccupied by any native animals. From the initial few, certainly no more than 100, the buffaloes spread through the monsoonal lowlands until 150 years later — in 1981 — the count stood at two hundred and eighty thousand.

Water buffaloes (*Bubalis bubalis*) have destroyed large areas of Australia's monsoonal Top End. Their wallowing turns wetlands into muddy bogs, and their regimented wanderings — always to individual daily and seasonal routines — create new water channels that allow salt water to extend much further into the normally freshwater floodplains.

In some places they were as dense as 70 per square kilometre, and the damage they did was enormous. Their wanderings — always to individual daily and seasonal routines — create new water channels that allow saltwater to extend much further into the normally freshwater floodplains, and ruin the breeding places of native fishes and birds. Their wallowing turns the wetlands into muddy bogs where plants and other animals struggle to survive.

But the buffalo damage may be helping to keep a worse menace at bay: where there are many buffaloes there are few pigs, and vice versa. Pigs too have established themselves in many places in the monsoonal lowlands since their first release last century. Though well adapted to the tropical heat, pigs rely on shade to keep cool, shade provided by the kind of vegetation that buffalo activity destroys. Now there is a new type of plant taking root in the Top End that offers them shelter, and which may help them spread. *Mimosa pigra*, a prickly bush originally from South America, forms dense thickets that choke off other plant growth. Introduced accidentally, it established itself swiftly in the disturbed country that buffaloes leave in their wake.

The Top End of today can be likened to the rest of Australia in the middle of last century, when much of the continent still lay untouched, and the drive to colonise and exploit was still to gather speed. The difference is that whatever challenges the Top End faces, lack of information is not one of them. The dilemma of the buffaloes and feral pigs shares its complexity with many similar problems across the continent. Tampering with one element, such as eliminating buffaloes, can alter the course of many others. More often than not now, those courses can be predicted.

The European invasion of Australia was launched from a base of total ignorance, for science itself was in its infancy and, tied as it was to European ideas and concepts, anything Australian was totally outside its ken. But this century — and especially in the past few decades — there has been a great leap in understanding. Researchers in many fields, from archaeology to botany and zoology, have pieced together a store of knowledge about how the ecosystems that make up the Australian environment actually work. That store stands available to underwrite the search for the best ways for Australians to manage their common wealth.

Knowing the answers is not enough, of course: the knowledge needs to be put to work. Too often, political and economic considerations formulated in a less informed age must still catch up with ecological realities. The devastation that would follow the workings of that Tasmanian copper mine last century could not be imagined at the time. That ecological damage will flow from a misfortune in the Top End's uranium mines into the priceless Kakadu region can be predicted with confidence.

A byproduct of uranium mining is waste water contaminated with radioactive material. It is supposed to be kept in storage ponds, but should it find its way — either through an accidental floodout or deliberate release — into the rivers and creeks of the wetlands, there is a high probability the reproductive systems of many forms of aquatic life will be affected, and that the effects of that will flow through to all related life.

What the precise effects will be may not be known in detail, but that they will not enhance the quality of life there is a certainty. It might be termed environmental management by calculated risk, with science reckoning the odds.

The Top End is also the showcase for a different experiment in environmental management: one that involves returning to the (recent) past. Responsibility for large parts of the region has been handed back to its traditional owners, who had been managing it reasonably successfully for tens of thousands of years.

But the clock can only turn back part of the way: Aboriginals' traditional ways employed simple weapons and tools, their transport was walking and their pressure on the land and its resources was light. European technology provided four-wheel drive vehicles and rifles, enabling a month's hunting and gathering to be done in a day, so greatly increasing the pressure on the environment, perhaps to the point where resources begin to be depleted. Their ancient firing patterns, too, may no longer mesh with changing conditions.

In a more general sense, Aboriginal people have many more options now — sharing in mining wealth, for example — and while their affinity with their land will no doubt remain strong, their objectives and expectations may well change. In any case, the Aboriginal way can only work in those places that retain their pre-European character. Elsewhere in the continent, other solutions have to be found and more complex choices made: there is no going back to some past Australia.

The future is uncertain, but some predictions can be made with more confidence than others. One is that the nature of Australia will be affected dramatically by the effects of human activity on the global climate. Even without considering the risk of nuclear winter, humanity's peacetime pursuits are rapidly becoming a major influence in the world's weather.

The destruction of forests and the burning of fossil fuels have caused a sharp increase in the level of carbon dioxide in the air. Before the industrial revolution, as measured from air bubbles trapped in ice cores in the Antarctic and in Greenland, the level was about 270 parts per million. Present levels are about 348 parts per million, and are rising at the rate of half a per cent a year. Other gases are also being poured into the atmosphere in increasing vol-

Scarce forest continues to fall, the inroads continue, but there is also a rising concern among Australians to preserve what is left of their natural heritage, a growing awareness that their ancient, wondrous land has more to offer than mere material prosperity.

ume, including the artificially produced freons used in processes from refrigeration to the manufacture of plastics; even methanes from increasing numbers of farm animals.

Carbon dioxide and the other gases together act like a thermal blanket covering the earth, trapping increasing amounts of solar heat. The earth's surface is beginning to warm up — but the average temperature rise will vary around the globe, from 1.5 degrees to 4.5 degrees. By early next century, that will cause major shifts and changes in rainfall regimes; more rain in some parts of the world, less in others.

The effects are likely to be felt in Australia by the year 2030. In inland areas, temperatures will rise around 2 degrees in northern Australia, and up to 3 or 4 degrees further south. Near the coast, these increases could be moderated by the lagging behind of sea-surface temperatures, and it is probable that winter and overnight temperatures will warm more than summer and daily maximum temperatures.

Rainfall changes will vary with season and location. In general, the summer rainfall regime will intensify and push further south. This has already happened through central New South Wales from the Hunter Valley west past Dubbo, where average spring, summer and autumn rainfall in some months has increased by 30 to 40 per cent since early this century. At the same time, winter rain associated with the fronts embedded in the westerlies at middle latitudes is expected to occur further south, leading to reduced rainfall in the southern parts of Australia, including the southwest of Western Australia, where average rainfall has already dropped 10 to 20 per cent so far this century.

What will happen in southeastern Australia is not clear yet: the Great Divide will be an important influence, and the effects of other factors, such as increased humidity and greater cloud cover, will have to be calculated before it can be predicted whether the net result will be more or less rain.

What *is* clear, however, is that as surface temperatures rise, the warmer air will be able to hold more water vapour, and so generate much heavier rainfall and greater maximum rainfall rates. There will be much more flash flooding as a result, accelerating rates of erosion. Higher rainfall inland will mean a rise in groundwater tables, and an increase in associated salinity problems as more salts are flushed to the surface.

There will be dramatic changes in the high country, too: it has been calculated that for every 1 degree increase in average temperature, the winter snowline will rise 100 metres. A 4 degree temperature rise may well see the snowfields melt away permanently.

As the earth's surface warms, much of the heat will be absorbed by the oceans, which will expand and increase in volume. Sea levels may rise by as much as 1.2 metres as a result. It is not as great a rise as Australia has experienced in the past, but it will be enough to see most of the present beaches, mangroves and other fore-shores disappear.

The effects of these climatic changes, as they flow through the living systems that make up the nature of Australia, can only be predicted in the most general terms. Increased levels of carbon dioxide will favour some plants more than others and, combined with the effects of changes in rainfall regimes, may well lead to rapid and dramatic changes in plant and animal communities.

Some species may flourish, others may become extinct. The changes may be especially marked in limited areas of sharp climatic gradients such as national parks, often selected to preserve rare and endangered species. And what the effect of a metre's rise in sea level will be on Australia's marine treasure, the Great Barrier Reef and the other coral reefs, still remains to be calculated. In theory, they should expand in the long term. But disruptions caused by changes in currents and tidal patterns may well work against them in the short term.

Toward a New Australia

Homo sapiens is a restless, questing species. It is this quality that gave it evolutionary success, that brought it to Australia in the first place, and that it will have to draw on in large measure to keep Australia a place worth living in.

Australians, too, have a responsibility to the rest of the world. Theirs was the last continent to be colonised by Europeans and their technology. Although the changes triggered by that invasion have rolled across the continent with great speed, the opportunity still exists for their course to be altered for the long-term benefit of both the land and its people. For the wellbeing of one cannot be divorced from that of the other: Australians have both the wealth and the opportunity to find solutions to problems that for various historical, economic and political reasons are intractable else-where. They can devise systems of environmental management that might serve to a greater or lesser degree as models for the rest of the world. The knowledge, the wealth, the opportunity — all exist. What is needed now is the communal will to make them come together in a formula for action.

There is growing popular concern about the degradation of the environment. Australians have always had a love-hate relationship with their land: many early settlers looked upon it with fear, but from the beginning there has been affection and fascination, too.

Laws to protect wildlife were early entries in the statute books of the young colonies, and the world's second national park was established in Australia; Royal National Park, south of Sydney, was proclaimed in 1879. Those early enthusiasms helped generate what is today a powerful conservation movement: forests continue to fall, but the bulldozers no longer have unimpeded passage.

The public and dramatic battles between the forces of exploitation and conservation, even if they do tend to reduce the debate to just those terms, at least focus society's attention on the choices facing it, and so serve to mobilise the political will.

Beginnings have been made, helped by a fusion of economic and ecological realities. Development is now judged for its environmental impact as well as its economic potential, even if profit is often still the most powerful argument. Farmers, concerned about declining productivity, are turning to the repair of the land, working it in ways that take into account new knowledge about what it can and cannot stand.

A new Australia is in the making — the next phase of the continent's long journey from Gondwana. Australians are fortunate that the nature of that new Australia is in large measure still a matter of choice . . . their choice.

BIBLIOGRAPHY

Chapter One

Archer, Michael (ed.). *Carnivorous marsupials*, Vols 1 and 2. Royal Zoological Society of New South Wales, Sydney, 1982.

Archer, Michael, and Clayton, Georgina (eds). *Vertebrate zoogeography and evolution in Australasia*. Hesperian Press, Perth, 1984.

Dawson, Terence J. *Monotremes and marsupials: the other mammals*. Edward Arnold Ltd, London, 1983.

Eisenberg, John F. *The mammalian radiations*. University of Chicago Press, Chicago, 1981.

Hume, Ian D. *Digestive physiology and nutrition of marsupials*. Cambridge University Press, London, 1982.

Hunsaker, Don (ed.). *The biology of marsupials*. Academic Press, New York, 1977.

Lee, Anthony K., and Cockburn, Andrew. *Evolutionary ecology of marsupials*. Cambridge University Press, London, 1985.

Rich, P.V., van Tets, G.F., and Knight, F. *Kadimakara: extinct vertebrates of Australia*. Pioneer Design Studio, Melbourne, 1985.

Simpson, George Gaylord. *Splendid isolation: the curious history of South American mammals*. Yale University Press, New Haven and London, 1979.

Tyndale-Biscoe, Hugh. *Life of marsupials*. Edward Arnold Ltd, London, 1983.

Tyndale-Biscoe, Hugh, and Renfree, Marilyn. *Reproductive physiology of marsupials*. Cambridge University Press, London, 1987.

White, Mary E. *The greening of Gondwana*. Reed Books Pty Ltd, Sydney, 1986.

Chapter Two

Budker, Paul. *The life of sharks*. Columbia University Press, New York, 1971.

Dakin, William J. *Australian seashores*. Angus & Robertson, Sydney, 1973.

George, David and Jennifer. *Marine life*. Lionel Leventhal Ltd, London, 1979.

Hughes, Roland (ed.). *Australia's underwater wilderness*. Weldons Pty Ltd, Sydney, 1985.

Martin, Richard Mark. *Mammals of the oceans*. Hutchinson Australia, Melbourne, 1977.

Matthews, L. Harrison. *The natural history of the whale*. Weidenfeld & Nicolson, London, 1978.

Newbury, Andrew Todd (ed.). *Life in the sea*. Scientific American, W.H.Freeman & Co., San Francisco, 1982.

Smith, Marcus Lincoln (ed.). *Sharks of Australia*. Jack Pollard Publishing, Sydney, 1981.

Stonehouse, Bernard. *Animals of the Antarctic: the ecology of the far south*. Peter Lowe – Eurobook Ltd, London, 1972.

Talbot, Frank (ed.). *The Reader's Digest Book of the Great Barrier Reef*. Reader's Digest Services, Sydney, 1984.

Thomson, J.M. *A field guide to the common sea and estuary fishes of non-tropical Australia*. William Collins, Sydney, 1971.

Thresher, R.E. *Reproduction in reef fishes*. T.F.H. Publications, Sydney, 1984.

Chapter Three

Armstrong, J.A., Powell, J.M., and Richards, A.J. (eds). *Pollination and evolution*. Proceedings of Symposium on Pollination Biology, 13th International Botanical Congress, Sydney, 1981.

Australian Heritage Commission. *Tropical rainforests of north Queensland*. Australian Government Publishing Service, Canberra, 1986.

Barlow, Bryan A. *The Australian flora: its origin and evolution, Flora of Australia*, Vol. 1. Australian Government Publishing Service, Canberra, 1981.

Breeden, Stanley and Kay. *Tropical Queensland* William Collins, Sydney, 1970.

Breeden, Stanley and Kay. *Australia's South-east* William Collins, Sydney, 1972.

Keast, A., Recher, H.F., Ford, H., and Saunders, D. (eds). *Birds of eucalypt forests and woodlands*. Royal Australasian Ornithologists Union, Surrey Beatty & Sons Pty Ltd, Chipping Norton, NSW, 1985.

Pate, J.S., and Beard, J.S. *Kwongan — Plant life of the sandplain*. University of Western Australia Press, Perth, 1984.

Pate, J.S., and McCromb, A.J. (eds). *The biology of Australian plants.* University of Western Australia Press, Perth, 1981.

Rowley, Ian. *Bird life.* William Collins, Sydney, 1975.

Smith, Andrew, and Hume, Ian (eds). *Possums and gliders.* Australian Mammal Society, Sydney, 1986.

Tyler, Michael J. *Frogs.* William Collins, Sydney, 1972.

Chapter Four

Barker, W.R., and Greenslade, P.J.M. (eds). *Evolution of the flora and fauna of Arid Australia.* Peacock Publications, Frewville, SA, 1982.

Davey, Keith. *Our arid environment.* Reed Books Pty Ltd, Sydney, 1983.

Grigg, Gordon, Shine, Richard, and Ehmann, Harry (eds). *Biology of Australian frogs and reptiles.* Royal Zoological Society of New South Wales, Sydney, 1985.

Heatwole, Harold. *Reptile ecology.* University of Queensland Press, Brisbane, 1976.

Morton, S.R., and James, C.D. 'The radiation of lizards in arid Australia: A new hypothesis' (in press).

Serventy, Vincent. *The desert sea: the miracle of Lake Eyre in flood.* Macmillan Australia, Melbourne, 1985.

Chapter Five

Blainey, Geoffrey. *Triumph of the nomads: A history of ancient Australia.* Macmillan, Melbourne, 1975.

Breeden, Stanley and Kay. *Australia's North.* William Collins, Sydney, 1975.

Elkin, A.P. *The Australian Aborigines,* revised edn, Angus & Robertson, Sydney, 1979.

Gill, A.M., Groves, R.H., and Noble, I.R. (eds). *Fire and the Australian biota.* Australian Academy of Science, Canberra, 1981.

Hallam, Sylvia J. *Fire & hearth.* Australian Institute of Aboriginal Studies, Canberra, 1979.

Jones, Rhys (ed). *Archeological Research in Kakadu National Park.* Australian National Parks and Wildlife Service, Canberra, 1985.

Mulvaney, D.J., and White, J. Peter (eds). *Australians to 1788, Australians: a historical library,* Vol. 1. Fairfax, Syme & Weldon, Sydney, 1987.

Ovington, Derrick. *Kakadu: A world heritage of unsurpassed beauty.* Australian Government Publishing Service, Canberra, 1986.

Ridpath, M.G., and Corbett, L.K. (eds). 'Ecology of the Wet-Dry Tropics'. Proceedings of the Ecological Society of Australia, Vol. 13, Darwin, 1983.

White, J. Peter, and O'Connell, James F. *A prehistory of Australia, New Guinea and Sahul.* Academic Press (Australia), Sydney, 1982.

Chapter Six

Birrell, Robert, Hill, Doug, and Stanley, John (eds). *Quarry Australia?* Oxford University Press, Melbourne, 1982.

Blainey, Geoffrey. *A land half won.* Macmillan Australia, Melbourne, 1980.

Bolton, Geoffrey. *Spoils & Spoilers.* Allen & Unwin Australia, Sydney, 1981.

Breckwoldt, Roland. *The Last Stand — managing Australia's remnant forests and woodlands.* Australian

Government Publishing Service, Canberra, 1986.

Cannon, Michael. *Life in the country.* Thomas Nelson, Melbourne, 1973.

Davis, Peter S. *Man and the Murray.* New South Wales University Press Ltd, Sydney, 1978.

Department of Arts, Heritage and Environment. *State of the environment in Australia in 1985.* Australian Government Publishing Service, Canberra, 1985.

Messer, John, and Mosley, Geoff. What future for Australia's arid lands? Proceedings of the National Arid Lands Conference, Broken Hill, 1982. Published by Australian Conservation Foundation, Melbourne, 1983.

Powell, J.M. *Environmental management in Australia 1783-1914.* Oxford University Press, Melbourne, 1976.

Recher, Harry F., Lumney, Daniel, and Dunn, Irina (eds) *A natural legacy — ecology in Australia.* Pergamon Press (Australia), Sydney, 1979.

Rolls, Eric C. *They all ran wild.* Angus & Robertson, Sydney, 1969.

General

Keast, A. (ed). *Ecological biogeography of Australia.* Junk, The Hague, 1981.

Schodde, Richard, and Tidemann, Sonia (eds). *Complete book of Australian birds* Reader's Digest, Sydney, 1986.

Serventy, Vincent, and Raymond, Robert. *Australia's wildlife heritage,* Vols 1 to 105. Paul Hamlyn Pty Ltd, Sydney, 1974.

Strahan, Ronald (eds). *Complete book of Australian mammals.* Australian Museum/Angus & Robertson, Sydney, 1983.

PICTURE CREDITS

Picture research by Maggie Weidenhofer

page ii inset top, D. Parer; centre, Jean-Paul Ferrero; **ii–iii** E. Parer-Cook; **vii** cycads, Palm Valley, Northern Territory, E. Parer-Cook; **viii** Antarctic beech *Nothofagus cunninghamii*, Kathie Atkinson; **x** E. Parer-Cook; **xi** Reg Morrison, courtesy of Weldon Trannies; **xii** Richard Woldendorp; **1** Ken Stepnell; **2–3** E. Parer-Cook; **4** Glen Carruthers; **5** M. Unkovich/National Photographic Index of Australian Wildlife (NPIAW); **6–8 (A)** E. Parer-Cook; **8 (B)–9** D. Parer; **11** E. Parer-Cook; **12** Stan Lamond, The Book Design Company; **13** Reg Morrison, courtesy of Weldon Trannies; **14** based on an illustration from M. Archer and G.Clayton (eds),*Vertebrate zoogeography and evolution in Australasia;* **15** D. Parer; **18** E. Parer-Cook; **20** Reg Morrison, courtesy of Weldon Trannies; **21** E. Parer-Cook; **22** Peter Schouten; **23** top, Glen Carruthers; **23** bottom and **24–5** E. Parer-Cook; **26** D. Parer; **27, 30** E. Parer-Cook; **33** Jan Aldenhoven; **34–5** bottom, Stan Lamond; **35** top, Kathie Atkinson; **37–8** E. Parer-Cook; **39** H. and J. Beste/NPIAW; **40** L.F. Schick/NPIAW; **45** Neil Rettig; **46** G.B. Baker/NPIAW; **47** E. Parer-Cook; **49** Rod Scott, courtesy of Weldon Trannies, from *Kangaroos*, Weldon Pty Ltd, 1985; **50** top, E. Parer-Cook; bottom, Peter Schouten; **51** Glen Carruthers; **52–3** E. Parer-Cook; **54** D. Parer; **55** E. Parer-Cook; **56** D. Parer; **57** E. Parer-Cook; **58, 60** Bruce Reitherman; **63** Jan Aldenhoven; **64** Stan Lamond; **65–72** D. Parer; **73** E. Parer-Cook; **74–5** Rudie H. Kuiter; **76** left, E. Parer-Cook; right, Rudie H. Kuiter; **77** D. Parer; **81** E. Parer-Cook; **82** Ken Stepnell; **83** E. Parer-Cook; **86** Stan Lamond; **89–90** D. Parer; **91** E. Parer-Cook; **93** D. Parer; **94** top, E. Parer-Cook; bottom, Jan Aldenhoven; **95** E. Parer-Cook; **96** D. Parer; **97** E. Parer-Cook; **98** Jan Aldenhoven; **99** D. Parer; **101** left, Kathie Atkinson; right, E. Parer-Cook; **102** top, D. Parer; **102** bottom and **103** Glen Carruthers/Mantis Wildlife; **104** B. Willis; **105** E. Parer-Cook; **106** D. Parer; **107–8** E. Parer-Cook; **112** top, D. Parer; centre E. Parer-Cook; **115** D. Parer; **116** Stan Lamond, based on the vegetation map in Mary White's *Greening of Gondwana;* **117** Ford Kristo; **119** Bob Miller/NPIAW; **120** E. Parer-Cook; **122** top left and right, Kathie Atkinson; **122** bottom and **123** Jan Aldenhoven; **124** Kathie Atkinson; **126** Jim Frazier/Mantis Wildlife; **127–8** Jan Aldenhoven; **129** top, E. Parer-Cook; bottom, H. Ehmann/NPIAW; **130** D. Parer; **131** Andrew Dennis/Australasian Nature Transparencies; **132** Y. Dymock/NPIAW; **134** left, Ford Kristo; right, G. Suckling/NPIAW; **135** Jan Aldenhoven; **137** P.R. Brown/NPIAW; **139** C.A. Henley/NPIAW; **141** D. Parer; **144** Robin Smith; **145** left, Ford Kristo; right, Ralph and Daphne Keller/Australasian Nature Transparencies; **146** Ken Stepnell; **147** D. Parer; **148–9** Jean-Paul Ferrero/Auscape International; **151** A.G. Wells/NPIAW; **152–3** Jan Aldenhoven; **154** G. Rogerson/NPIAW; **155–6** Jan Aldenhoven; **158** A.G. Wells/NPIAW; **161** E. Parer-Cook; **162** Robin Smith; **163–70** E. Parer-Cook; **171** Dick Whitford/NPIAW; **172** Mike Gillam; **173** E. Parer-Cook; **174** top, Jan Aldenhoven; bottom, Densey Clyne/Mantis Wildlife; **175–6** E. Parer-Cook; **177** D. Parer; **179** E. Parer-Cook; **180** Jan Aldenhoven; **181** E. Parer-Cook; **182** Jan Aldenhoven; **183** Ken Stepnell; **185, 188–9** E. Parer-Cook; **190** left, Kathie Atkinson; **190** right and **191–2** E. Parer-Cook; **193, 196** Jan Aldenhoven; **197** D. Parer; **198** E. Parer-Cook; **201** Densey Clyne/Mantis Wildlife; **203–4** Jean-Paul Ferrero/Auscape International; **207** D. Parer; **208** Neil Rettig Productions; **209** Stan Lamond, based on an illustration in White and O'Connell, A *Prehistory of Australia, New Guinea and Sahul* page 45; **210** Des White; **211** Kathie Atkinson; **212** after Alderson, Gangali and Haynes ©1979, adapted from 'Seasonal calendar of NE Arnhemland' © Morris 1978; **213** top, Jan Aldenhoven; bottom, Jim Frazier/Mantis Wildlife; **214–15** Jan Aldenhoven; **216** top, Glen Carruthers; **216–17** bottom, Stan Lamond; **217** top, Neil Rettig Productions; **218** Glen Carruthers; **219** Jan Aldenhoven; **220** top, Neil Rettig Productions; bottom, Glen Carruthers; **221–2** E. Parer-Cook; **223–4** Glen Carruthers; **225–7** Jan Aldenhoven; **229** Glen Carruthers; **230** Jim Frazier/Mantis Wildlife; **231** Glen Carruthers; **232** Ronald Rose; **234** Jan Aldenhoven; **236–7** Des White; **238** Glen Carruthers; **239** C. and S. Pollitt/Australasian Nature Transparencies; **240** Frith Foto/Australasian Nature Transparencies; **241** Glen Carruthers; **243** Reg Morrison, courtesy of Weldon Trannies; **244** Kathie Atkinson; **245** J. Brownlie/Australasian Nature Transparencies; **246** Greg Parker; **247** H. Gee/Wilderness Society; **251** based on Recher, Lunney and Dunn (eds), A *Natural Legacy;* **254** Alan Gibb/Australasian Nature Transparencies; **256** top, Barry Golding; bottom, Australian Museum/NPIAW; **257** Rex Nan Kivell Collection, National Library of Australia; **258** Australian Conservation Foundation; **259** J. Christesen/NPIAW; **260–1** Kathie Atkinson; **262** based on Powell, *Environmental Management in Australia 1783–1914;* **263** D, Parer; **264** Kathie Atkinson; **265,** top, D. Parer; bottom, Kathie Atkinson; **268** Densey Clyne/Mantis Wildlife; **270** top, G. Wheeler/Australasian Nature Transparencies; bottom, Ern Mainka/Australasian Nature Transparencies; **272** Otto Rogge/Australasian Nature Transparencies; **273** E. Parer-Cook; **274** D. and T. O'Byrne/Australasian Nature Transparencies; **275** D. Parer; **278** Glen Carruthers; **280** D. Parer.

INDEX

ACKNOWLEDGEMENTS

*T*his book is based on the television series of the same name. Many people contributed to the making of the series, and therefore to this book, and I am grateful to them all.

The series production team is listed below. I owe special thanks to my colleagues David Parer, whose tireless pursuit of excellence was a constant source of inspiration, and Dione Gilmour, who contributed greatly in many discussions. David Parer and Elizabeth Parer-Cook's exhaustive research provided a rich store to draw upon, and Dr Jan Aldenhoven, Glen Carruthers, Roy Hunt, Martin Stone, Jeremy Hogarth, Graeme O'Neill, Dr David Smith and Mary White also helped gather the material on which the series and this book are based.

The source of most of that material was Australia's talented community of natural scientists — the biologists, zoologists, botanists and workers in related fields, who gave so unstintingly of their time and expertise to add to our understanding. I am especially grateful to those who read draft chapters of this book to keep me from error and to save me from foundering on the wilder shores of speculation: Professor Anthony Lee (who also generously gave me access to some as yet unpublished manuscripts), Dr Marilyn Renfree, Professor Roger Short, Dr Peter Jarman, Dr Bryan Barlow, Dr Ron Thresher, Dr Peter Doherty, Rudi Kuiter, Dr Steve Morton, Dr Graeme Griffin, Dr Heather Aslin, Dr Harold Cogger, Dr Dick Braithwaite, Professor Sylvia Hallam, Dr Dean Graetz, and Professor Geoffrey Bolton. I also thank Dr Michael Archer, Dr Richard Schodde and Dr Len Webb for stimulating ideas and insights.

A selected bibliography is included; it can only begin to indicate the wealth of knowledge now available through the endeavours of our scientific community, and a book of this kind can only aspire to draw together the main themes of what is an immensely rich, complex and exciting story.

John Vandenbeld
July 1987

NATURE OF AUSTRALIA TELEVISION PRODUCTION TEAM

Executive Producer

John Vandenbeld

Producers

David Parer
Dione Gilmour

Photography

David Parer
Neil Rettig
Keith Taylor
Bruce Reitherman

Glen Carruthers
Jim Frazier
George Murahidy
Malcolm Ludgate
Rory McGuinness
Don Hanran-Smith

Film Editing

Jeremy Hogarth
David Luffman
Peter Vile

Production Assistance and Research

Elizabeth Parer-Cook

Martin Stone
Jan Aldenhoven
Jeremy Hogarth
Roy Hunt
David Smith
David Lloyd

Sound

Elizabeth Parer-Cook
Chris West
Paul Freeman

Music

Kevin Hocking
Melbourne Symphony Orchestra

Production Managers

Richard Campbell
John Winter

Designer

Dale Mark

The television series 'Nature of Australia' was produced by the Australian Broadcasting Corporation in association with the Australian Heritage Commission and the British Broadcasting Corporation. Associate producer for the BBC: Dr John Sparks.